T0331068

Changing Organizational Culture

How is practical change work carried out in modern organizations? And what kind of challenges, tasks and other difficulties are normally encountered? In a turbulent and changing world, organizational culture is often seen as central for sustained competitiveness. Organizations are faced with increased demands for change but these are often so challenging that they meet heavy resistance and fizzle out. *Changing Organizational Culture* encourages the development of a reflexive approach to organizational change, providing insights as to why it may be difficult to maintain momentum in change processes. Based around an illuminating case study of a cultural change programme, the book provides 15 lessons on the entire change journey; from analysis and design to implementation and how organizational members should approach change projects. This updated and enhanced third edition considers the most recent studies on organizational change practice, with new examples from businesses and the public sector, and it includes one empirical study which uses the authors' own framework, enriching their practical recommendations. It also draws on the latest theoretical developments, including ideas of power, identity and storytelling. *Changing Organizational Culture* is vital reading for students, researchers and practitioners working in organizational studies, change management and HRM.

Mats Alvesson is Professor of Organization Studies at University of Bath, UK and Business Administration at Lund University, Sweden.

Stefan Sveningsson is Professor of Business Administration at Lund University, Sweden.

Changing Organizational Culture

Cultural Change Work in Progress

Third Edition

Mats Alvesson and Stefan Sveningsson

Routledge
Taylor & Francis Group

LONDON AND NEW YORK

Designed cover image: GettyImages. Credit: bayshev. Creative
#:669060294

Third edition published 2025
by Routledge
4 Park Square, Milton Park, Abingdon, Oxon, OX14 4RN

and by Routledge
605 Third Avenue, New York, NY 10158

Routledge is an imprint of the Taylor & Francis Group, an Informa business

© 2025 Mats Alvesson and Stefan Sveningsson

First edition published by Routledge 2007

Second edition published by Routledge 2016

British Library Cataloguing-in-Publication Data
A catalogue record for this book is available from the British Library

ISBN: 978-1-032-75563-2 (hbk)
ISBN: 978-1-032-75561-8 (pbk)
ISBN: 978-1-003-47455-5 (ebk)

DOI: 10.4324/9781003474555

Typeset in Times New Roman
by Apex CoVantage, LLC

Contents

List of illustrations   vii
Preface   viii

PART 1
Perspectives on organizational and
cultural change   1

1   Introduction   3

2   Organizational change   14

3   Organizational culture and change   42

PART 2
Change work in practice – a close-up study   65

4   The case – and how we studied it   67

5   A cultural change project I: background, objectives
    and design   74

6   A cultural change project II: implementation, reception
    and outcomes   94

PART 3
Crucial issues in cultural change work   113

7   'It is not so damn easy': lack of consistency and expressiveness
    in cultural change work   115

8   Disconnected work: cultural change efforts decoupled   125

9   Hyperculture   137

PART 4
Getting into the substance of organizational change work 149

10 Working with culture versus culture working on change workers 151

11 Working with change 166

12 Lessons for cultural change actors and others 183

Bibliography 203
Index 213

List of illustrations

Figures

2.1	A cultural web	29
5.1	Draft of target culture	86
6.1	Jigsaw puzzle	98
10.1	Levels of culture	161

Tables

2.1	The six positions	37
2.2	Common causes of resistance	38
5.1	The cultural change process and how we have tried to capture it	75
10.1	Concepts of culture	152
11.1	Situated identity constructions of key actors	176
11.2	Levels of culture	179
12.1	The images used	193

Preface

Why another book on organizational change? This is a question that the potential reader may ask him or herself – and with good reason. There is an abundance of studies and textbooks on the topic. Perhaps most things have been said already?

In this book – based on a case study – we investigate how people work with, interpret and make sense of, and act in change processes. This book is aimed at locating and drawing upon the experiences of living with organizational change efforts among various groups of organizational members. We thus try to get close to the people involved and illuminate their assumptions and reasoning. Arguably, close-up studies of change efforts are necessary in order to understand what is happening, and to produce insights for much more thoughtful and realistic change work than is common. We feel strongly that our study opens up unexpected and novel insights and ideas. We hope and believe that this text gives additional depth and richness to the understanding of why change is so difficult, what can go wrong, and what can be done in order to make change work more reflexive and productive. The book provides a rather profound critique of many common assumptions and recommendations in the change literature and offers a rich case, new concepts and some new ideas for thinking and acting in change work, partly focused on cultural change, but also with relevance for all kinds of change projects in organizations.

We are very grateful to Julia Balogun, Patrick Dawson, Emmanuel Ogbonna, Jens Rennstam and Nadja Sörgärde for reading and commenting upon previous versions of the manuscript. We are also grateful to the Jan Wallander and Tom Hedelius Research Foundation and the former Swedish Research Council for Working Life and Social Science for research grants funding the research projects of which this study is a part.

In this updated third edition of the book a number of additions have been made to the second edition. We have also considered recent research and literature in the field.

Lund, September 2024
MA SS

Part 1

Perspectives on organizational and cultural change

1 Introduction

According to most present-day writings on change, we live in a time of turbulence and radical change. We are frequently informed about how changes in consumer and labour markets and in technologies, pressures of financial markets, globalization and new values and orientations from employees all act as key drivers for change. In recent years, we have also seen increased political instability in many parts of the world and the emergence of a pandemic that boosted an improvement in digital communication technologies and facilitated the development of the hybrid workplace. It is also often said that organizations must learn to adapt to changes or otherwise risk failure. This risk is regularly emphasized by contemporary authors of change. For example, Ibarra (2020: 13) suggests that: 'Most leaders today are trying to do the same things: help their organizations becomes more agile, more innovative, more digitally savvy, and more customer-centric.' A call for change that has been repeated many times. Already twenty-five years ago, Beer and Nohria (2000: 133) suggested that the modern societal conditions are exceptional in terms of change: 'Not since the Industrial Revolution have the stakes of dealing with change been so high. Most traditional industries have accepted, in theory at least, that they must either change or die.' Understanding and managing change has developed into a virtual industry, encompassing consultancy firms, management and leadership gurus, mass media, the business press, high-profile corporate executives, politicians and business schools, as well as management writings and management rhetoric and practice. In most writings, change is seen as good or necessary or both, often however with limited critical reflection on the subject matter (Sturdy and Grey 2003). Contemporary ideas of change stress that managers must be adept in working with planned organizational change as well as be responsive to changes in the environment. External pressures are manifold and there are many popular topics that need to be acknowledged. For example, an increasing awareness of the impacts of global warming and the roles corporations play when it comes to greenhouse gas emissions intensify demands on many organizations. To an increasing degree, organizations also need to be able to demonstrate that they care about corporate social responsibility (CSR). PwC conducted a study in 2018 on how companies globally prioritize and report on the sustainable development goals (SDGs) for their businesses. The study showed that 72% of companies mentioned sustainable development goals in their annual report or their sustainability

DOI: 10.4324/9781003474555-2

report, and that 54% of those that prioritized the goals also included them in their business strategies (PwC 2018). These figures are likely higher today. Consequently, efforts to change organizations are numerous and take a large proportion of the time and energy of many managers, staff and other employees. Even though change talk may be more common than ambitious change work, it is still likely that there are more change initiatives.

Many of the existing writings and projects of organizational change involve organizational culture in one sense or another. Culture is often seen as either the key issue to be changed or something that is crucial to take seriously in order to make change possible. Indeed, many authors of change suggest that a major reason for why organizational change efforts usually fail to materialize as planned is the frequent neglect of aspects of organizational culture (Balogun and Johnson 2004; Pettigrew 2012). In line with that, one could argue that few if any organizational changes are 'culture-free' or can navigate around culture. Also, technical changes such as in the digitalization area are about understandings, meanings and values about the necessity, design and acceptance of these changes. It is often the cultural context and how people relate to technical changes that determinate if they are successful or not. (Often there is a range of problems, not all entirely about technological issues.) One author argues that 'organizational change involves confronting the persistent pattern of behaviour that is blocking the organization from higher performance, diagnosing its consequences, and identifying the underlying assumptions and values that have created it' (Beer 2017: 388). At minimum, culture may create problems and need to be considered. It is thus an important aspect and something to carefully consider for any person trying to change an organization.

Even several decades after organizational culture was viewed as *the* ultimate way of addressing organizational problems – combining efficiency and focus with flexibility and engagement, through values and conviction – culture is still broadly seen as a key aspect of organizational competitiveness. In terms of the possibility of accomplishing change, Carl-Henrik Svanberg, at the time CEO of Ericsson, has said that 'culture always defeats strategy'. Lou Gerstner, former president of IBM, concluded that 'I came to see, in my time at IBM, that culture isn't just one aspect of the game, it *is* the game' (cited in Palmer *et al.* 2022: 358). Accordingly, the belief seems to be that, unless culture, at a minimum, is seen as an integral part of change, efforts at the latter will fail. Many organizations work with, plan or contemplate organizational culture changes – often as an important element in other changes. In the present book, we elaborate extensively on organizational change efforts where culture was claimed as a key theme. More specifically the book offers an in-depth investigation of a cultural change programme in a high-tech firm.

This means that we go beyond surface issues and look at the meanings, definitions and identities of the people involved. How change work is organized (and disorganized), how people define themselves and others, and what the entire project is basically about emerge as key themes to explore, and for actors in change projects to address and work with. Part of our case story is that key actors in many ways had little knowledge of what was going on and produced a mismatch between their self-understandings and the expectations of others. Developing new metaphors for change work is part of a suggested approach for how to deal with this in more thoughtful ways than seem to be common.

Understanding organizational change

Organizational change is a very broad area. It addresses a variety of time spans, interests in broad patterns (industrial/professional trends) or organization-specific transformations, and types of changes (technological, mergers, digitalization, downsizing, etc.). There is a lot of variety concerning the theoretical perspective employed; some emphasize agents of change, others environmental driving forces. Here we will raise a few issues that are usually seen as important in understanding organizational change and position our study.

Change typically, but not necessarily, implies an interest in *time*. Some say that we cannot understand changes through a snapshot and instead emphasize a longitudinal approach (Pettigrew *et al.* 2001; Pettigrew 2012; Sminia 2016). Different time spans can be focused on, however. At one extreme we have an interest in how changes take place over history, and here a decade may be a fairly short unit of analysis. At the other extreme we have a limited time period, where one may even study what is happening over a few hours, for example when a work group develops a new idea or solution that subsequently affects its work. But sometimes time is disregarded and there is no focus on what is happening during the change process. Except for a few studies such as Mirfakhar *et al.* (2018), Stensaker *et al.* (2021) and Todnem *et al.* (2018), it is still quite common in many studies of change projects to focus on outcomes, for example on the difference between before and after the change intervention or period, thus downplaying what actually happens over time, that is, the process (Dawson 2014). Many authors observe that, although there is some recognition of the temporal (before and after changes) aspect, many still ignores focusing upon the micro-processes of change at work. This is probably a consequence of the significant requirements for close access and intensive ethnographic field work needed to follow change processes in depth. Consequently, in many change studies the actual change work is put in the notorious black box – before and after are studied, but not much is known about the actual change at work. Interviewing people at a distance may not say that much about what takes place.

We have been fortunate in terms of having very good opportunities for access to carefully and deeply follow change efforts in real time, and to interview a variety of people involved and observe different events.

Another interesting dimension concerns the presumed *need* for change, including espoused or 'real' motives for change. As indicated earlier, it is frequently assumed that an organization, in the face of changing contextual circumstances, 'must' adapt or face great problems. However, we can also study people's constructions of the 'need' for change or how rhetorical and other resources are mobilized in change projects. Many academics emphasize the need to address how contexts not only shape actions but also can be employed by individuals for pursuing certain changes. Researchers sometimes draw attention to how people interpret and make use of various logics and drivers behind changes. Ogbonna and Wilkinson (2003) for example noted how management in one firm emphasized new forms of competition and an increased need for customer orientation, while many of the employees interpreted the motives of top management as being about cutting costs in order to appeal to investors and analysts. Talk about new values was seen as a smokescreen for less noble considerations.

In this book we encounter an interesting example where there was some agreement that there were good reasons for change, but where initiative, action and engagement around the change programme still faced problems of mobilization, apart from at a superficial level.

A third issue connects to the significance of *context* and *levels* of analysis. An interest in organizational change may lead to an extension of contexts to broad trends or macro- and business-level changes, for example changes in an industry and how fashions affect an entire set of organizations at an aggregated level. At the other end, there may be a focus on micro-level changes in a specific part of an organization, for example on how a new manager or an emergent expression of discontent among a group of employees or a customer triggers reactions within a department.

We take a primary interest in specific events and acts, and follow the micro-processes of change efforts involving different groups as communicators, translators, interpreters and receivers of change messages. An idea is to take the varieties of people involved seriously. However, we also connect to broader trends in order to make change processes intelligible. It is for example important to relate the content of organizational change, such as customer orientation and quality programmes, to broader institutional and fashionable scripts and recipes. What is happening locally is sometimes best seen as imitations of trends and recipes circulating more broadly in business and amongst consultants.

Fourthly, a change typically involves a wide set of different phenomena and aspects, sometimes understood as the *content* of change: these may be the means and/or the outcomes of change projects. Candidates include everything from meanings, emotions and values to behaviours, technologies, systems and structures, as well as knowledge, objectives, strategies, vocabularies, systems, identities, social relations, networks and power relations. Many of these themes go together, and changes often involve several of these, but they may be given different emphasis – by the actors involved and by researchers trying to study what is happening.

This book mainly focuses on the cultural level, which means that we emphasize informal meanings, beliefs and understandings. We also consider values, but more in terms of how people relate to – and often become confused by – talk about (managerially invented) values, than what kind of values people in organizations 'really' have. Generally, meanings are more significant than values – people generally like what sounds good ('values') but it is more interesting and important to think about what they actually mean.

A fifth theme regards the possible interest in *actors* of change. Which actors are being focused on in the study? Are these institutions, such as the state, large companies initiating pressures on for example partners or suppliers to modify their operations, or industrial or professional bodies, or are local actors, for example a new top manager, of key interest? Or are we less interested in a centralized agent and want to know more about what is happening amongst those supposed to be targeted for change, their values, identifications or ways of working? There are many options. It is, of course, possible not to take any closer look at specific actors and their ways of initiating change or making sense of what managers try to encourage them to do. One may look at the operations of structural forces of change and their possible effects on behaviours and performances as if these worked in a 'mechanical way', thus black-boxing those supposed to create these new outcomes through modified practices.

Most research on organizational change tends to be management-centric, that is, focused on the management or the change agent's point of view and actions (By 2020), although there are some notable exceptions discussed in later chapters. Our approach is that it is very important to carefully consider the experiences, meanings and actions of all involved. It is not just those communicating objectives, messages and instructions who are of interest but also those supposed to be affected by these, and how they interpret and accept, reject or downplay the goals, values and behaviours they are encouraged to take on board. Not only the managerial and subordinate, but also the intermediary, levels are worth taking seriously. We thus give some space to the sandwiched person's, that is senior and junior middle managers', point of view.

Finally, we have the matter of *theoretical perspective*. This of course is closely interrelated with many of the other issues: a population ecologist is typically interested in the overall outcomes of developments in large samples of organizations over long time periods and does not care about actors and their meanings. A sense-making theorist takes the opposite stance, and pays attention to how people reason and act based on their identity and perception of the situation. But many theoretical approaches can be aligned with a span of different empirical foci. Concentrating on a particular kind of empirical theme does not in detail determine the theoretical perspective used: one can study a change process in a specific organization at close range and use for example a functionalist, an interpretative, a critical or a post-structural approach. Studying how people interpret and respond to a change programme can, within an interpretative approach, emphasize sense-making, psychodynamic or culture theory. The study of organizations is a field with many theoretical options – not so suitable for the researcher with severe decision anxiety.

We are proceeding from an interpretative perspective, on which the meaning-creating activities and the cultural background of such activities are focused. As will be made clear in the next section, anthropological culture theory is significant here.

Studying change in depth

There are thus many options within an interest in change and we will take one specific route. Our study focuses on what is happening in, rather than with, a specific organization. Geertz (1973) suggests that anthropologists do not study villages, but *in* villages, and we see this as inspirational also for organization research-ers. As mentioned previously, we are interested in process issues, not so much in before and after scores on various variables (attitudes, behaviours, performances). We are not neglecting the latter, but are mainly interested in following an entire organizational change process in real time. We are perhaps not so much inter-ested in organizational changes as change *efforts* and what these consist of. As the case that is the focus of this book indicates, change efforts and change are hardly the same.

The concentrated approach we take means that a number of organizational actors are targeted. We pay secondary attention to structural forces, fashions or institutional changes, and focus on how people try to improve their organization in what they perceive to be some key respects. We note that our research subjects construct a certain organizational context in which they motivate change efforts, but we do not try to make any objective assessment of this construction. We study what people do when they engage in change work and what this seems to lead to in an organization. A possible strength of the study is that we have studied a broad spectrum of people involved in or exposed to, and more or less successfully called upon by the initiators of, the change efforts: in the text we will encounter top- and middle-managers, HRM people, consultants and low-level employees. We have had direct access to change activities and have listened to the thoughts, intentions, sense making and responses of people involved in and/or targeted by the change project.

The change project focused on culture or, rather, what those involved defined as 'culture'; values and 'drivers' behind success were targeted for change and improvement. This means that we tried to follow this project and the people more or less involved in it: looking at meanings, ideas, lines of reasoning, emotional responses, identities, etc. But we also looked at change design issues: how manage-ment operates and how managerial ideas inform and perhaps misinform actors in organizations.

In terms of theoretical framework we draw upon cultural thinking focusing on meanings and symbolism (Alvesson 2013; Geertz 1973; Martin 2002; Smircich 1983a). This is a broad and varied field, which still allows sufficient focus and sup-port on in-depth inquiries and readings to allow for direction and the production of research results well beyond the case of finding results emerging inductively out of data and thus only 'surface patterns'. We are also inspired by Latour's (1986, 2005) idea of change and influence as translation, emphasizing how social institutions and interactions are contingent upon how various actors pick up and reinterpret the elements presumably linking people and social elements together. We focus on what the people involved tried to do, the micro-processes as indicated earlier. We raise questions such as 'What is going on here?' and 'What do these people think they are up to?' In addition, we draw upon the organizational change literature, with an emphasis on process and the dynamics of change.

The organization studied here was formed as an independent company (subsidi-ary), having previously been a large R&D unit within a very large, internationally leading firm. The challenge as seen by management and consultants is a classical one: to make the company more market oriented and also to make the organization work better internally, through better leadership and teamwork. The cultural change programme was conceived of and designed by top management together with consultants. Besides planning and design, we follow the implementation phase and also uncover how various people related to and made sense of the programme as well as its outcomes. We have followed the change programme in detail and in real time.

We think that this makes the study quite original – there are enormous amounts of texts on organizational change. Some researchers report in-depth studies of cultural change projects (e.g. Helms Mills 2003; Ogbonna and Wilkinson 2003), but few follow the entire process of cultural change from intentions and aspirations to the outcomes via change practices and the responses to these in real time. It is much more common for studies to look at the output of a process or follow it in a broad, overall way (e.g. Murdoch and Geys 2014). It is probably even more common with consultancy or here-is-how-to-accomplish-great-results kinds of texts. These are seldom based on thorough studies and tend to report superficial and partly misleading examples as 'proofs' or illustrations. They make their readers happy and optimistic when reading the text, but often an imperfect world less inclined to respond quickly to recipes for change projects lies ahead.

For some readers, looking at one single change project may appear limited. In line with a long and increasingly popular case study tradition, we argue that getting a rich and detailed picture, sensitive to local context and the meanings of the people involved, is necessary in order to understand the phenomenon – and to learn something that can encourage more reflective and realistic change work.

It is important to study several different groups within an organization, as one cannot assume that people relate to the change project and the outcomes in similar ways. As we need to know the context, the actors, their interactions and practices, how processes unfold and how people make sense of what is happening, we realize that a single case can be sufficient for learning a lot. As mentioned, this case involves part of a large, internationally leading firm. The consultancy firm mostly involved is also one of the internationally most high-profile ones. The case should be of some general interest. It may in some respects appear as rather idiosyncratic and deviating from what is generally presented as organizational changes in management textbooks and pop-management writings full of positive examples with happy endings, but we think that it exhibits many common themes and offers very good learning opportunities.

The purpose of the book

This book is directed at undergraduate as well as postgraduate students, academics and practitioners interested in organizational change, management consultancy, leadership and organizational culture. These are diverse audiences but we have tried to written the book so that a variety of groups may be interested and can benefit from it. The purpose of the book is to investigate and discuss a range of questions such as:

- How do managers, consultants and HRM people *work* with cultural change projects? How do they design and execute such projects? How do they think, get information and follow up their work? Is there a set of shared meanings making coordinated work possible or are there varieties of interpretations and meanings among those engaged in the change work producing difficulties?
- What is happening in terms of *processes*? Are the intentions of the design of change projects realized in the implementation events? Are instruments of change used as intended? How do those involved in these processes, for example the managers and employees seen as the recipients and carriers of change initiatives, make sense of this and what do they do?
- What are the outcomes in terms of *responses and consequences*? Do the change projects lead to changes in values, meanings, beliefs, identities and sentiments and, if so, which? Do they lead to changes in practices? Are the possible changes those initially intended or are the consequences unforeseen? If there are no changes, how can this be understood?
- What can be learned about culture change projects and other forms of organizational changes? What are the *traps and problems*? What do managers, consultants, HRM people and other people involved need to consider in planning, designing, executing and learning from such projects? We have in mind here the need to consider complexities and difficulties rather than come up with a blueprint for success. The ability to navigate and act in an interactive and responsive way in the process is perhaps at least as important as to engage in careful planning and then implement the plan.

Apart from addressing questions such as these, we find it important to investigate *the organization of change work*, for example how people position themselves in terms of being central in or moderately participating in, as opposed to distancing themselves from, the change project. We thus address questions such as: How do people connect themselves to and disconnect themselves from change objectives and change work? We note in the study that people move in and out of change work – not only in terms of behaviour but also in terms of identification. We also note that the division of labour between the persons involved seems to create some peculiar consequences. Change work needs to be better organized, calling also for attention to the more implicit aspects of this, including the assumptions, images and identities of those involved.

We find the area of association with, commitment to or *identification* with themes and projects a) of great significance in organization studies more broadly and b) of clear interest for change projects. People relate to projects in terms of showing commitment to and sympathy with the ideas and ambitions, but also in terms of distancing themselves from projects. In some cases this means taking a fairly consistent position, but often people switch between positions. Interest and optimism may vary over time and sometimes even fluctuate from day to day.

This book then aims to make contributions in the following areas of, or related to, organizational culture and organizational change:

- *managing culture*: management thinking and action in relation to the engineering or influencing of values and beliefs;
- *organizational change project work*: the workings and problems of cultural change programmes, including connections to and disconnections from various phases and elements of change work;
- the *ambiguity*, fragmentation and disconnectedness of much organizational life;
- *cultural meaning creation in organizations*: the subtleties of meaning creation, and breakdowns and difficulties in understanding values;
- *paradoxes of change*: elements in change work that, ironically, reinforce what the work is supposed to change;
- *identities and identification in organizations*: how people define themselves in relationship to potential tasks and lines of action.

The structure of the book

The purpose of this introductory chapter has been to try to position the book in terms of some common and significant issues in organizational change and on that basis to raise some questions that we aim to discuss in detail throughout the book. The chapters of the book are organized in four parts.

In the first part, 'Perspectives on organizational and cultural change', we set the stage for the study in terms of elaborating on important issues in organizational and cultural change that need to be investigated, for example the emphasis on the experiences and sense making of those involved in the change process. We also review the concepts and frameworks within organizational and cultural change in order to bring some clarity and to position our study in the fields under investigation.

Chapter 1 offers a variety of questions that are commonly raised in connection with organizational change. In Chapters 2 and 3, we review some of the concepts, key issues and frameworks in the field of organizational and cultural change. In Chapter 2, we identify the why, what and how of change by primarily discussing the planning and process approaches, respectively, to organizational change. We relate this to cultural change in Chapter 2, but extend that discussion in Chapter 3. There we connect the discussion to some of the central perspectives and key debates in writings on culture. We elaborate on the debate about whether organizational culture can be managed and discuss two perspectives on organizational cultural change, the grand technocratic and the local emergent.

In Part 2, the objective is to present the reader with an account of the conduct of the study as well as a detailed, rich and intimate narrative of organizational change work in practice – a close-up study. In Chapter 4, we detail the organization in focus and how the study of it was conducted. We also outline an investigative model of change that guided us in our attempts to organize the collected data. This model involves a few stages, such as background and context, intentions and strategy, design, practices (implementation and interaction), reception (interpretation) and outcomes. The model is intended to show how we tried to capture the change processes as they evolved in the studied case.

Chapters 5 and 6 follow the organizational change efforts over time. In Chapter 5, we investigate how managers perceived the situation prior to the conception of a change programme and what they wanted to achieve with the programme. We also investigate how they worked with issues of design and interaction with the rest of the company in preparing for implementation. In Chapter 6, we explore in detail what happened with the carefully designed programme as it met the managers and employees it was supposed to target. We look at how the targeted people addressed the programme and its outcomes or effects.

Part 3 consists of three chapters on what 'really' happened in the process. The part offers deeper interpretations of the major problems and challenges that were raised throughout the change work. We listen to a variety of participants involved in the change process and how they experienced this in terms of some, for them, crucial issues. In this part, we come close to the change work from the actors' point of view.

In Chapter 7, we begin to more thoroughly report and analyse the change efforts based on interpretations from those experiencing it. We address why things went wrong in the process and here we focus on the absence of strong emotional engagement and lack of high-powered commitment or expressiveness from those in charge of the process.

Chapter 8 focuses on the organization of the change work. It does so through an account and analysis of how the change programme unfolded in terms of collaboration, interaction and division of labour between the participants involved in the change process – the top managers, consultants, HR people, middle managers and other employees. In the chapter we consider problems of integration between these individuals, partly based on diversity of understanding of the cultural change work, something that made the change efforts disconnected and fragmented.

In Chapter 9, we proceed to reporting on how the participants looked at the change process by investigating culture as what we call 'hyperculture'. In the chapter, we discuss the culture programme as a package, as something manufactured, as ceremonial talk and as an ideal fantasy creation. We treat these aspects as contributing to making the formulated and designed culture more real than the reality, ideal or existing, it was supposed to mirror. We discuss this hyperculture as something used in the marketing and image building of the organization.

In Part 4, we get into the substance of organizational culture and change. We set out to investigate more in depth what assumptions and values govern people in their change efforts and change work. The idea here is not primarily to focus on how the activities of those involved produce a new culture but rather how the activities express a culture in terms of more deeply held beliefs and assumptions.

Chapter 10 provides an analysis of the organizational culture informing the cultural work in the studied organization. The idea in the chapter is to move beyond what the individuals talk about as culture and interpret their activities as expressing deeper, non-realized cultural assumptions and meanings. We confront the cultural values being talked about with meanings and ideas informing action. In doing this we suggest that many of the cultural change activities in fact reproduced and strengthened existing organizational culture.

In Chapter 11, we proceed from the analysis made in Chapter 10 and discuss specific problems and possibilities in working with cultural change. In particular we discuss problems involved in working with change efforts based on a technocratic approach to organizational culture. In this chapter we also deepen the analysis of the meaning constructions made by various involved participants and connect these to identity issues. We also discuss the cultural programme as a relay race and introduce an alternative metaphor of the change work as a football game. The latter challenges some conventional notions of managerial work in organizational change.

Chapter 12 addresses issues of practical relevance for those interested in change management. The chapter is based on our case but extends the discussion and offers a consideration of common traps in organizational change, and the need for and possibility of creating a shared language, and also directs attention to some lessons that can be drawn from the case analysis. The aim of the chapter is not to list a collection of how-to-do-it recommendations but rather to point to some considerations of practical value that broaden awareness and insights into the complexities of organizational and cultural change. Working with change calls for critical thinking and being receptive to people's responses and sense making; following a cookbook recipe seldom works in this often complex and messy field.

2   Organizational change

Organizations are generally faced with a variety of expectations and demands to engage in change in order to maintain focus on changing customer preferences, market and industry dynamics, technological development, political and cultural shifts, globalization, and fashionable management concepts and ideas. To this list of forces, one should also add unexpected pandemic outbreaks such as Covid-19 between 2020 and 2022 as well as wars like Russia's attack on Ukraine 2022. To some extent following this, the field of organizational change consists of a large number of concepts, labels and models. There are numerous writings on the content such as structure, culture, leadership and strategy; the process whereby change is accomplished; the various internal and external forces that trigger, accelerate and obstruct change; the scope and magnitude of change; implementation problems and so on. For example, during the last twenty-five years, there has been a barrage of three-letter-acronym improvement programmes, such as BPR (Business Process Re-engineering), BSC (Balanced Score Card), JIT (Just-In-Time), TQM (Total Quality Management), CSR (Corporate Social Responsibility), ISO (International Standardization Organization programs), and various models of organizational cultural change, organizational learning, authentic and agile leadership. It is interesting to note that while we see more and more models of how to accomplish organizational change effectively, studies also show that a majority of change programmes score high in failure rates (Beer and Nohria 2000). Change efforts may occasionally worsen things since they often entail significant time- and resource-consumption that could have negative consequences for other organizational processes, and in general cause disruptions and other disturbances in work.

In this chapter we will undertake an overview and assessment of research on and recommendations for organizational change programmes.[1] We will focus upon concepts and theoretical reasoning of change that put a single organization and its formulated change ambitions in focus. We will thus not, or only very marginally, draw upon evolutionary or institutional theories – such as, for example, life cycle reasoning – of change (Van de Ven and Poole 1995). Even with these limitations the research on change is vast and varied. This is not surprising given the pluralistic nature of both academically oriented research and more practitioner-oriented studies of organizational change in terms of perspectives, methodologies and epistemological and various philosophic and moral commitments.

DOI: 10.4324/9781003474555-3

We start the chapter with the forces behind change, and discuss conventional ways of classifying change. We then discuss what is usually understood as planned change and relate the discussion to why so many planned change efforts seemingly fail. This is followed by a discussion of change as an ongoing process. Here we connect to employees', managers' and other people's experience and interpretations of change that are not seldom marginalized in discussions of planned change. Linked to that we continue with a discussion of the politics of change and resistance.

Forces of organizational change

External and internal triggers for change

In many cases organizational change is seen as a direct result of external changes. Among these external forces we often see the following (based on Child 2015):

- political;
- technological;
- cultural;
- demographic;
- economic;
- market.

Political forces can for example refer to deregulation or the liberalization of legislation in the international trade of consumer products and services. This is often characterized as how competition has developed from being local to becoming more global. Globalization is often mentioned as a key aspect of the contemporary development, usually referring to the intensity with which companies engage in an international presence. There are frequently demands on organizations following this globalization to centralize, standardize and make their operations more transparent and efficient, partly through the use of management control systems such as balanced scorecards and quality management systems. We could also see the strength of political forces during the Covid-19 pandemic, as political regulations such as strict travelling regulations led to various supply-chain disruptions and out-of-place shipping containers in international trade, amongst many other problems requiring swift organizational adaptions.

The Covid-19 pandemic also triggered technological development as organizations increasingly had to offer hybrid (blend of in-office and remote working) and virtual workspaces. The development of digital communication facilitates new products and services, such as when people are no longer obliged to go to the bank in order to manage transactions (reducing the need for bank offices). The increase in mobile commerce, online transaction processing and internet marketing have enabled a significant development in e-commerce that has impacted traditional retailing.

Societal and cultural norms about what is politically and morally appropriate are increasingly pressuring organizations to change in certain directions. Of course, many companies pay lip service to some of these issues in order to appear more legitimate, but some changes may still be triggered. Organizations follow fashionable trends and change according to what seems popular at the moment, often by benchmarking and imitating what they perceive to be significant for success in other organizations. For example, in recent years it has been hugely popular to talk about sustainability in environmental or social terms (CSR) and about being a corporate citizen. Demographic forces can impact on an organization's recruitment possibilities and the competence profile of the labour force. It is often claimed that millennials are an increasingly important demographic group with impact on workplaces, recruitment, and views on change and leadership. Millennials are sometimes said to demand more flexibility in terms of workspace and influence over work tasks. However, similar statements have been made also about other generations – so we need to be careful about (over)emphasizing the novelty and uniqueness of a 'new' generation.

It is perhaps self-evident that organizations are also highly sensitive to events in the wider economy. Economic factors include the causes and effects of business cycles and what in an international world leads to growth and stagnation. Changes in gross domestic product lead to changes in the rate of growth of sales and output for organizations. All these forces mix with market forces consisting of existing and potential customers. For example, deregulation is often said to lead to the emergence of new markets and opportunities for organizations to expand to new territories through local alliances or acquisitions (Child 2015).

There are also internal triggers to change. These may be related to the emergence of new technology, the revision of the primary task following from new products and services, new people in key positions (or people getting new ideas, interests or ambitions) or pressure to modify administrative structures. Rapid expansion might lead to demands on organizational changes such as when organizations divisionalize as a consequence of diversification. It can also be a matter of leading individuals trying to realize personal interests and agendas. For example, it is difficult to imagine the enormous product and service development taking place at Apple for the last twenty-five years without recognizing the role of Steven Jobs. Also, more 'average' persons in CEO positions may be interested in trying to put their stamp on the organization and thus initiate change projects to show that they make a difference.

It is often difficult to make a clear distinction between external and internal drivers for change. They tend to mix and overlap in shaping the orientation of change, although some conditions tend to dominate more than others. As we shall see later, we had, in our particular case, a situation where a few internal circumstances – perceptions and reports about low confidence in management and a technologically biased organization – produced the motivation to try to change the organizational culture. As a consequence of the organization being transformed from an internal unit to a (quasi-independent) firm (subsidiary), the sudden presence of an external market and demanding customers on the company doorstep led to an objective of improving relations with customers and thus avoiding an unfavourable technological orientation. This new external situation also offered an opportunity to address internal problems.

Making sense of drivers of change

Contextual drivers do not unequivocally determine change in a particular direction. There is always room for action based on how people interpret and make sense of what is happening around them (Fine and Hallett 2014; Tsoukas 2005). A processual view of organizational change directs attention to how people interpret and understand what is happening in the environment and occasionally draws upon this in order to push for organizational change (Sminia 2016; Todnem *et al.* 2018).

External and internal drivers are interpreted by people, creating a certain variation in terms of change between organizations. The way managers make sense of the organizational context is related to personal interests, educational background, organizational culture, history and how one perceives that managers in other organizations engage in change (Balogun *et al.* 2015). Some authors suggest that organizations should strive for originality in interpreting their contexts in order to sustain creative problem solving and innovation. However, it seems more common for organizational changes to follow fashions and trends. The eagerness among managers to benchmark towards what they perceive others do might explain the common trend among organizations to adopt whatever change programme is advanced by business schools, consultants or commonly known pop-management writers. Helms Mills (2003) refers to these as 'serial change companies'. The ambition to benchmark what one believes other organizations do contribute to that various version of many popular change models – formulated by academics, practitioners and consultants – that often gain widespread circulation among organizations, frequently without any critical review of its substance or effects (Alvesson 2013).

Since fashion changes all the time there are never-ending possibilities for managers and others to identify gaps between fashionable ideals and current practices, and thus for the need to accomplish change. Unfortunately, however, these fashions, and thus change ambitions, are not always very well grounded or motivated (Collins 1998). This does not however, prevent practitioners from jumping on ideals that are in vogue. Ideals that make lofty promises if the recipes of change are followed. New ideals often sound better than old ones – sometimes seen as ancient – and few are willing to take the risk to appear too passive and rigid. However, it is seldom possible to manage and control the real-life complexities of organizations with recipes for success. Indeed, this is clearly shown by our case study.

Views on organizational change

As briefly introduced in Chapter 1, there is a variety of different ways of looking at change. Key dimensions include the scale of change, the sources of change, its content and the political aspect.

The scale of change

A change is normally characterized in terms of two extremes – as revolutionary or evolutionary. Revolutionary refers to changes that affect several organizational dimensions simultaneously. These involve large-scale changes that radically affect organizational culture, management control systems, organizational structure, reward systems and leadership. These are often seen as strategic changes such as the result of product development or mergers and acquisitions triggered by external forces like technological development, internationalization or changes in industry competition. It is not uncommon to have mergers between organizations as markets mature and pressure on cost-cutting and efficiency increases. In contrast, evolutionary changes refer to what is understood as operational changes that affect a limited part of the organization. These changes take place within existing strategy and organizational culture, and involve modification of products such as design or distribution, recruitment of additional personnel or improvements in service quality. The scale of change is sometimes related to the rhythm or tempo of changes. Revolutionary changes are usually seen as occurring during relatively distinct and delimited periods of change activity, sometimes called discontinuous change, while evolutionary changes are seen as occurring gradually and incrementally during a longer and less distinct period of time, also referred to as continuous change. Burke (2018) mentions some concepts used in order to distinguish the scale of change:

- revolutionary versus evolutionary;
- discontinuous versus continuous;
- episodic versus continuing flow;
- transformational versus transactional;
- strategic versus operational;
- total system versus local option.

These labels and distinctions often mean roughly the same.

The sources of change

It is also common to make a distinction between planned and emergent change. These terms indicate that the sources of change vary. When talking about planned change, managerial ambitions and plans are central, while emergent change emphasizes the significance of organizational members outside management, and acknowledge the contextual and often the rather messy character of change. Planned change has – by far – received most attention in the change literature, as it also includes models for how to accomplish change successfully. Among planned change models we find the many broad and elaborate change programmes designed by managers, usually with the help of HR staff and external consultants, as in the case this book is based upon. The idea here is to look upon change as a rational pattern consisting of a sequentially organized and distinct activities. Models that are often referred to as n-step change models. The idea is that a number of necessary steps need to be gone through, systematically and in the right order, to bring about the aimed for outcome. Here we find many of the contemporary change programmes of re-engineering, downsizing, restructuring, quality programmes, mergers and acquisitions, outsourcing and networking. As already suggested, these change programmes that have received enormous attention. However, it is not unusual to talk of successful changes emerging from the bottom up in the organization. Among emergent changes we find continuous improvement projects, and spontaneous experimenting and development by lower-level managers and employees 'on the floor' that are often seen as characterizing learning organizations.

The politics of change

Depending on their political intensity, change efforts may take different forms in terms of participation, negotiation and resistance. Organizational strategies are the result of a political process where bargaining, negotiating, persuasion, convincing and the pushing of personal interests are key factors (Edmondson and Besieux 2021). The pushing of interests is usually facilitated by the use of power means such as expertise, formal position and reward as well as the manipulation of symbols, language, ideologies and organizational culture (Pettigrew 1985). A central political dimension is the opportunity to advance interests as legitimate in the eyes of significant others. This involves framing personal interests in terms of more rational and analytically accepted terms, which is more important when the change is challenged. A change initiative that is challenged calls for forceful change work. In change projects broadly viewed as acceptable by those concerned, extensive participation is possible (Buchanan and Badham 1999).

The content of change

This dimension refers to the 'what' of change such as strategies, organizational cultures, rationalization, re-engineering, reward systems, management control or new production systems. Often many aspects of change are related to each other and it may be difficult to target one area of change as distinct from another. For example, changing corporate culture is usually regarded as affecting more or less the whole organization and many of its constituent elements. It is difficult to imagine a cultural change as a separate and distinct activity without any effect on strategy, structure and other management control systems. Next, we turn to a classification of changes that to some extent integrates some of the preceding discussion.

Four change metaphors

Organizational change can also be characterized by the help of metaphors, which contribute to increased understanding. Drawing on different metaphors influences how we understand and interpret the world and has been used quite extensively in organizational analysis (Morgan 1997). Metaphors are occasionally drawn upon more explicitly but often also taken for granted. When for example talking about an organization's environment, life cycle and niche we employ a biological metaphor of an organization, viewing it as an organism. When focusing upon the designing and structuring of an organization we may view the organization as a machine (Beech and Macintosh 2012). Based on this reasoning, Marshak (2009) distinguishes between organizational changes in terms of four metaphors that refer to how radical a change is and whether it can be seen as planned or emerging:

1   Fix and maintain.
2   Build and develop.
3   Move and relocate.
4   Liberate and re-create.

1   Fix and maintain may not sound like a change but refers to adjusting existing organizational conditions in order to avoid larger-scale change. Organizations are here seen as machines that need regular maintenance and repairs such as simplifying changes that enable the current strategic orientation. This refers to smaller-scale, so-called operative, changes within existing supporting systems and structures.
2   Build and develop is a question of a somewhat more advanced change that involves building on the existing, adding to existing strategies, structures and systems in contrast to just repairing these. This can amount to recruitment of new competence or expansion of markets through the use of advertising campaigns. This form of change involves achieving what is sometimes labelled single-loop learning and allude somewhat more to seeing organizations as organisms in need for also learning and development.
3   Move and relocate means changing the systems per se and portrays change more as a journey – to move from one point to another. It is more about radical change that is often seen as a transition. This form of change involves questions about whether an organization should outsource an internal function, change the organizational structure, such as adopting a network structure or consolidate organizations in connection with an acquisition. This refers to planned changes initiated and formulated by top management levels.
4   Liberate and re-create is the most advanced form of change and is seen as a transformation of an all-encompassing and a profound kind. Transformations are here about the renewal of an entire organization which connects to several organizational sub-systems such as strategy, structure, culture, management control systems, etc. simultaneously. This occurs through research and development, radical and innovative thinking, creativity and fantasy, commonly among the employees. This is change not necessarily planned beforehand or seen as implementation of formulated goals or objectives. These changes usually challenge many of the existing systems and are seen as forms of double-loop learning that usually comes also with a lot of tensions and political game playing.

Although these metaphors (and the concepts of what change is generally) offer some understanding of organizational change activities there are problems in categorizing these.

Images of organizational change

As indicated, organizational change activities are not unambiguously captured in neat and well-ordered conceptualizations. Changes look different depending on whose perspective they are seen from. Changes viewed as minor and incremental from someone's perspective might be construed as radical and revolutionary by someone else (Palmer *et al.* 2022; Sörgärde 2006). The preceding concepts and metaphors help us make sense of organizations but this is never done independently from personal interests, background, education, hierarchical position, etc. Constructions of how radical or significant a change is are part of the bargaining, negotiating, persuading and political game playing that is inherent in organizational processes in general and in organizational changes in particular. We will return to the variety of ways in which people construct images of organizational change in the case under examination.

Whether a change is revolutionary or evolutionary is also a matter of levels of analysis. At a macro level and distance, it might look like a change is revolutionary and episodic but at a closer micro level the same course of action could be seen as evolutionary and continuous. A common assumption among writers on change is that stability is the norm and that change occurs in successive states, as a result of managerially initiated and planned change programmes. Organizations are constructed as stable entities which on specific occasions undergo change as movements from A to B. Organizational change is here seen as occurring discontinuously. However, many suggest that organizations change continuously (such as in the fix/maintain, build/develop and liberate/re-create models, for example) and that change rather than stability is the natural state. After all, people enter, mature and leave organizations; customers and suppliers change; new products and technologies are developed and used and so on. Based on such a perspective the idea that organizations are stable is merely an illusion; seen at a distance most organizations seem stable but, looked at more closely and with regard to events such as fixing, building and re-creating, organizations can be seen as constantly changing.

The planning approach

A major topic in organizational change and certainly in our case revolves around the possibility of accomplishing planned change. There is a substantial number of (more normatively informed) writings on the possibility of accomplishing managerially planned organizational change programmes. These are often designed in terms of successive stages and occur at specific instances, a view of change Weick and Quinn (1999) term as 'episodic' (sometimes also referred to as 'revolutionary', 'discontinuous', 'transformational', etc., as seen previously).

Within the planning approach, in a loose sense, there are numerous writings and models, some of which share similar characteristics, such as a belief that change benefits from some rational design. Here we discuss a few of the most popular models and ideas that also informed much of the change design and work in the case studied in this book.

Within the planning approach it is common to elaborate on two approaches depending on levels of analysis. One approach is the Group Dynamics school, with its origin in the writings of Lewin and its focus on the work group level and its later development into Organizational Development (OD). The other is the Open Systems school, with its origin in organizations as open and living systems and its focus on the organizational level. First, a short review of Human Relations approach as background of the Group Dynamics school and OD in particular.

Background in human relations

The Human Relations approach emerged as a response to widespread discontent with working conditions, alienation and general worry among employees in many organizations, especially in connection to changes in the US in the 1930s. Organizational changes, especially technological ones changing working conditions, frequently lead to resistance and even sabotage. The so-called Hawthorne studies and other research projects suggested that the social dimension of work was not taken into sufficient account in understanding the dynamics behind changes and the prospect of achieving change without also creating discontent, resistance and sabotage. Many authors suggested that the problems with employees' discontent and resistance did not involve the technical content of the changes but rather were about social and personal issues. According to Burnes (2017: 82), the Hawthorne experiments contributed to the 'Economic Man/Woman' being challenged by the 'Social Man/Woman' and to an increased understanding of the significance of social relations – human relations – for motivation, work satisfaction and change. Following this, the interest in leadership and communication related to managing organizational change was amplified. This development also created an increased interest in leadership and communication as significant means in accomplishing successful change work. Researchers suggested that managers should listen to and appreciate the experience and knowledge of employees in change projects. In this context, Roethlisberger and Dickson (1950) also developed the advantages of what they called a democratic and more participative leadership, which was later further refined by Lewin (1951) and the Group Dynamics school and OD.

The Group Dynamics school and OD

A central problem in planned change efforts is to make changes more sustainable in people's thinking and actions. Organizational changes often fail because people return to old ways of thinking and doing things in their smaller work group once the change work or a particular change process is ended. Scholars here argued that human thinking and actions are primarily influenced by the work group's norms and dynamic, which is why changes of external stimuli, such as individual rewards, are less productive in changing people's behaviour at work. Strong forces in work groups are rather the desire to perform in line with others and subsequently be confirmed as belonging to the group. Numerous experiments have demonstrated that individuals tend to stick to the view of the group even if it is obviously wrong or against the individual's personal convictions. The Group Dynamics school thus targeted change at the group level, based on the idea that most employees are engaged in smaller work groups within organizations (Burnes 2020; Endrejat and Burnes 2022). Lewin proposed a three-step model in order to target group norms and values in change projects:

1   unfreezing;
2   change;
3   refreezing.

The first step is a preparatory and planning stage where employees can be included, partly in order to reduce friction and resistance. Unfreezing means destabilizing the status quo of group norms and values and can include activities such as projects, education or inspiring talk from significant persons. This entails making co-workers understand that change is necessary in order to survive in the longer term. Often this process involves unlearning assumptions that are taken for granted. Something that can include enough presenting convincing data that disconfirms the belief that everything is alright the way it is. By demonstrating misalignments, current thinking could be undermined and people would recognize that there is a problem.

The second step is about moving the organization to a new and, for organizational members, acceptable state. This implies developing new concepts and learn new meanings. For instance, it could be a transition from being an 'internal engineer' to become an 'external expert consultant' and learn to see yourself also as a market person and not only as an engineer.

The last stage involves stabilizing the new state and preventing it from regressing into previous behaviour. Returning to their ordinary work group, people easily return to their old way of thinking and acting. This is why it is necessary to continue working with changing the norms and behaviour of a group and to ensure that the new ways of working also harmonize with these as is suggested by Burnes:

> Lewin saw social change as a group activity because, unless group norms and routines are also transformed, changes to individual behavior will not be sustained.

> (Burnes 2020: 50)

A central theme is that through knowledge, commitment and learning it is possible to reduce resistance to change and create a need or will to change among employees: 'Managing change through reducing forces that prevent change, rather than through increasing forces that are pushing for change' (Dawson 2003: 30). Organizations are seen here as containing forces of change and stabilization. Change is accomplished by continuously undermining the stabilizing forces. Unfreezing should create a disequilibrium that facilitates the implementation of change activities that re-create equilibrium in the direction perceived as healthy and effective for the organization. A key insight from the reasoning is that a change not only implies a change *to* something but also suggests a change *from* an original state. Thus, it is not enough to focus on the future, but also to break free of the present. The collaborative, humanistic and democratic view of change that Lewin proposed means that managers work together with employees and consultants and jointly diagnose the state of the organization. Much of the reasoning of Lewin was later developed by the OD movement and is still considered important to recognize in change processes (Burnes 2020).

The initiative to embark on change is, however, usually taken by top managerial levels. When an initiative has been taken, change efforts are usually thought to be implemented first at the higher hierarchical levels and then progressively involve lower levels. Considering the progressive involvement of employees, OD implies that changes are to be seen as long term rather than a quick fix. Some approaches of OD also suggest that organizational change could benefit by drawing on an external change agent that continuously applies scientific behavioural knowledge in the process. Change in this tradition involves an explicit ambition to integrate theory and practice, an idea that has contributed to the development of professional change consultants. This view of change is seen as linear and evolutionary, changes occur incrementally in order to continuously review improvement and progression.

As suggested previously, the legacy from Lewin is still very strong in the academic field and among the practitioners and consultants of OD. This is well illustrated when looking closer at the following list of the activities that are suggested to contribute to efficient change implementation (Cummings *et al.* 2020):

1   Motivating change – creating readiness for change and overcoming resistance to change.
2   Creating a vision that describes the core ideology and the envisioned future.
3   Developing political support – assessing the power of the change agents and identifying the key stakeholders and other possible influencing stakeholders.
4   Managing the transition with the help of activity planning, commitment planning and management structures.
5   Sustaining momentum – supporting the change through resources, developing support systems to help the change agents, developing new competencies and skills, reinforcing new behaviours and maintaining the course.

Much of Lewin's and the early OD model's focus on group-level, evolutionary and participative change has developed into more organization-wide change approaches that use more integrative and managerially oriented views of change.

Lately, OD has developed into two conceptually distinct directions, and it is common today to talk about a diagnostic versus a dialogical orientation of OD.

Although sharing ideas of humanism, participative decision making, developing members of an organization as a basis for development and expressing a strong facilitative orientation on how to accomplish change are evergreens, an increased emphasis of focus on sense making and interpretation contrasts somewhat to the classics. The classics – the diagnostic OD – are seen as treating organizations as open and objective systems where change is seen as more episodic, the dialogical OD focus more on seeing organizations as social constructions where meaning-making is central and change is understood more in continuous terms (Bushe and Marshak 2015; Hastings and Schwartz 2022).

In general, OD as an overall approach to change is seen as radically different from the more instrumentally oriented 'change management' approach that also has been highly popular for more than a couple of decades and that usually entails suggestions of downsizing and trimming rather than growth and renewal (Sveningsson and Sörgärde 2023). Some of the development in OD has, however, come to reorient itself towards a stronger focus on cultural, strategic and more revolutionary change. This development has laid the ground for many of the popular practitioner-oriented n-step models towards change that have been developed in the last fifteen to twenty years and made OD more similar to the Open Systems school.

The Open Systems school

This school emphasizes the importance of having an organization-wide view of organizational change. It is thus important to see the organization in its entirety rather than just in groups, as was the case in the Group Dynamics school and early OD. Open Systems thinking views organizations as being composed of a set of various interconnected subsystems that together constitute the whole organization. From this it follows that in a well-functioning organization there is fit and harmony between these various subsystems. The subsystems are open to each other in terms of impact, but the organization in its entirety is also to be seen as an open system in constant interaction with the larger system of which it is a part, the multifaceted macro environment. The idea is to align the subsystems together so that they create a harmonious whole rather than optimize certain distinct subsystems. A central assumption in the systems theory is that the different parts are mutually dependent on each other, creating a complex and historically emerging web of relations. Based on this assumption, one could argue that even seemingly rather confined change projects are quite complex and usually entail a variety of long-term and often unpredictable organizational consequences.

The idea among many writers is thus to try to acknowledge that change work needs to appreciate a variety of different aspects in order to succeed, and since its emergence many open systems models have been established. Much focus has recently been directed towards strategy, structure and organizational culture, besides the traditional focus on leadership and individuals. It is argued that the change process should be systemic and that an alignment between the 'softer' elements of people, leaders and values and the 'harder' elements of technology, strategy and structure is necessary. An early and influential system framework is the

TPC theory by Tichy (1982). The theory suggests that organizations can be seen as consisting of three mutually dependent systems: the technological (production), political (allocation of power and resources) and cultural (normative glue). It is argued that an organization is effective to the extent that there is alignment within and across the subsystems. As suggested, these system models usually involve both the harder and the softer systems and have as their aim the facilitation of the change work, both the diagnosis and the implementation. Another popular model is McKinsey's '7 S', which characterizes the organization on the basis of seven systems. These include the 'hard' subsystems of strategy, structure and systems, and the 'soft' ones of shared values, skills, staff and style. Whittington *et al.* (2020) developed an influential alternative that employs a metaphor called a 'cultural web' that portrays organizations as consisting of nine subsystems, including a central paradigm (the web) that functions as a set of integrative and coordinating taken-for-granted assumptions for the various subsystems. These assumptions are expressed in reward systems, control systems, communication, rites and routines, histories and myths, symbols and power structures. It should be repeated that a central idea is that a change in any of these systems always affects other systems since they are interdependent. Any change effort is thus necessarily a complex, long-term, politically messy and arduous change task that requires a broad understanding of the interdependence of subsystems. This is change that develops incrementally as new ideas and thoughts are aligned and 'muddled through' within existing organizational subsystems (Lindblom 1959).

In most of these models, culture is often treated as something an organization has along with other organizational dimensions, usually understood as a 'variable view' of culture (Smircich 1983a). Culture is thus treated as a variable that needs to be managerially aligned with other organizational variables (structure, strategy, technology, etc.) in order to implement organizational change effectively. There are some variations within the field, however, and in some recent studies of OD – especially the more dialogical approach – the view of culture has developed in terms of the metaphoric view that sees organizations as cultures (compare to the systems view of organizations as organisms or systems, with a cultural 'subsystem' or part of the whole). See more about this in Chapter 3.

Change as a sequential process

The subsystems as described earlier are supposedly managed through a sequential and linear process usually consisting of the following elements: analysis and diagnosis, planning, implementation and evaluation. Although there are some variations, the rationalistic assumption underpins them all (for a review of these models see Palmer *et al.* 2022). Dawson (2003: 32) summarizes these processes in five steps:

1   identifying a need for change;
2   selecting an intervention technique;
3   gaining top management support;

4 overcoming resistance to change;
5 evaluating the change process.

This kind of model, a heritage from Lewin and early OD, is used broadly within clinically oriented action research and popular practitioner-oriented writings on organizational change. A model that has gained substantial influence in this respect is Kotter's (1996/2012a, 2018) eight-step reasoning that aims to establish employee commitment and reduce scepticism:

1 *Establish a sense of urgency.* Commonly, organizations experience too much self-satisfaction (we are good as we are) when a change process commences, so they often fail to communicate to others about the need for change. It is therefore important to investigate the competitive environment and identify threats and opportunities.
2 *Form a powerful guiding coalition.* Organizations need to create a powerful coalition to steer through the change work and reach a momentum in the change process. Soloists rarely produce results in organizational change processes. So, that demands creating a group that has the mandate to drive the change process and to see to that the group work as a team.
3 *Create a vision.* Creating a vision as a source of inspiration and drive for change is often central in change processes. In addition, the organization needs to develop strategies that make the possibility of reaching the vision apparent.
4 *Communicate the vision.* It is central to communicate the vision every time an opportunity to do so emerges. Failing to communicate the vision weakens the chances of keeping the change work alive. That also demands that the guiding coalition act as role model for the kind of behaviour expected of those impacted by the change.
5 *Empower others to act on the vision.* It is also highly significant to get rid of mental and structural barriers that often block the power of the vision and momentum of change work. This demands that one change the systems that undermine the vision for change and encourage some risk-taking and non-traditional activities.
6 *Plan for and create short-term wins.* Many organizations fail to make the results of change visible, and thereby risk losing momentum in the change work. Following that, it is important to emphasize progress early in the process and reward those who achieve quick wins.
7 *Consolidate improvements and produce still more change.* Organizations frequently claim victory too early and thus fail to embed the change work effectively in the organizational culture. Following that it is central to draw upon early wins in order to intensify changes in organizational systems and structures that are seen as blocking changes. It is also important to recruit and promote people who is in favour of the change and that can participate in its implementation. It is also of central importance to revitalize the change continuously through new projects and people.

8   *Institutionalize new approaches*. Organizations regularly fail to entrench the change work in their organizational culture, meaning that to be able to create long-term change it is important to work with also with customers and productivity-oriented behaviour, improved leadership and more effective management. Here it is also suggested that one should make the connection between new behaviour and organizational success more explicit. Also develop means for leadership development and succession.

Successful organizational change draws upon these steps in one way or another according to Kotter, who emphasizes that change takes time and that skipping any of the mentioned steps never produces change.

In a slightly different approach, the significance of organizational culture is stressed (Heracleous 2001; Heracleous and Langham 1996). Based on the cultural web model (see Whittington *et al.* 2020) and the idea that culture can be seen as deeply held assumptions related to espoused beliefs and concrete artefacts, Heracleous argues that change is difficult because of existing cultural assumptions. The taken-for-granted nature of these often precludes them from being problematized and part of the planned change agenda, frequently making change superficial and not lasting. In order to produce lasting change, it is necessary to bring the assumptions to the surface and recognize their expressions and legitimacy in organizational artefacts (or subsystems) such as symbols, power structures, organizational structures, incentives, control systems, communications, rites/routines and stories/myths. The cultural web is suggested as a diagnostic tool for this task (see Figure 2.1).

The cultural web should be employed in a process of five steps (from Heracleous 2001):

1   *Situation analysis*: Where are we now? The cultural web should facilitate understanding of the basic assumptions and beliefs of core business (often historically anchored).
2   *Policy and strategy making*: Where do we want to go? This is to clarify how assumptions and beliefs govern existing strategy when contemplating strategic reorientation or organizational change triggered by some internal or external incident.
3   *Organizational implications*: Which values need to be changed in accordance with new strategy and which do not?
4   *Change management*: focusing the organizational dimensions that should be changed in order to accomplish strategic change.
5   *Monitoring and evaluation*: tracking the progression of ongoing organizational change.

These steps are employed in one study of organizational change in a consultancy firm (Heracleous 2001). Based on changes in the market the firm perceived a need to change strategically and organizationally. To understand their existing culture they made a situation analysis that showed perceptions of a strong professional

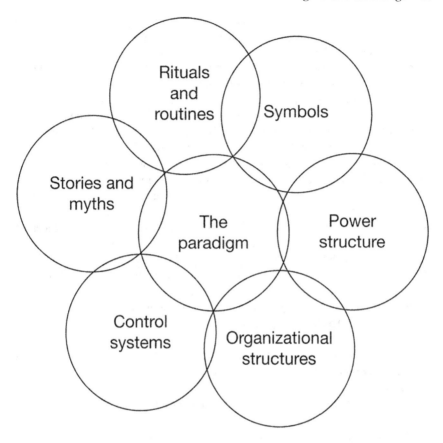

Figure 2.1 A cultural web
Source: Johnson (1987); Whittington *et al.* (2020)

culture based on six assumptions: 1) that the core business was 'job evaluation', 2) a strong client orientation, 3) individualism and high autonomy among the consultants, 4) that change is incremental and consists of mainly institutionalized routine without any deeper organizational effects, 5) that generalist expertise among consultants is significant and 6) that managers take no real decisions nor effect any real changes. These beliefs reinforced each other. The strong belief in individualism and autonomy of consultants meant that managerially proposed changes were seldom followed in practice, but just seen as rhetorical decisions without deeper organizational effect.

However, the cultural web also suggested that, in order to transform the company, most of these assumptions, except for the strong client orientation, had to change. The company needed to 1) pursue an understanding of how to work with integrated human resource services rather than just job evaluation, 2) maintain ideas of its client orientation, 3) complement the idea of high autonomy of consultants with an idea of the productivity of team orientation, 4) establish beliefs that change can be transformational with significant effects on strategy and organization (changes can be substantial), 5) replace the idea of having generalists with an idea of expert consultants in certain areas and 6) install an idea that managers make real decisions with significant organizational effects.

The use of the web for understanding the implications of the proposed changes suggested that these challenged the existing assumptions, beliefs and interconnected artefacts. One issue was the idea that the consultants worked more effectively individually rather than in teams. This idea rested on an assumption that human beings are self-motivated and self-governing and prefer to work individually. This assumption was expressed in the behaviour of the consultants and routines such as the incentive system (individually based), communication (informal), myths (hero consultants and legends who always worked individually) and organization structure (decentralized). Work methodology, recruitment processes, organization structure and incentives were all aligned to the assumption of the significance of individualism, thus strengthening and legitimating these. The cultural web thus showed how assumptions and practices mutually reinforced each other, creating a very tight web that was very difficult to change.

Based on the change management in the case, four themes are suggested by Heracleous (2001) as being important:

- *Visible, active and clear leadership of the change process.* Leaders' actions are highly symbolic and it is suggested in the case that leaders took visible steps towards the new culture by frequent and clear communication, meetings, and personal and group interviews with employees about their attitudes towards the proposed changes.
- *Making it possible for those targeted by the changes to participate in the planning of changes.* It is suggested from the case that many participated in internal projects aimed at improvements of processes and systems. Attention was also paid to integrating small-scale initiatives into the strategic change efforts.
- *Communication facilitating a clear understanding of the change efforts.* The rationale for change was clearly communicated in the case. Employees reportedly understood why they had to change. It is also suggested that communication in meetings and groups addressed the employees' potential concern over the changes in order to motivate participation.
- *Developing new skills.* The most important new role in the case was that of the 'regional team manager', who was responsible for allocation of work, consultant development, coaching, etc.

In particular the authors emphasize the importance of clear managerial communication and encouragement of managers to become role models for desired behaviour. They also emphasize the need to change many practices in order to support the new culture, for example ceasing practices that symbolize individualistic behaviour such as praising individual 'billing achievers' at Christmas parties.

In terms of following change processes closely in order to gain deeper under-standing, the case goes beyond many of the pop-management stories that are based primarily on anecdotal secondary data. But even in ambitious cases there are problems. Even though the authors present a variety of tools for working with change it is difficult to judge whether these contributed to actual cultural change in terms of changing deeper assumptions. The authors claim they saw signs of the unfreezing of the existing culture but we don't know whether this refers to people really loosening up in their traditional sense making about how they work. Even if people comply with certain behaviours such as working in teams, we don't know whether this has any thorough impact on how they think and make sense of their work. It is the deeper meanings rather than surface behaviour that are important. This is a general problem in studies of cultural change. Even when cultural aspects are addressed, they are typically played down in terms of fine-tuned meanings. People's sense making, feelings and experiences are typically not stressed enough since we don't come close to the actual change process. In the case discussed, it is not clear how the changes were communicated and how the consultants involved thought about the suggested changes or how they responded in terms of meaning and significance. Although there is acknowledgement of the cultural issues, the actual change process remains rather elusive regarding the thinking, feeling and acting of those targeted for change.

The planning approach – a critique

Many change models assume that it is possible to control the change process. The process and outcomes of changes are then seen as predictable and susceptible to detailed planning. If a sufficient amount of information is collected and applied in a sequential, stepwise manner, changes will follow. While this logic might explain the popularity of the models it says relatively little about how changes emerge in real-life organizational settings and how people interpret change efforts and relate to these based on their various interests, backgrounds and work tasks (Pettigrew 2012).

Many change models imply a simplistic view of organizations and claim that their models apply for any organization, independent of industry, business, prod-ucts and organizational culture. Some models however suggest that context should be taken into account (see Heracleous and Langham 1996; Tichy 1983), but this is usually reduced to instrumental management tools such as organization structure or management control systems.

Clichés are abundant, as pop-management authors use them frequently in sim-plified recipes for communication, leadership, participation, etc. (Collins 1998). Many of the suggestions may intuitively appear adequate but might not say more than that one should do what seems positive and avoid what seems negative. If one takes Kotter's model (see pp. 27–28), for example, it suggests that one should get rid of obstacles for change and have good leadership, but this should be obvious to anyone. Moreover, the empirical material in the many practitioner-oriented texts is often of anecdotal character and usually disregards the variety of persons involved in the change process, how relations develop or how people make sense of change efforts. Real-life complexities that are connected to change processes are reduced to banal recommendations that hardly help us understand the complexities and depth in change processes.

A difficult circumstance with planned programmes is of course the high failure rate. According to Beer and Nohria (2000, see also Bodell 2022), 'the brutal fact is that about 70% of all change initiatives fail'. This may be an exaggeration and also express a rather naïve view of the failure/success dichotomy– often the outcome is not so clear-cut and there are degrees of success and failure (Hughes 2011, 2016). However, Gleeson (2017) has a point when suggesting that that most change programmes fail to yield benefits proportional to the various resources put into them. People are often tired of trying to engage in yet another change initiative, suggesting that the central reason for failure can be seen as change battle fatigue among employees. Beer and Eisenstat (1996) state that the majority of companies report that neither TQM nor re-engineering efforts live up to the promises made at the outset of the change efforts. These disappointing outcomes are often seen as related to poor implementation. In order to defeat implementation problems and better understand organizational change many writers suggest a rethinking of change as being a continuous process rather than episodic.

The process approach

Partly based on the fact that many programmatic organizational change efforts – informed by rationality ideals – have a tendency to produce failure, there is a growing interest in trying to rethink change as emergent, processual, local and also characterized by continuous learning (Hart 1999). For example, Beer and Nohria (2000) contrast E-type changes – emphasizing economic value – and O-type changes oriented towards organizational capacities. The former changes are characterized as classic planned social engineering with centralized control and focus on structure, systems and financial factors while the latter changes focus on local interpretation, understanding and translation. E-type represents instrumental rationality, while O-type represents a form of OD with emphasis on broad employee participation and commitment (Norbäck and Targama 2009).

The process perspective of change has its roots in social constructionism and can be related to how people understand and make sense of the world. Instead of assuming that people live in an objective, 'ready-made' reality, this perspective emphasizes that people – by making sense – create and sustain understandings of reality. A characteristic of the process approach is the interest in how people interpret a particular change situation and how that interpretation potentially guides their actions (Jabri and Jabri 2022; Weick 1995). Rather than primarily focus on top management and their change ambitions, this approach thus broadens the picture by including a larger number of employees at different organizational levels and by acknowledging that change is a complex process including a variety of different process elements. It is thus important here not only to study the initial managerial change plans and design but also to focus on process elements such as implementation, interaction, reception and outcomes based on the interpretations of those involved in and targeted by the changes (Murdoch and Geys 2014).

It has become more common to talk about organizational change as an open, continuous and unpredictable process, without any clear beginning or ending. Based on this, organizational change is seen as a result of a variety of operational and administrative decisions and actions taken daily by organizational members. These decisions and actions involve the aim of adapting the organization to changes in the environment, or political struggles between departments over what needs to be prioritized in the development of new products, or the advancing of an alternative view of how to work by some organizational members. The process approach takes seriously managerial ambitions to accomplish planned change but acknowledges that executed plans are always modified, reinterpreted and altered in unpredictable ways. As plans are set in motion they blend with many other organizational circumstances (if they take hold at all, that is) rather than operate like the mechanical clockwork according to which a complex organization is governed.

Organizational change seen as processual involves applying an understanding of a complex and chaotic organizational reality. Unforeseen consequences of planned organizational change, resistance, political processes, negotiations, ambiguities, diverse interpretations and misunderstandings are part of this (Balogun *et al.* 2015; Dawson 2003; Pettigrew *et al.* 2001). Based on this organizational change is seen as a continuous process emerging in relations where sense making constitutes a central dimension (Alvesson and Sveningsson 2011a; Stensaker *et al.* 2021). This is in contrast to the idea of changes taking place in specific and well-confined episodes between which organizations remain stable (Jian 2011). Consequently, organizational change is not mainly a matter of carrying out a sequential list of steps.

Sense making, translation and identity

A processual perspective has emerged because of the difficulties in executing ideas according to previously made plans. A central dimension here involves the experiences, feelings and sense making of those mobilized in change processes, something less considered in much of the popular writing on change. Balogun (2006: 43) suggests that 'We need to move away from reifying change as something done to and placed on individuals, and instead acknowledge the role that change recipients play in creating and shaping change outcomes.' By acknowledging local and emergent interpretations, experiences and sense making, a more thorough understanding of the politics, context and substance of change might be gained.

In subsequent chapters we investigate how the content and process of a particular change programme in a technology-intensive firm was locally interpreted and made sense of by a variety of individuals. Interpretation here means taking seriously how people ascribe meaning to a particular phenomenon and find ways of defining and aligning their interests and themselves (and their identities) with others. A way of studying this process is suggested by Latour (1986, 1988, 2005) in talking about movements of ideas and objects as translation.

In explaining a spread or move in time and space of an idea or object, such as a planned change programme, Latour (1986) contrasts a *diffusion* model with a *translation* model. In the diffusion model it is generally assumed that an object, such as a change plan or command, order, wish or claim, is bestowed with an inner force. An object will spread and move according to its initial force, which triggers the move and 'constitute[s] its only energy'. The power of the initial force may lessen because of friction, such as bad communication, or resistance, such as opposition, which can deflect or slow down the initial force (see section on 'Resistance', p. 37). This model fits with and shares the assumptions governing the planned approach to change. Formulate a plan, mobilize resources and switch the button, and the plan will start to execute according to its commands. The focus here is on the initial force behind the movement. A manager makes a decision and subordinates' actions follow like billiard balls that are pushed in irreversible directions. It is typically assumed that the managerial rule is sovereign and shared by subordinates. The latter are seen as passive receivers of their roles and identities (interests) by following the sovereign rule (Callon and Latour 1981). Subordinates' interaction and involvement with a change process are thus seen as a mechanical execution of predefined tasks. People are here expected to behave as what Latour (2005) calls intermediaries, that is people (or things) transporting a force and meaning according to its initial definition. An intermediary is a black box, and 'defining its inputs is enough to define its outputs' (Latour 2005: 39): hence the emphasis on the design and disregard of implementation in the planning approach, although of course considerable initial force (resources, instructions, persuasion, rewards and sanctions) is needed to produce the wanted outputs.

This model is contrasted with a translation model. In this model an object, order, command or change programme will move according to how people actively align with and make sense of the order and command. The move of an object or an element is seen as residing in the hands of individuals, or actors, and their sense making, interest and identity projects. People (or things) are here seen as mediators that 'transform, translate, distort, and modify the meaning or the elements they are supposed to carry' (Latour 2005: 39). A movement of an idea or object is contingent upon how people work with it, how they appropriate and invoke it, and modify and adjust it, and generally how they make sense of it according to their own interests and ambitions, the latter contingent upon sense making (Weick 1995) and identity constructions (Alvesson and Willmott 2002). The idea in this model is that people do something actively with ideas, claims and plans; the chain of individuals is made of actors who shape the ideas, claims and plans according to their different projects such as identity or career progress. Translation thus emphasizes the active transformation of ideas rather than passive transmission as is suggested in the diffusion model. Following the model of translation in our particular case we think it becomes important to understand local interpretation, sense making and active identity positioning in order to understand the dynamics of organizational change. Here inputs – strategies, messages, instructions – are not seen as forces but as inspiration for a kind of series of restarts of the process. What happens with a planned change programme is according to this not primarily a result of the initial force given to the programme but rather the constant renewed energy given to the planned programme by people who do something with it: 'as in the case of rugby players and a rugby ball. The initial force of the first in the chain is no more important than that of the second, or the fortieth' (Latour 1986: 267). Interaction and involvement with a change project are thus contingent upon how one associates and identifies with for example a change programme and its content.

This view of course leads to an interest in following change processes at close range and takes seriously the views – and the language used – of those who somehow become involved in them, something rarely done (Bartunek *et al.* 2006).

The significance of language in change

In recent years much research on organizational change has emphasized the significance of language in change processes. This involves questions of how change occurs – or is opposed and contested – in daily organizational interactions among people and to what extent language, stories and communication in general is significant in planned organizational efforts (Grant and Marshak 2011). Language is here seen not just as a means for expressing thought and ideas but also as something that involves talking and thinking in particular ways (Brown *et al.* 2009). In terms of organizational change this emphasizes the importance of investigating the creation and meaning of stories and narratives in change work. People normally create more or less coherent stories – narratives – of organizational change processes and how they view historic events and the present organizational situation. These stories and narratives both express and form people's sense making and understanding (Brown and Humphreys 2003). Of course, only certain stories become influential and have a wider impact on broader sense-making in an organization. Normally it is more resource-strong individuals whose stories get more air-time in company descriptions, talks, annual reports and media and may dominate. However, these stories are not necessarily shared among many of those involved in change situations, nor do they necessarily influence people very much. Besides the plausibility to the story itself, the status and credibility of the storyteller may also often be quite significant for its impact (Thurlow and Helms-Mills 2015).

Organizational change situations often present some uncertainty about consequences and outcomes and this normally produces sense-making activities among people wanting to explicate and understand – by means of language, narratives and other expressions – their own situation in relation to the changes. This often involves reflections about one's own capacities as well as relationship to the work group and organization at large. Individuals and groups create stories about who one is and what one stands for – about individual, group or organizational identity – in contrast to how one interprets what the organizational change stands for or can be expected to entail (Sörgärde 2006). Occasionally a change idea may present an opportunity to mobilize resistance and make one's own identity more explicit, something that may motivate organizational continuity rather than change. Organizational change processes and its results are thus hardly objective facts but rather different stories created on the basis of different experiences, purposes, career ambitions, background and identity (Thomas *et al.* 2011). The complexity of organizational changes normally permits such storytelling and narrative processes that often also involve power and politics as suggested earlier (Thurlow and Helms-Mills 2015).This includes not only senior managers but also other organizational members experiencing having a stake in a specific change which may potentially influence a process by, for example, spreading rumours, gossiping about people, taking a passive or more active – open or concealed obstructing – position with regards to the changes (Buchanan and Badham 2011).

It is frequently difficult to unambiguously determine the outcomes of specific change processes and most of those involved are most likely eager to construct a positive view of their own efforts, even if the change at large is viewed as less successful (Alvesson and Sveningsson 2011a). Listening to or taking part of only very few individuals' experiences and views – as a participant or as an observer – of a process normally provides a rather limited understanding of the course of a change project (Buchanan and Dawson 2007). This suggests that the understanding of storytelling and language use among a variety of different individuals and stakeholders involved in change work may be a significant part of leading change more effectively, or at least counter some ineffectiveness. We will return to this theme more in depth in the next chapter about organizational culture.

Organizational change work

Given the importance of sense making, interpretation and translation, many suggest securing organizational change by having organizational members take the initiative (cf. experimentation and improvisation), a form of engagement that can be triggered by changes in the environment but also be an outcome of internal changes such as product development, innovations or unexpected developments such as key personnel leaving the organization. The ideal is engaged, motivated and knowledgeable employees who have the confidence to act.

Palmer *et al.* (2022) identify a number of possible positions or images of managers engaged in change work. They proceed from two key dimensions: way of managing and the outcome of change. The former can either be about *controlling*, that is the manager through top-down acts putting a strong imprint on the change work, or about *shaping*, which is more about managers trying to involve people, influence opportunities and provide encouragement. Shaping is close to what many authors refer to as leadership. Change outcomes may be *intended*, that is, there is a strong similarity between goal or ideal and actual outcome, *partially intended*, where aims are reasonably well realized, or *unintended*, that is, the outcome differs from the original goal or image (if there was one). Unintended outcomes may mean failure, but new ideas or initiatives or adaptations to new conditions may lead to positive although unplanned or unimagined results.

Combining the two dimensions means that we get six positions, which Palmer *et al.* (2022: Ch. 2) label in metaphorical terms, as shown in Table 2.1.

The framework is not unproblematic. A change manager wanting and believing in control may be better described as a failed director or navigator with a flawed map

Table 2.1 The six positions

		Ways of managing	
		Controlling	*Shaping*
Image of	Intended	DIRECTOR	COACH
change	Partially intended	NAVIGATOR	INTERPRETER
outcomes	Unintended	CARETAKER	NURTURER

or compass than as a caretaker. This seems to be an unwanted kind of position. One could also argue that most people active in change work mix controlling and shaping elements and that there is a combination of intended and unintended outcomes. As intentions shift over time, this distinction is difficult to maintain. In addition, one can discuss whose image is of interest – particularly as various people involved may have different views of the change manager. But on the whole this framework has its value and we will use it in parts of our discussion. In particular we will draw attention less to the view of the single change manager him or herself, and more to the variety and incoherence of various images held by actors in change projects.

Another view of roles or types argues that different phases of (continuous) change call for different types of managers (or champions) of change during the various phases: evangelists (using influence to sell ideas), autocrats (using authority to change and direct practices), architects (establishing routines and embedding change in technology) and educators (shaping intuition and fuelling the cycle of change in subtle ways on an ongoing basis) (Lawrence *et al.* 2006). The last category is arguably often overlooked:

> The work of educators is perhaps the most overlooked. Evangelists, autocrats and architects all tend to attract significant attention as highly visible proponents of change. In contrast educators often depend on subtlety, leading others to work in ways that indirectly shift their perceptions and understandings.
> (Lawrence *et al.* 2006: 64)

A problem here of course is how to recruit and mobilize such a wide spectrum of people/skills and create a change process involving such disjointed competences, behaviours and personalities. As our own case study will show, the involvement of diverse people is not without its problems.

Resistance

Based on seeing organizational change in terms of the diffusion model, it is common to point out forms of friction that may slow down and obstruct the natural progression of plans and ideas. The focus here is on how people might disobey or deviate from planned change and managerial sovereignty. This is seen as a distortion, or resistance, according to the diffusion model (Callon and Latour 1981; Latour 1986). Resistance can often be the result of a variety of different things

Table 2.2 Common causes of resistance (adapted from Sveningsson and Sörgärde 2023)

Innate dislike of change Low tolerance of uncertainty	Psychological reasons	Resistance towards the substance of change
This is not in my interests Perceived breach of psychological contract	Political reasons	
Perceived ethical conflict Attachment to organizational culture and/or identity	Cultural reasons	
Lack of conviction that change is necessary Lack of clarity as to what is expected Belief that the proposed changes are inappropriate Perception that the timing is wrong Too much change The cumulative effects of other life changes The legacy of past changes	Lack of sense making or readiness for change	
Disagreement with how the change is managed	Resistance towards the process	

depending on perspective and purpose (from Palmer *et al.* 2022; Sveningsson and Sörgärde 2023). Table 2.2 lists some of the common causes of resistance.

The list in Table 2.2 is quite comprehensive and includes many different logics and reasons behind what is understood as resistance by those behind a change initiative. More specifically related to the change discussed in the coming chapters is that resistance may follow from actors having another opinion about what is in the best interest of the organization, and what the nature and ideals of it are that are worth pursuing. According to Sennett (1998) older employees are often more loyal to the firm than to their superiors and may resist the plans of the latter if not seen as serving the firm. It is thus important to avoid treating employees as a group expressing similar interests. Dawson (2003) displays how a group of celebrated and respected workers who resisted a specific change initiative were not only pressed by managers to comply but also isolated by other workers, eventually leading to separation and seclusion. Those resisting the changes were labelled outsiders and their former celebrated behaviour was reinterpreted as deviant and old-fashioned, a process that created conflicts and controversies. Also, geographical work-location can be a source of resistance. In a Nordic oil company, resistance to an organizational change took different forms following two contrasting identity constructions based on location – offshore versus onshore – among employees (Stensaker *et al.* 2021). It is suggested that a better understanding of how the employees made sense of the change efforts based on might have been more productive. Resistance may also be a result of different professional or occupational expressions. People occasionally differentiate quite distinctively between various occupational cultures and identities. Pieterse *et al.* (2012) suggest for example that differences in occupational language use may obstruct communication between groups of employees in change processes. Different ways of expression may cause confusion and trigger negative feelings and a distancing from other groups' ideas and change suggestions.

Techniques used in order to reduce resistance include involving organizational members in the planning of change, generally being open to participation, trying to reduce uncertainty through information and also encouraging experimentation. To be open about one's owns assumptions of change processes, ambitions and expectations of outcomes of change may be one way of trying to reduce friction and resistance – at least a way of trying to clarify contradictions and the positions of resistance among those involved. A focus on the 'obvious facts' may sometimes be too myopic and make it difficult to recognize and focus on the more basic assumptions behind the so-called facts.

A problem in much popularly oriented writings is that those in favour of changes are usually portrayed in a positive light while those less convinced are usually portrayed negatively (Erwin and Garman 2010). Change authors take sides with the corporate elite, often implicitly so. Even if changes are presented as important and necessary there are often reasons to be sceptical. There is a myth about the inherent good in changes just because they are changes. As Wallander (2003) remarks, changes often destroy the intricate network of relations that form an organization and it may take a long time before it is re-created. We discussed earlier how many companies change because others seem to do so but often these changes, or talk about changes, remain at a highly symbolic level without any real or substantial effects. Wishful thinking about what can be accomplished and exaggeration of the need for and possibilities of change are common. So are failed attempts. There are thus good reasons to remain sceptical about the talk of the need for organizational change and be cautious about embarking on all the change trends that regularly crop up. There is a serious risk of producing cynicism and frustration among organizational members if one fails to create something more substantive, sustainable and meaningful.

Resistance is, however, not only or mainly about being directly oppositional to a change initiative. Often people have mixed feelings about new ideas and objectives. They may accept some transformation but resist too drastic changes. They may favour the goals and new proposed arrangements in principle, but in practice find it difficult to implement or work according to these and at various stages in the implementation process prevent the change initiative from materializing or modify it considerably. One interesting example of change efforts concerned the BBC. The objective of top management and external consultants, after pressure from the government, was to restructure this large organization substantively, but only fairly marginal changes were accomplished.

The restructuring projects had been adopted and paid lip service to, but the goals and interests of top and middle managers, their cultural values and situated

practices were too deeply embedded within the BBC not to influence the outcome of the transformation.

(Magala 2005: 44)

Resistance here does not come through as such, but as an ingredient in bend-
ing the change project into accommodation with previous values, practices and
arrangements.

Conclusions

Organizational change is driven by a variety of external and internal conditions
and actors. These do not automatically force change in a particular direction but
are always interpreted by organizational members based on, for example, personal
interests, educational background and perceptions of what is fashionable. Hence,
managers often imitate various organizational trends, promising a lot but unfortunately neglecting real-life complexities. The latter tend to complicate efforts to use
many fashionable ideas.

However, in spite of many change initiatives failing, much writing on change
suggests that it is possible to control change through various forms of planning and
design. The idea of planning organizational change has its roots in ideas of participative and incremental change central in OD. The idea developed into more comprehensive Open Systems models depicting organizations as consisting of a variety
of subsystems that need to be carefully aligned in order to implement organizational change successfully. These models constitute the basis for many of the n-step
guides for change developed in the last twenty years. These rational models are
representative of a social engineering that thrives as long as the models remain
where they are conceived: on the drawing board. If they leave the drawing board
and get set in motion in an organizational setting, a variety of problems occur that
make planned change problematic. A highly significant, but commonly ignored,
circumstance is that people tend to interpret and make sense of change efforts in
quite diverse ways (sometimes this is explained as forms of resistance). Based on
this circumstance it is very difficult to plan and execute change by assuming managerial sovereignty independently of how elaborate the change initiative might seem
for those involved in its design. Those targeted for change often see things differently, and cynicism is not an uncommon reaction (Reichers *et al.* 1997). Change is
thus not quite the neat, apolitical and linear process suggested by the rationalistic
orientation and expressed in the various recommendations to follow a number of
predefined steps as a guide to successful change ('n-step' thinking).

As an alternative, the process approach provides a general framework for understanding the messy and disordered character of organizational change. Broadly
speaking, this approach emphasizes the significance of studying and practising
change from a micro perspective, making it possible to focus in depth on local
interpretation and identity positioning among those participating in change processes. In this approach changes are treated as more or less continuous. Most
research on this approach takes an interest in not only change initiatives formulated

by a managerial elite but also how change is accomplished by all organizational members on a daily basis. This focuses on the complexity and dynamics of organizational change as well as on the political and cultural context within which it takes place.

In the process approach the ideal is to follow individual and collective sense making by those involved as it happens, and how people translate, react to and feel about change initiatives. Uncertainties, confusion, anxieties and feelings of inadequacy surround change work. An important element here is how people relate to change initiatives in terms of their identity positioning, that is, how they understand themselves and their interests as related to the change programme. This focus on identity constructions and sense making constitutes a micro perspective on change that is central to this study, where we follow change processes in depth and in detail.

Note

1　For other reviews see Burke (2018); Collins (1998); Dawson (2003); Hughes (2010); Palmer *et al.* (2022); Pettigrew *et al.* (2001); Preece *et al.* (1999); Sveningsson and Sörgärde (2023); Tsoukas (2005); Weick and Quinn (1999).

3 Organizational culture and change

The term 'organizational culture' has been around since the end of 1970s and the beginning of the 1980s and is still considered to be of key significance for organizational performance and competitiveness (Pathiranage *et al.* 2020). It is understood that organizational culture can either facilitate or obstruct the possibility of implementing strategy and accomplishing change. Cultural change is part of a set of changes: in organizational structure, new ways of enforcing and monitoring behaviour, lay-offs or changes of people in key positions. Basic assumptions are seen as governing behaviour and organizational practices through more visible values and norms that are expressed in various organizational subsystems as rituals, organization structure, leadership and management control systems. One view of cultural change is everyday reframing, which is mainly an informal, ongoing, culture-shaping agenda, involving pedagogical leadership in which an actor exercises a subtle influence through the renegotiation of meaning. Local initiatives are also frequently constrained by broader organizational culture as well as by relations of power.

The somewhat exaggerated view of the significance of organizational culture for performance and change that was common in the 1980s and 1990s has since been revised substantially, although there is agreement that organizational culture remains a central aspect behind a range of organizational topics such as commitment and motivation, prioritization and resource allocation, competitive advantage and change (Nikpour 2017; Pathiranage *et al.* 2020). It is often understood that organizational culture can either facilitate or obstruct the possibility of implementing strategy and accomplishing change (Ibarra 2020). As seen from the previous chapter, organizational culture is often seen as one, sometimes the most significant, element in organizational change efforts, including in those cases where culture is not directly targeted for change.

A problem in much of the literature on organizational culture is that the potential value of the culture concept easily disappears behind rather thin and superficial descriptions. Organizational cultural characterizations are often used as slogans, wishful thinking and fantasies rather than as a way of gaining a deeper understanding of organizational life. It is very common among managers and others to characterize the organization as unique and special but then to characterize it in simple and standardized terms such as 'We are customer- [or market-]

DOI: 10.4324/9781003474555-4

oriented'; 'We are leaders in digitalization'; 'We treat employees with respect and see them as our most valuable asset'; 'We provide excellent service'; 'We are an agile organization'; 'We are in favour of change'; and 'We support sustainable development.' These are vague and sweeping expressions. Sometimes they mean something; often they don't. Organizational culture can be difficult to get a grip on; the phenomenon doesn't lend itself to measurement. Characterizing and understanding culture normally requires good language skills – people often tend to get stuck in the aforementioned rather clumsy and insipid terms. They lead to a kind of 'pseudo-meaning' – a misleading feeling of saying something.

Understanding also requires not only distinctiveness but also a certain degree of imagination and creativity. Dimensions of cultural analysis focus on lived experiences and representations, implying a focus on people, relations, meaning and emotions, while things like systems and structures are seen as secondary. Many aspects of culture are often taken for granted and therefore particularly difficult to capture. We usually become aware of our own culture when confronting alternative cultures. This is sometime referred to as breakdowns in understanding – frustrating but also providing an occasion for learning and enrichment (Agar 1986).

In this chapter we initially elaborate briefly on organizational culture and relate this to some ideas and problems of organizational change as discussed in the previous chapter. We then review specifically some ideas on organizational change and, in relation to that, discuss two views of how organizational culture change is accomplished. Finally, we discuss how culture change is related to substantive changes.

What is organizational culture?

When talking about culture we usually think of people sharing something, whether this sharing refers to traditions of doing and thinking in particular ways or systems of meanings or basic assumptions governing people in certain directions. In the variety of culture studies conducted in the last thirty years in organizational research, a broad array of definitions of organizational culture have been produced and most of these definitions connect to some form of shared meaning, interpretations, values and norms. It is common to talk of the following seven characteristics when referring to culture (Hofstede *et al.* 1990):

- Culture is holistic and refers to phenomena that cannot be reduced to single individuals; culture involves a larger group of individuals.
- Culture is historically related; it is an emergent phenomenon and is conveyed through traditions and customs.
- Culture is inert and difficult to change; people tend to hold on to their ideas, values and traditions.
- Culture is a socially constructed phenomenon; culture is a human product and is shared by people belonging to various groups. Different groups create different cultures, so it is not human nature that dictates culture.

- Culture is soft, vague and difficult to catch; it is genuinely qualitative and does not lend itself to easy measurement and classification.
- Terms such as 'myth', 'ritual', 'symbols' and similar anthropological terms are commonly used to characterize culture.
- Culture most commonly refers to ways of thinking, values and ideas of things rather than the concrete, objective and more visible part of an organization.

Accordingly, culture does not refer to social structures and behaviour but in contrast to mental phenomena such as how individuals within a particular group think about and value their reality in similar ways and how this thinking and valuing is different from that of people in different groups (occupations, tribes, etc.). Culture refers to what stands behind and guides behaviour rather than the behaviour as such (Bate 1994; Geertz 1973; de Rond *et al.* 2019).

Smircich (1983a) organized the cultural research in two broad directions, one drawing upon culture as a variable and the other drawing upon culture as a root metaphor. Research treating culture as a variable sees organizational culture as something the organization has, while the root metaphor refers to culture as something the organization is. Bate (1994: 12) suggests that culture 'is a label or metaphor *for*, not a component *of*, the total work organization'. Here organizations are cultures (as well as systems, machines, organisms, etc.): 'Organizations exist as systems of meanings which are shared to various degrees. A sense of commonality, or taken for grantedness is necessary for continuing organized activity so that interaction can take place without constant interpretation and re-interpretation of meaning' (Smircich 1985: 64).

A slightly different view from this is taken by Schein (1985), who developed a fairly influential model of organizational culture consisting of three interrelated levels.

The governing *assumptions* constitute the core of the organizational culture and consist of taken-for-granted beliefs about the nature of reality, the nature of the organization and its relations to the environment, the nature of human nature, the nature of time and the nature of people's relations to each other. The governing assumptions are the beliefs that guide everyday thinking and action in organizations. On a more conscious level are what Schein refers to as the *values* and norms that prescribe how the organization should work. This refers to principles, objectives and codes that the organization values as significant. Norms and values that guide behaviour effectively can over time become taken for granted and an aspect of the less visible governing assumptions. At the most concrete levels are the expressions for the governing assumption, what Schein terms artefacts, such as physical, behavioural and verbal manifestations, some of which becomes very entrenched in daily organizational life, what Ibarra (2020: 13) refers to as 'iconic practices'. In Schein's cultural model the various levels influence each other mutually. While governing assumptions expressed in norms, for example, influence, Schein also suggests that new forms of behaviour and new norms could change the governing assumptions over time. Schein's model thus opens up the possibility of analysing how deeper assumptions and beliefs are interconnected to espoused values and organizational symbolic and material artefacts, as was discussed in Chapter 2 in regard to Heracleous and Langham's (1996) analysis of change in a consultancy firm. As was suggested, cultural change is difficult to accomplish since it usually requires, at minimum, that the normally hidden and less conscious assumptions are made explicit and targeted. Basic assumptions are here seen as governing behaviour and organizational practices through more visible values and norms that are expressed in various organizational subsystems as rituals, organization structure, leadership and management control systems.

While Schein's model is inclusive and broad in terms of the various levels of analysis, we will apply a perhaps somewhat stricter view of organizational culture involving construction of meaning and sense making. This way of looking at culture also includes how organizational culture is expressed in terms of language, stories and rituals (Thurlow and Helms-Mills 2015).

Language, stories and rituals

It is often understood that people ascribe a subjective meaning to everything non-trivial they meet. Feelings, fantasy, emotions and expressions of belief that affect people are central elements in this. Culture can be seen as that which is created and sustained through shared experiences by the use of shared symbols. In economics it is common to talk about Homo economicus, but the culture theorist would rather talk about Homo symbolicus. The latter points towards topics such as beliefs, values and symbols rather than rational economic calculation. If we take high salaries, for example, one can say that those who adhere to the idea of Homo economicus would suggest that this is a matter of buying power, while culture researchers would point to its symbolic value. The symbolic value is here connected to how one looks at oneself in terms of status and self-esteem. Culture is expressed in behaviour and can be seen in actions, events and other material aspects but does not refer to these exterior elements per se but to the meaning and beliefs these have for people. Culture is thus behind and beneath behaviour.

Culture is expressed in language, stories and myths as well as in rituals and ceremonies and in physical expressions such as architecture and actions. In terms of language one can say that different vocabularies used in organizations express and shape different organizational cultures. Even slogans can be important to the extent that they can signal what the company stands for, if they are shared among the organizational members. An IT company, for example, had a slogan that said 'fun and profit', signalling that the result, as well as having a positive workplace climate and experiencing enjoyment at work, was seen as important in the firm (Alvesson 1995). The risk that such expressions becomes empty jingles that make employees react negatively is significant (cf. Fleming 2005) but in this IT company people took it quite seriously, suggesting it had an influential effect as well as expressing a common feeling of the 'soul' of the organization and guiding managers and subordinates across a variety of situations.

Stories can also be important in that they can convey values, ideas and beliefs. They commonly circulate in organizations and can give clues about how to think and act in various circumstances. It is also increasingly common among organizations to hire people as storytellers, the title Chief Storyteller is a rather popular development in many industries for new hires or as part of line managers' job descriptions. For example, at Nike some senior executives are titled Corporate Storytellers as they are expected to tell a story of the founder of Nike, Phil Night. Storytelling often works to maintain or reproduce organizational culture, but can also be vital in change work. Buchanan and Badham (2020) observe that leaders of various kinds draw from a well-established 'storytelling catalogue' in order to: *spark action* by telling 'springboard stories'; *generate trust* by communicating who you are through personal narratives; *transmit values* through parables in order to ingrain new codes of conduct, and remove destructive behaviours; *foster collaboration* by using an emotive 'trigger' story to help stimulate others to create and listen to their own stories; and *tame the grapevine* by developing counter-stories to show the incongruity of destructive rumours. Of course, stories can't accomplish anything and are often difficult to craft and tell in a convincing way, but are still key part of organizations – and as part of organizational culture they are important sources of resistance to change.

Another form of cultural expression is rituals, carefully staged and executed in order to create a certain atmosphere and to express the right values and ideas. Meetings can often be quite ritualistic, as can specific work practices that people have got used to and provide them with a sense of security and predictability. When Jean-Philippe Courtois took charge of sales and marketing at Microsoft in 2016, he wanted to change what he saw as the company's inspection culture to a more learning and coaching culture. In terms of practices and rituals, the inspection culture included presenting yourself as always having the right answer to all kinds of detailed questions and providing impressions of always being the smartest person in the room. This culture also meant never admitting any mistakes or failure under inspection from others, typically superiors. An old-style mastery of details based culture going back to the days of Bill Gates. In contrast, Courtois aimed at developing a learning and coaching culture that could facilitate Microsoft's move into partly new terrain of increased digitalization and cloud engagement. This move suggested an organizational culture that encouraged experimentation and asking questions about how to tackle different challenges without knowing everything in detail or feeling it necessary to provide the impression of being knowledgeable about everything. Courtois talked about moving from a kind of knowing-it-all culture to a culture of learning-it-all. Embarking on the change Courtois initially restructured the sales force, changed the compensation scheme and also implemented a variety of digital tools to be used by employees in their daily work. However, most of those structural changes didn't seem to change the mindset of people and how they understood the work – the organizational culture – as people still clung on to the inspection culture of always having the right answer and providing the impression of being the smartest person in the room.

Following those ponderings Courtois related the strength of the old culture to a particular practice at Microsoft, the annual review meeting among managers known as the January midyear review. This meeting represented perhaps the most visible manifestation of the inspection culture. The January meeting was said to have a fear impact on people and it was generally looked upon as a kind of examination meeting where managers were judged personally rather than for what they could contribute. People were said to prepare for the meeting weeks in advance and it usually took up all the energy long before Christmas. The meeting was a kind of ceremony that drained valuable resources for weeks and installed a large amount of fear in people. Upon evaluating the significance of this annual ceremony for the maintenance of the inspection culture, Courtois concluded that he needed to kill the ritual and rather focus company meetings on learning and development. This resulted in meetings that came to be called quarterly business connections, a sort of shorter and more interactive session focusing on asking questions without any prefabricated answers and with a focus on learning. According to Ibarra (2020: 14):

> Leaders were encouraged to behave more like coaches than inspectors, asking questions like: 'What are you trying? What's working? What's not working? How can we help?' In the Europe, Middle East, and Africa region alone, one of Courtois's managers calculated that they saved 4,000 hours of preparation – in their view, time better spent with customers and employees.

Although difficult to evaluate in detail the case seemingly suggests that working with structural everyday means such as killing a ritual – with extraordinary symbolic value – may trigger changes with broader cultural consequences.

Subcultures and identity

We have discussed culture as something that provides coherence of meaning among a group of individuals. However, it is also important to take cultural variety, differentiation and fragmentation seriously.

Cultural variety and differentiation

It is not unusual among writers on culture to assume coherent organizations where all organizational members share a similar kind of unique value. This is a rather fragile assumption, however, since different groups in organizations usually express different values. People hardly interpret everything in organizations similarly, partly because organizations are characterized by a rather complex differentiation of work tasks, divisions, departments and hierarchical levels that potentially also foster strong differences in terms of meanings, values and symbols. In addition, organizations inhabit a variety of generations, genders, classes, departments and occupational groups that produce and sustain cultural variety and fragmentation rather than overall organizational cultural unity and coherence (Alvesson 2013; Martin 2002; Van Maanen and Barley 1984).

Thus, there are good reasons to be a bit sceptical towards the idea of an overall and uniting organizational culture. Indeed, the concept of culture is often used to refer to top management beliefs of organizational culture (ideas of a specific culture can often be seen as a senior management subculture) that marginalize the (sometimes contrasting) meaning creation of other groups in an organization. It is possible of course that management, more than others, influences meaning making and the formation of values and ideas in an organization but much of what managers do and say might also be left unnoticed in many cases, not least in circumstances of planned change, as was seen in Chapter 2. Occasionally cultural efforts produce negative reactions. In a call centre where the management in a paternalistic manner tried to form a playful, warm and personal spirit many of the employees interpreted the efforts as if they were treated as children. The employees turned against the idea of taming the company into what they saw as a kind of kindergarten (Fleming 2005).

Organizational culture and identity

The extent to which organizational members identify with the organization is important for whether a more distinct organizational culture emerges. What is important here is whether the organization is experienced as being distinct or not and whether it stands for anything unique in terms of style, orientation, history, etc., that is, whether the organization is perceived as having a salient and significant identity (Gioia *et al.* 2013). Conditions that affect the degree to which organizational members identify with an organization include (Ashforth and Mael 1989):

- *how distinct the values of a particular group are*: more distinct values may potentially provide for a more distinct identity;
- *the status that is connected to a particular group*: higher status offers more attraction;
- *how salient other groups are*: a more salient 'other' provides for the construction of a more salient 'we';
- *the presence of social processes that sustain the creation of groups*: more interpersonal interaction, experienced similarity and common goals or history offer a more distinct identity.

Hence, an organization that is distinct in terms of material practices (production, localization), symbolic expressions (architecture, slogans, logotypes) and values and that is also experienced as successful, unique and distinct from its environment, and sustains interpersonal interaction, provides a specific social identity for its members. A requirement here is that the organization is seen in a positive light. To the extent that an organization (as identity) is a significant source for identity work, people tend to view themselves as part of an overall 'we' and experience unity and closeness with the whole organization. If the organizational identity is ambiguous and less pronounced people tend to look for (in relation to the whole organization) alternative sources of identity, such as a department, project, specific work tasks or professional affiliation. It is not uncommon to identify oneself with hierarchical status (top, middle or bottom) or department (production or marketing) rather than the whole organization, the latter often being a more abstract and ambiguous entity. This sustains the emergence of subcultures and further fragmentation of an organization. It should also be noted that there is a more problematic – or darker – side of organizational identification and culture, as it can foster problematic outcomes such as, for example, narcissism, burnouts, ingroup bias, tribalism, identity conflicts, confusion and so on (Caprar *et al.* 2022). Some appear to some extent also in the study we present in this book.

Organizational identity is thus closely related to organizational culture. Some suggest that culture is more of a context, implicit and emergent, while identity, as related to culture, is more language oriented, explicit and more directly emphasized (Hatch and Schultz 2002). Perceptions among organizational members that an organization stands for something unique and positive in terms of identity can increase the inclination to appropriate common organizational values and meanings, i.e. organizational culture. One can also say, however, that a common organizational culture can sustain a distinct organizational identity. Distinct values, ideas and symbols can provide for a common identity even if the orientation of the business is more blended and lacks uniqueness.

Organizational cultural change

A large part of research and writings on organizational culture has addressed organizational change. Some people seem to think that organizational culture is of interest to the extent that it is possible to intentionally and systematically change it. Quite a lot of energy has been put into answering the question: can organizational culture be managed and changed?

Three views

There is a wide spectrum of positions around the possibilities of managing culture, that is, for management being able to have a strong, systematic, intended influence on the values, beliefs, ideas and meanings of the subordinates, including being able to change culture. Broadly, three views on the manageability of organizational culture can be identified. One is that organizational culture, at least under certain conditions and with the use of sufficient skills and resources, can be changed by top management. (This corresponds with what Palmer *et al.* (2022) see as the director, navigator and coach images, as presented in Chapter 2.) A second view is that this is very difficult. As indicated earlier, there is a multitude of values and meaning-influencing groups, and 'depth' structures are not easily accessible for influencing. People do not respond predictably to efforts to change their orientations. Still, change takes place and management is one resourceful group exercising influence. One could therefore assume that senior managers exercise a moderate influence on some values and meanings under certain circumstances such as in the case of Microsoft discussed where changing meeting rituals triggered larger change (Ibarra 2020). (This would resemble the interpreter image of the change manager.) A third view emphasizes that culture is beyond control. How people create meaning in their work experiences is related to local culture,

contingent upon educational background, work tasks, group belonging and interpersonal interactions, etc. This means that senior actors' efforts to exercise influence will often have limited impact and will typically be reinterpreted, so that
intended and received meanings may not overlap (Ogbonna and Wilkinson 2003:
1154). (This would push managers to positions corresponding to the caretaker and
nurturer images, as reviewed in Chapter 2.)

So far there are different views on the questions of whether organizational culture can be changed and whether top management can change organizational culture. One may say that this a matter for going out and investigating change efforts
and their consequences. However, there is no easy answer to the question for a
variety of reasons.

One is that the answer is in the question, in the sense that what a person means
by culture will give quite different possible answers. If one views organizational
culture as a matter of 'deep structures', associated with basic assumptions (Schein
1985) or sacred values and beliefs (Gagliardi 1986), then it is very tricky indeed
to change culture in a predictable way. This is also the case if culture is viewed
as a rich, holistic and integrated net of meanings and symbolism (Alvesson 2013;
Geertz 1973; Smircich 1983a, 1983b). But if one defines culture somewhat more
superficially and narrowly, then it becomes a more open matter what will happen
if top management or another powerful group tries to affect the values, norms and
understandings of organizational members.[1]

Another problem concerns the difficulties of studying cultural changes in organizations. Culture is a phenomenon difficult to grasp and study – it calls for in-depth
interpretations which typically take a long time. Studying the effects of change
programmes is not easy, as it would, in principle, call for two in-depth studies
at different periods. Another difficulty is that, as indicated earlier, it is frequently
difficult to sort out cultural change from material and behavioural changes. Often
cultural change is part of a set of changes: in organizational structure, new ways of
enforcing and monitoring behaviour, lay-offs or changes of people in key positions.
Behavioural changes may reflect heightened surveillance and instrumental compliance rather than changes in values and meanings (Ogbonna and Wilkinson 2003).
In Heracleous and Langham's (1996) study of change, as discussed in Chapter 2, it
was difficult to judge whether the changed norms and behaviour also reflected an
actual change in basic assumptions and beliefs. Frequently it is difficult to sort out
what is revised talk – perhaps reflecting a desire to look good as a loyal employee
or a kind of surface adaptation – from revised values and beliefs.

Cases of cultural change in very large organizations are spectacular and receive a
lot of attention, but are often especially problematic. Illuminating top management
efforts to manage or change an organization of several thousand people, belonging
to a large number of different groups, calls for a rather broad-brush approach. It is
very difficult to say anything about what actually happens and how meanings are
transformed, as this takes place in a variety of different specific contexts that tend
to form various subcultures. There is sometimes a tendency for organizations to be
treated more or less as unitary wholes and almost exclusively from a top management perspective. Simple stimulus – response thinking, in line with the diffusion

model discussed in Chapter 2, is common: management makes an intervention and the organization responds.

An illustration is given by Brown (1995), who reports a mini-case of 'culture change at Nissan'. Nissan, one of the world's largest manufacturers of cars, ran into problems at the beginning of the 1980s, mainly owing to economic causes, but to some extent also owing to deteriorating labour – management relations. A new CEO put forward the motto that 'Management and the labour union should both discharge their duties properly.' He encouraged a downplaying of hierarchical relations and a stronger focus on the marketplace. He made attempts to improve communication and encouraged all employees to address each other as 'Mr' or 'Ms', regardless of rank, which was a break with an earlier practice of using titles in communication. He also removed pattern-maintaining symbols such as the wearing of uniforms by female employees and introduced flexible working hours.

The interesting thing is, however, how people reacted – how they interpreted the changes – and whether the changes led to anything other than behavioural compliance. The case does not address this. A cultural change is not when management tries to impose new behaviours (or talk), but a change of the ideas, values and meanings of large groups of people. Whether addressing other people as 'Mr' or 'Ms' led to a softening-up of rank-related interactions and understandings, or not, is impossible to say without thoroughly listening to various people encouraged – or forced – to adopt this new habit. But it is uncertain to what extent even this can accurately evaluate whether their ideas and values have changed or not. Part of the problem is that trying to grasp cultural change in a heterogeneous company with 100,000 employees is difficult. The sheer size and heterogeneity of the object of study make it difficult to avoid trivializing organizational culture.

There are, however, some studies looking at outcomes of cultural change projects.

The possibility of intended cultural change

Although cultures are always, at least in contemporary 'late capitalistic society', in motion, intentional and systematic organizational cultural change is a difficult project. In pop-management writings, there is much optimism, but most reflective writers treating this topic downplay the chances of intended large-scale cultural change (Brown 1995; Fitzgerald 1988; Lundberg 1985; Ogbonna and Wilkinson 2003). Cultural manifestations shared by a larger collective constitute a very heavy counterweight to the possibilities of a top figure exercising influence on people's thinking and feelings. Such a task is of course severely constrained by the rich variety of work conditions, group identifications and commitments producing cultural differentiation and fragmentation in most organizations (Van Maanen and Barley 1985). There are also cultural constraints, held not only by a large number of the employees, but also by many top executives themselves, especially those promoted from within. Much reasoning on cultural changes takes the position of how to change 'it' (the organizational culture) or 'them' (the masses), but rarely asks the question of how we should change 'us', that is, top management and staff.

There are a number of studies of cultural change initiatives. Siehl (1985) found that a new manager's efforts to change values in the organization studied had no major effects that could be registered, although they did influence the expression of values. Such an impact on the level of the espoused rather than on the 'deeper' level is probably the most common.

Ogbonna and Wilkinson (2003) noted that most studies focused on low-level workers, especially shop floor workers. Their study focused on middle managers, viewed as central, both as a group whose values and convictions are crucial for what is happening in an organization and a group expected to persuade others. Important questions are then: how do middle managers respond to cultural change programmes and how do they act and communicate to their subordinates based on their reception of the change messages? In the change programme studied, the intention was to introduce a new management style and organizational culture characterized by openness, delegation, learning, cooperation, trust and mutual exchange. The findings suggested that the managers studied were at best ambivalent about the culture change programme. They were positive to the new values, such as openness in communication and greater involvement of subordinates, but also expressed fear about increased policing from headquarters. Changes in action seemed at times to reflect changed convictions, but probably even more often the result of heightened surveillance. It is concluded that the presence of a variety of different beliefs about the intentions behind change initiatives can result in 'attempts to impose top management derived values on employees are fraught with difficulties and unintended consequences' (Ogbonna and Wilkinson 2003: 1171).

Ogbonna and Harris (1998: 286) found in their study of an organizational culture change project in a large UK food retail firm 'considerable and significant variance' amongst organizational members who reinterpreted and reinvented the espoused values communicated by top management. While top management emphasized that the change was about developing 'a more customer-focused organization', store managers thought it was mainly about reducing their numbers and power, and many shop floor workers believed the new conditions and practices were introduced in order to increase their exploitation. Whilst the various views were not in direct conflict, the authors conclude, 'it seems inherently logical that there is serious potential for unintended consequences hampering change efforts'.

According to these researchers, efforts to change culture 'frequently degenerate into changes to behaviour, commonly leaving higher levels of culture untouched' (Ogbonna and Harris (1998: 274). People often respond in an ambiguous way to a cultural change programme – accepting to some extent new messages, but also being suspicious about the relationship between new espoused values and various intentions not fully in line with or even deviating from these.

A senior middle manager in a large high-tech company, interviewed by us in another context than the one reported in this book, expressed her experiences of the possibilities of radical change as follows:

I believe that change must come from both directions, i.e. there must be an organization that is mature; there must be people who are affirmative and open in their organization; there must be a clear will amongst managers. A will amongst the employees alone, or the affirmation of the organization and a will amongst managers, is not sufficient.

This makes sense. Cultural change calls for receptiveness amongst the collective for new ideas, values and meanings. Without such openness – which may be facilitated by cultural changes in the society, business or occupation or by a growing awareness of fundamental problems in the organization – cultural change is very difficult. Some shared notion of problems and feelings of significance and urgency is probably necessary for radical change.

Views of organizational culture change

It is common to talk of accomplishing organizational culture change in terms of either a grand plan according to which the changes are engineered or a locally grounded, more emergent process.

Change as a grand technocratic project

The most popular view in the literature, and probably what most people have in mind when thinking about cultural change, is the view of change as a grand technocratic project (Alvesson 2013), akin to the rationalistic versions of planned organizational change as seen in Chapter 2. Most descriptive and even more normative models of large-scale cultural change are of this type (see reviews in, for example, Brown 1995). It portrays or promises the possibility of an intentional large-scale transformation from a particular cultural situation to another, more superior and profitable one, although it is recognized that this is not easy and often takes place slowly. It is this way of looking at cultural change that those investigated in this book embarked upon.

The overall plan for accomplishing this is often a version of the following general scheme:

Step 1: evaluating the situation of the organization and determining the goals and strategic direction;
Step 2: analysing the existing culture and sketching a desired culture;
Step 3: analysing the gap between what exists and what is desired;
Step 4: developing a plan for developing the culture;
Step 5: implementing the plan;
Step 6: evaluating the changes and new efforts to go further and/or engaging in measures to sustain the cultural change.

The common means for accomplishing cultural change seem to be a combination of the following ingredients:

• new recruitment and selection procedures so that people supportive of a desired culture will be hired, sometimes combined with laying off and/or replacing people;
• new forms of socialization and training programmes to signal the desired values and beliefs;

- performance appraisal systems in which the culturally correct ways of being and behaving are rewarded and encouraged;
- promotion of people expressing and symbolizing the desired culture;
- leadership which communicates cultural values in talk, actions and material arrangements, for example vision talk and for-public-consumption acts by the top manager;
- the use of organizational symbols – language (slogans, expressions, stories), actions (use of meetings in a ritual way, the visible use of managers' time to signal what is important) and material objects (corporate architecture, logo-type, dress code).

A more process-oriented view is expressed by Beer (2017), who advocates 'seven sub-principles for organizational change':

1   Mobilize energy for change such as when leaders articulate challenging goals, standards of behaviour or expose employees to model organizations.
2   Develop a new compelling direction by facilitating discussions in managements teams in order to arrive at understandings about what such directions means.
3   Identify organizational barriers to implementing the new direction. For example, identify resistance and other barriers such as unclear strategies, conflicting priorities, poor coordination in different directions and inadequate leadership.
4   Develop a task-aligned vision. Based on identifying barriers to change managers must also design an encouraging vision for employees, something that inspires and encourage.
5   Communicate and involve people in implementation. Articulate links between existing and new competitive realities and the new organization may that enable commitment to the changes.
6   Support behaviour change such as developing the needed skills and attitudes. For example, coach individuals in order to facilitate development and identification with change direction.
7   Monitor progress and make further changes. Regard change as a learning process in need of constant focus and monitoring.

According to this view, culture change is a project emerging from and run from above. It is assumed that top management is the agent from which superior insight about the needed change emerges and also the chief architect behind the plan for change. Apart from planning and allocation of resources to change projects and making decisions in line with the desired change, the dramaturgical acts of senior executives – public speeches and highly visible acts drawing attention to the ideals – also symbolize the reframing of how people should think, feel and act in accordance with the new ideals and values. Consultants are frequently used to back up senior managers in this kind of change project.

These kinds of recipes can be described as n-step models, as the models are similar but differ in the number of steps the successful change manager is supposed to take.

Limitations with the grand technocratic project – a critique

Connecting to the discussion on organizational change, one can say that the models of culture change such as Beer's try to compensate for the mechanical orientation typically characterizing n-step guides in that they acknowledge that people's thinking and mental programming are important in order to accomplish change more effectively. Change management must accordingly include the problem of changing people's beings in addition to their behaviour. But, as discussed, this might require a more sophisticated understanding of the existing culture (and subcultures) and how people see themselves in organizations. The latter often produces variety since there are significant organizationally internal differences in terms of values, beliefs and symbolism based on the diversity of groups associated with organizational differentiation between divisions, departments, occupations and hierarchical levels that often produce and sustain cultural differentiation and sometimes conflict rather than integration. Research has also shown that the cultural patterns in organizations are often fluctuating, inconsistent and ambiguous rather than clear, consistent and unambiguous, partly as a result of the interplay between various subcultures. Authors talk about a fragmentation or ambiguity view on culture (Martin 2002). This suggests caution in addressing culture as a homogeneous object which can be changed through the employment of a homogeneous set of messages and practices. It is likely that these will trigger unexpected and diverse responses, in particular in complex organizations with a diversity of occupations and units with partly different histories and orientations.

Considering these features it is clear that managers and other change agents do not easily impose their ideas of how to think and what to accomplish on others. As framed by Ackroyd and Crowdy (in Collins 1998: 126): 'The findings of a good deal of case study work in industry, and particularly that with an ethnographic or an anthropological focus, have suggested that cultures are highly distinctive, resilient and resistant to change.'

But, as said earlier, this does not mean that managers have no influence over organizations. Organizations do change and there are good reasons to believe that managers, as a resource-strong group, do have an impact on the direction of changes, although in a more complex and multifaceted way than previously suggested.

Cultural change as the reframing of everyday life

Another view of cultural change is everyday reframing (Alvesson 2013). This connects to the view of leadership as the management of meaning (Smircich and Morgan 1982). This is more about local initiative than a big, grand project in which what is perceived as an inferior state is transformed to a superior one through the heroic acts of top management, assisted by consultants and other managers.

Everyday reframing tends to be driven by one or a few senior actors, frequently a manager, but informal authorities and small groups of people may also be central. It is most typically mainly incremental and informal, for example, not clearly espoused or signalled as a project or a campaign with a set of distinct activities which are supposed to accomplish a predefined ideal. It is a matter of local cultural change. The actors engaged in everyday reframing regularly influence the people they directly interact with, although this may create wider effects as these people in the next instance may affect those they interact with (Bate 1994; Ibarra 2020). Everyday reframing is mainly an informal, ongoing, culture-shaping agenda, involving pedagogical leadership in which an actor exercises a subtle influence through the renegotiation of meaning.

Local initiatives are also frequently constrained by broader organizational culture as well as by relations of power (van Marrewijk *et al.* 2010). Everyday reframing is, on the other hand, strongly anchored in interactions and 'natural' communication. It is also better adapted to the material work situations of people and thus has stronger action implications. It means that there is analytic depth in terms of making clear the meanings and interpretations involved. Compared with the frequently rather lofty and managerially idealistic ambitions of efforts to transform a whole large organization, everyday reframing has a potential 'realism' and a better connectedness to the level of meaning. For the large majority of managers not at the top of large organizations, everyday reframing is often a more relevant mode of cultural change than being mobilized as implementers of grand projects. It calls for creativity, stamina, insights into one's own beliefs, values and ideas, communicative skills and some courage and will in making sacrifices, as drawing attention to and underscoring certain ideas and conditions may call for paying less attention to others, for example if one wants creativity and learning then one cannot emphasize quality and short-term efficiency consistently and strongly, as new ideas and experimentations will usually involve some errors and additional resources.

Combining the grand and the local

In order to understand organizational-level, planned cultural change efforts it is probably necessary to address both designed programmes and the overall change practices, on the one hand, and the local (in)actions and influencing processes that guide the meaning making that ultimately determines the belief in the communicated values, ideals and understandings. One can imagine a top management initiative that inspires, legitimizes and supports local initiatives and change work. This would call for tolerance for local discretion rather than top management insisting on a carefully defined content or form of working with culture. One could also imagine a local initiative being picked up by top management, trying to use this as an exemplar for a broader programme, in which the diffusion of the local initiative would be a key source of inspiration.

One may of course not totally rule out the option of a broad, organizational-level project with limited local variation being pushed on or more voluntarily gaining foothold in the whole organization, as assumed in the grand projects idea. People may broadly buy the message – interpret this is in similar ways – and fairly uniformly let this affect thinking and acting. One may also imagine local initiatives not necessarily coming into contact with senior levels or large segments of an organization. Units and groups may be loosely connected to other parts and may develop local cultures. But we believe that in most cases there is an interaction, and in order to understand grand-scale change programmes, which is the focus of this book, it is typically important to consider what is happening at the local level and what kind, if any, of everyday reframing takes place. Without local initiative (and thus some variation within the organization), top manager-initiated cultural change is probably difficult.

Power

Accomplishing change is very much a matter of power and politics. This is neglected or marginalized by authors having a technocratic, planning mindset as well as people focusing on learning and cognitions, seeing cultural change as transformations of meanings and values. Both approaches tend to assume consensus. Often there are various interests and priorities at stake in change work. Material interests (resource allocations), status, identity, preferences and more or less demanding and challenging pressures to change mindsets and work practices are part of organizational changes. Organizations are, in addition to everything else, political arenas, and various groups aim for maximizing their individual or group interests or they at least are eager to protect themselves from moves from other groups or general changes that may be perceived as harmful in one way or another. Also changes that may seem uncontroversial and broadly benefitting most people may be perceived differently by various groups. Often initiatives and 'developments' may lead to time-consuming or emotional pressures on various groups. HRM initiatives around equity, diversity and inclusion or well-being may not be viewed positively by managers supposed to implement activities or see employees spending time in training on issues they view as unimportant and competing with a focus on deliveries. Leadership development programs may benefit units and consultants that can expand their work and influence, but engineers or sales-oriented people concerned with core work may be resisting these programs and have doubts of the value of the learning. Increased customer orientation may be presented and at a superficial level applauded as a generally good thing in everybody's interest, but may in everyday life be more embraced by marketing people than the rest of the organizations more inclined to give priority to employee orientations or technical excellence. Our point is that few things are entirely neutral, and more or less manifest or implicit power and political issues are part of organizational life, including change work (Buchanan and Badham 2020). This often triggers political conflicts and activates power work.

As the change program we studied did not exhibit so strong signs of political conflicts – there was little overt conflict and resistance – and the use of power was quite weak, we don't focus much on power and politics in this book. However, given its general significance and the need to be aware of also subtleties of power and politics we briefly address this theme. We also believe that the absence of acts – such as strong use of power – is of interest in order to illuminate practices and outcomes, including the lack of the latter.

Often, researchers refer to four major perspectives or 'faces' of power (Fleming and Spicer 2014; Lukes 1974) formal/coercive power, agenda setting/restriction, ideology/domination and subjectivity regulation. These perspectives provide a useful framework for this study.

Coercion is the direct exercise of power to achieve certain political ends by getting someone to do something. This type of power is for the most part episodic, aiming at securing specific behavioural outcomes. Senior people may give instructions to subordinates or they may decide upon policies and rules. They may also initiative change programs with a set of prescribed actions for people to follow.

Agenda setting is about putting things on – and preventing them from appearing or removing them from – the table and framing them in a specific way (Bacharach and Baratz 1962). Power is then much about gatekeeping or controlling the agenda. In change work certain issues are then highlighted and focused, while others implicitly are downplayed or dropped. Training in a specific form of leadership for managers may mean that other forms of leadership become less prominent and discouraged from being addressed. Co-workership and other alternatives to leadership – professional control, teams and autonomy – may also be downplayed, as the leadership training aims to underscore the role of leadership and the doing of it in a specific way. Power then means sticking to the agenda and preventing alternative issues from being raised.

Ideological domination is how social order is made to appear inevitable, natural and/or simply 'good', and thus unquestioned. If subjects accept the proposed 'truths' or values, this exercise of control bears imprints of power; when successful it makes individuals comply without much consideration or protest as they buy into the prescribed world view and a specific set of values and orientations. Leadership training and an ideology of managerialism, where managers are seen as 'leaders' (not administrators or superiors) and a certain form of elitism become an overall ideology, forming beliefs and consciousness.

Finally, *subjectification* 'seeks to determine an actor's very sense of self, including their emotions and identity' (Fleming and Spicer 2014: 244). Through social definitions of what is normal and what characterizes an individual subject in a specific category, the individual is being imprinted with the sense of 'normality'. The discourse defines and constrains the individual, becoming produced as a specific type of subject regulating himself/herself. In the work context, this form of power is often linked to one's professional identity or logic, but more general prescriptions for being a good organizational citizen are also part of the picture. Being a 'team player' (not too autonomous or insensitive to others), a loyal employee being much into corporate citizenship or having a high degree of 'customer orientation' (adjusting to the customer as a king) may exemplify subjectification. People are of course exposed to this all the time, not only from their superiors but also from all sources.

In change work all forms of power are typically more or less involved, even though different aims, projects and change workers may emphasize these in different degrees. There are almost some degree of coercion that pressure or force people to act in some direction that they would not otherwise have done. Top management makes decisions and does some orchestration of change procedures that others are expected to follow, often with more or less sanctions in cases of non-compliance (although sometimes much go under the radar).

Agenda-setting is of course a key element of change work; power often enters through preventing or marginalizing issues other than those being chosen for decisions and actions. Prevention from distractions or alternative routes are thus part of the agenda-setting exercise of power. As with coercive control, agenda-setting may not really 'reach' people; sometimes the response is only some behavioural surface behaviour – lip service or tick-the-box acts – and not much is happening beneath what can be directly observed and measured.

Ideological control is very much about getting positive responses and full buy-in. The right persuasive framing, with positive words, and the portraying of potential features in bright colour are commonly used. A part of this is often some negative portrayal of alternatives and the neglect of contradictions and conflict. 'Sustainability', 'authentic leadership', 'inclusion', 'well-being' and 'excellence' are typical examples of ideals that are difficult to object to, because it appears immoral or stupid not to accept and embrace these seemingly self-evident and positive things. However, they cover up tensions, for example, conflict between environmental concerns and profitability, authenticity as something all appreciate versus being a source of interpersonal problems when people demonstrate the 'wrong' type of authenticity (e.g. religious fundamentalism, sexism or impatience with people's performances), turning the authentic person into a work environment problem harming some people's well-being. Change work then is about how to create full ideological buy-in and adapt thinking and behaviour to the idealized version of the change initiative, for example more thinking of environmental sustainability that is not costly or forces people to do something uncomfortable (e.g. recycle, but not eating meat or flying) or being 'authentic' in selected politically or socially correct ways or simply playing 'authenticity'.

As with the use of ideology in exercise of power, subjectification influences people's beliefs and orientations and thus goes beyond coercion and agenda-setting. Change work then tries to make people see themselves in a different way than previously. There is some re-definition of who they are, often not so profound but still enough to make a difference in terms of inclinations to think, value and act somewhat (or more radically) differently. The norms or template for being is revised. An engineer turned into a manager is thus typically targeted for change efforts to embrace a managerial identity, for example in managerial group meetings and through training programs. Sometimes a new identity is partial as the work domain may still be technical, but a manager person is one who views doing leadership and administration as natural tasks to prioritize. Organizational changes may aim to make all (or at least sufficient number) people see themselves in line with a new corporate emphasis. In a move from up-market to less costly products and services change agents may try to get employees to be less of perfectionists or over-doing things and become more of pragmatists working for the average people or creating value for money and not overspending.

Cultural change: preceding, following from or intertwined with 'substantive changes'?

One important aspect of cultural change concerns whether this is a matter of primarily involving the level of values, ideas and beliefs or if it also, and perhaps mainly, involves more substantive matters, such as structural and material arrangements directly implying behavioural changes. One line of thought suggests that we must change people's ideas and values in order to make any 'real' change possible, thus giving priority to a cultural level. This is of course vital in organizational culture and sometimes less so in modifications of supply chains or introduction of new IT systems. The use of various forms of power will be different depending on the nature of the change target.

Another issue is that making people behave differently is what matters; cultural changes will follow from this. Reallocation of resources and rewarding different behaviour would then be sufficient. Most authors on organizational culture single out the cultural level as having the main interest (e.g. Lundberg 1985; Schein 1985). (This was also the case with the cultural change project that forms the main body of this book.) Here, it is mainly idealistic (ideology and subjectification) means – articulation of visions, creating organizational rites, initiating training programmes, what leaders pay attention to, control, reward and teach – that are relied upon, although more substantive changes also clearly matter. Occasionally, the more material and substantive side of organizations is emphasized more strongly. Anthony (1994: 60), for example, argues that 'cultural change that is not reinforced by material change in structure, reward systems, precept and policy is likely to be seen as unreal and any adjustment to be temporary'. Here ideological control and subjectification are seen as insufficient.

Ogbonna and Wilkinson (2003) showed that, although top management emphasized planned organizational culture change, middle managers saw this in relation to other structural and material changes and responded in relation to the combined impacts of cultural processes and organizational restructuring. Some elements of the latter undermined the autonomy of local units, centralized power and increased close monitoring and corrective discipline over middle managers. The researcher observed mixed reactions to the cultural change messages; many accepted these, but with a strong element of 'instrumental compliance' (see also Willmott 1993). Ogbonna and Wilkinson (2003) are therefore somewhat sceptical about cultural change really transforming values and thereby maximizing human asset utilization in the form of a positive and genuine belief in and a desire to 'voluntarily' act in accordance with promoted cultural values.

This is partly a matter of the question concerned. If it is a matter of core business with direct perceived links to production, performances and performance measures, then a 'pure' cultural change appears unrealistic. But if we talk about something like greater openness in the company or new ways of dealing with customers then the situation is different. If senior managers strongly favour this value, their personal example seems to have an effect on broader patterns in organizations (Hofstede *et al.* 1990, see also Alvesson 1995).

We think it is fair to recognize the variety of different issues and the possibility of cultural change involving mainly a change of meaning and values without directly presupposing substantive changes. However, interplay between the level of meaning and the level of behaviour and material and structural arrangement must often be considered in organizational change work. In order for behavioural change, unless referring to simple and technically easily controlled behaviours (such as mechanical smiling in service work), to be possible, it must be preceded by and accompanied by cultural reorientations. Cultural change efforts often call for anchoring in labour processes and work conditions in order to communicate effectively. Efforts to accomplish change in meanings and values incoherent with substantive arrangements exercising behavioural control are difficult.

On the whole, working with organizational change in a culturally sensitive way calls for interpreting and acting in specific unique contexts. Following recipes, as we shall see in later chapters, is seldom productive. Examples should be used to inspire learning and insight, rather than be directly copied.

Organizational culture and the hybrid workplace

Following the recent pandemic and the increased digitalization of the workplace through a variety of digital communications devices, many employees nowadays expect and also demand to be offered the possibility to work – to some extent – at remote locations, typically at home. A development that is most commonly understood as the emergence of the hybrid workplace – a blend of working in person at the office and working remotely – that naturally impacts on the possibility to maintain and develop organizational culture as a way of managing organizations and change (Howard-Grenville 2020; Spicer 2020; Trevor and Holweg 2023). Only in the US, people working primarily from home tripled, from 5.7% to 17.9%, between 2019 and 2021 (Allen *et al.* 2024). In spite of many organizations trying to get people back the work office, many employees want to maintain some hybrid work situation (Bloom *et al.* 2023), having the possibility to work some days remotely and some days at the office – typically two days remotely of a five-day week – as this provides flexibility while also countering feelings of social isolation.

Upon the pandemic and with digital communication becoming more commonplace the question of what all this means for organizational culture has become increasingly significant (Arena *et al.* 2023).

The continued significance of culture in organizations depends, of course, on a variety of elements such as the kind of task performed, industry and environmental demands, knowledge intensity, managerial ambitions, the importance of strong social capital that holds the organization together and so on. In a study by Choudhury *et al.* (2024) of a hybrid work situation where employees – professional service employees – had a medium blend work situation of working remotely around two days a week results showed that quality of work as well as creativity was enhanced. The employees could also report a more favourable work-life balance as well as lower feelings of isolation. Like many others, Trevor and Holweg (2023) maintain that the hybrid workplace is here to stay but that culture can be maintained if organizations manage to create alignment between the task performed and the environment. They suggest that some tasks can be easily conducted remotely, such as what they call 'procedural simple work', while more collaborative and creative work typically requires more personal contact. Naturally, when it comes to highly creative problem-solving, such as in research and product development, it is usually much more difficult to work remotely (individually), as such work normally demands more personal contact. Innovation is seen as a 'contact sport' that is strongly facilitated by meaning alignment and social capital in terms of togetherness and emotional ties. Following that they suggest organizations need to acknowledge the hybrid demands by managing time and space in ways that facilitate different kinds of tasks and the significance of culture for their performance. Accordingly, a hybrid workplace does not rule out the possibility to manage and work with cultural change. There are variety of means such as, reflection and experimentation (Elsbach and Stigliani 2018), that could encourage employees to critically reflect about the existing culture and assumptions (Alvesson and Spicer 2012). There is also a possibility to use the existing cultural tool-kits to in way that could potentially shape and form cultural change (Howard-Grenville 2020). However, the formation and continuation of organizational (group, department, unit etc.) cultures calls for interactions, and the richer and more intense these are, the easier it is to develop shared beliefs, understandings and meanings. There is a risk – or possibility – that remote or hybrid work leads to more fragmentation of cultures and sometimes more meaning variation, confusions and misunderstandings.

Conclusions

Arguably, the concept of organizational culture is significant for understanding deeper meaning and assumptions in organizations, which lie behind and guide behaviour. Organizational culture is commonly expressed in language, stories, myths and other forms of artefacts that are suggestive of deeply held meaning and beliefs. Changing organizational culture is seen as very difficult; in some instances culture is even seen as beyond managerial control, although a variety of uses of power may directly (agenda-setting, ideological control and subjectification) or indirectly (coercion controlling behaviour) affect culture. Studies of organizational cultural change seem to confirm that culture is, at the least, very difficult to change. Based on these studies it is generally believed that openness and receptiveness to new ideas, values and meanings are central to accomplishing cultural change. When it comes to views on how to accomplish change it makes sense to distinguish between cultural change as a grand technocratic project and as everyday reframing.

The grand technocratic project portrays cultural change as a more or less scheme-regulated stepwise activity. This is similar to the (under-socialized and standardized) n-step guides discussed in Chapter 2, although the primary target for change in a cultural context is people's thinking – as well as values and feelings – rather than behaviour. The (over-socialized) models focus on changing people's thinking and feeling, a kind of cognitive approach. By changing cognitions, behavioural change will follow. These ideas also characterized the cultural change programme in the present study to a certain extent. It was designed in order to create a new way of thinking, thus facilitating a kind of attitude change. It was based on an analysis of the existing organizational cultural situation and a (contrasting) desired future, thus producing a gap that managers wanted to close: hence a design and plan for the future.

However, the grand design more or less assumes organizational cultural homogeneity, something that rarely is the case. In contrast, many organizations exhibit cultural heterogeneity based on divisions, hierarchical levels, departments and other features. Such cultural heterogeneity is often underestimated in change models but it is important to take it seriously. Of course, a purpose may be to counteract various parts pulling in different directions, but sometimes there are unrealistic aims, and the communication of the same message may lead to diverse responses and thus fuel differentiation and fragmentation. The tendency in many managerially governed projects is to trivialize the deeper levels and neglect the differentiated character of organizational culture, something likely to make much change activity remain at a surface level, unable to target people's thinking and feeling. It is important here, as also elaborated upon in Chapter 2, to acknowledge the local character of meaning and interpretation and appreciate how identity positioning and construction often follow such local meaning and sense making. Sometimes cultural change projects may benefit from a more targeted approach, focusing a group or unit with a nuanced set of ideas and need for calibrated shared meanings rather than addressing the entire company with very broad and vague value talk.

In this study we take cultural heterogeneity, differentiation and local interpretation and sense making seriously. People's sense making cannot be assumed to follow managerially espoused organizational beliefs and values. The idea with a cultural analysis is to move beyond not only the behavioural level but also the espoused level and dig deeper into the meaning construction among organizational members. This meaning construction is sometimes governed by assumptions that are not easily reached but are nevertheless important for how people act in organizations; something clearly exhibited in the cultural change efforts that we shall explore in the chapters that follow.

Note

1   A related problem with organizational culture change is that many authors have an interest in the subject matter, meaning that they promote a particular view. Consultants and managers with an interest in consultancy tend to emphasize the great opportunities to change culture, while academic 'purists', eager to maintain an academic, perhaps anthropological, perspective, may be inclined to stick to a view making culture stand above efforts to manipulate it. Of course this overlaps the theoretical definition of culture, but adds to this the personal position of the academic, tending to lead to a pro-change or anti-change view in terms of the possibilities of planned change.

Part 2

Change work in practice – a close-up study

4 The case – and how we studied it

The company and its story

Technocom (TC)[1] was formally created as a separate legal entity as a result of an extensive restructuring of the parent firm Global Tech (GT). GT was founded at the beginning of the 1930s and established itself successfully in the international markets back in the 1980s and is still today – 2024 – seen as one of the most significant companies in its industry. In order to exploit what it believed to be a core competence within a particular product and technology development unit it decided to separate out that competence to an independent company, TC (with GT as the owner). TC produces technically very sophisticated and highly developed systems and applications for the high-tech industry. TC could thus potentially exploit this core competence and market it to other companies. The high-tech companies using software from TC would thus gain access to cutting-edge technology with limited investments in R&D. The CTO explains the background to the creation of the firm:

> The GT internal unit that became TC started relatively recently with the purpose of ensuring technical inventions for product development. The unit was thus very research oriented. It had a project culture that was research oriented and which focused more on technical advancement rather than [projects] being finished at certain times and at certain costs. In the new environment that we now have as a business it is much more important (not only) to have the right quality, but also to be finished in time to the right cost. These are new rules for us and we concluded that the culture or the mindset, the attitudes to enable us to achieve this, were not right. So, when we created TC we took the technical organization and added things one needs as an independent organization: finance, personnel, sales and marketing. These functions were new and got a fresh start; they were easy to fit in the new organization, while the technical development function was stuck in the old beliefs. From that came the initiative to start a culture programme. The purpose was to make people look in the mirror. It didn't concern shifting people's ways of thinking, which you don't do overnight. The strongest driving force is rather if you can make it obvious for people what is wrong and what we lack.

DOI: 10.4324/9781003474555-6

TC (for example, when we did the study) consists of more than 2,500 people (globally) of which about half are part of the project organization. While headquarters and the main research site, Titan, are located in Scandinavia, the company has a few research sites in Europe and Asia.

The formal structure of TC is a matrix organization; vertically it consists of the various key functions, and there is a project organization crossing these horizontally. TC has a cultural heritage from its days as an internal unit, with a strong focus on technological advancement and sophistication. Most people are occupied with rather advanced technological development tasks which influence broader cultural orientations. People in the project organization are mainly engineers with academic degrees, a few with PhDs. They are typically engaged in complex and sophisticated knowledge work. As a consequence, managing the engineers strictly through a focus on behaviour is difficult. The nature of the advanced work implies a high degree of self-organization (Rennstam 2007). Of course, and TC is no exception, there are significant elements of bureaucracy – although in a fairly loosely structured form – in most larger knowledge-intensive firms (kifs) (Hislop *et al.* 2018; Kärreman *et al.* 2002). Still, the difficulties of employing valid and reliable rules and performance measures on a detailed level has led many authors of kifs to emphasize cultural-ideological or clan control instead of – or in addition to – bureaucratic or market-like (output) forms of internal control (Kanter 1983; Mintzberg 1998; Newell *et al.* 2009; Wilkins and Ouchi 1983). Organizations like TC then typically form a mix of overall bureaucratic structural and cultural patterns as well as adhocratic project work and self-organization.

Although the talk was framed in other terms than forms of control (as the authors formulate it), the CTO similarly points towards the significance of creating a new 'culture' parallel to the creation of TC. The CTO talks of this as important in order to change the 'mindset' of the narrowly focused internal unit, to change cognitions through making it possible for people to 'look into the mirror' and reconsider what they are doing in the new organizational context. The 'mindset' of the former internal unit is here implied as being inadequate considering the new business situation that now purportedly emerges. The CTO implies that they now have to start doing the 'right' technology rather than the best, signalling a departure from always doing the technologically superior and most advanced things. The way to accomplish this is to make the existing insufficiencies obvious to people and to make them change the way they think, feel and act according to a larger 'cultural programme', implying they have to try to install a new form of cultural or ideological control.

This kind of talk and the underlying image of wrong values, beliefs and orientations are common in contemporary organizations. The measures to fix the situation employed in TC are also similar to what is suggested in the organizational and cultural change literature, as discussed in Chapters 2 and 3. What we can learn from the case is therefore of broad relevance and warrants a detailed study of the change efforts. To focus on the entire process and its complexities is important here. We have argued that reducing and simplifying complex change processes to a few steps or simple recommendations fails to elaborate many of the critical issues involved in the launch and trajectories of change programmes. We aim to go deeper than the many n-step manuals based on anecdotal material of 'successful' organizational change. Especially important is to take the experiences and views of those involved in the change processes more seriously than is common in many of the popular books on the subject.

In Chapters 5 and 6 we try to follow the entire process and the complexities by which this cultural programme was initiated, formulated, designed, implemented and interpreted by those involved and targeted by it. Before that we will briefly discuss the method used in the field work and a presentation of the model or framework guiding us in the study of the cultural change programme. The process is structured and broadly understood in terms of a particular investigative model of management process. This is used in order to grasp how the process evolved and the role of various participants. Next we present this investigative model.

Investigative model of management and cultural work

In this book we try to uncover the trajectory of a cultural change project from an empirically close reading and to thematize the process through deeper interpretations. We use an investigative model of management that captures the content of the cultural programme and the organizational context in which it took place. This model consists of six elements or phases:

1 *Background and context*: here we elaborate upon the perceived contextual background and problem definition that motivated the change efforts. The overall situation, as seen by the actors who were central in the change programme, is described.
2 *Strategy and intended line of action*: in this section we investigate ambitions, objectives and solutions as advanced by the managers and others in order to manage the problems discussed in the previous section.
3 *Design*: here we emphasize the overall design of a management change programme, for example its major components and the relationship between them, as well as the specific acts and arrangements, technologies and instruments (e.g. formal talks, workshops, documents, assessment instruments, etc.) forming the ingredients of a specific cultural programme.
4 *Implementation and interaction*: in this section we elaborate on how the designed practice is put into action in social contexts. The designed practice then gets a particular twist as those targeted to carry out the management change efforts, for example the change agents and/or their subordinates, are activated – or not activated – in change initiatives. Different actors may act according to plan, improvise and put their own imprints on what is happening or more or less strongly deviate from what is intended. Subjects can here, for example, a) validate and support the designed practice; b) try to influence,

change or even oppose or resist the designed practice; or c) show indifference, confusion or ignorance.

5   *Reception and interpretation*: here we focus on the interpretations and the responses of the subordinates on the management initiative (practices and/ or the strategy). How do they ascribe meaning or meaninglessness to specific elements? There are two elements here: one is about meaning (how do they understand it?); the other is about attitudinal or affective response. This aspect is less about overt behaviour or visible interactions – as in the previous theme – and more about acts of sense making and interpretation, which may not be expressed in espoused opinions, at least not in the semi-public situations in which the change programme is being carried out.

6   *Results and outcomes*: in this final section we elaborate on indications of the possible effects of the management initiative, for example on behaviour, turnover, productivity, climate, feelings and thinking. While reception and interpretation are best captured fairly closely in time to specific events and change practices, results and outcomes are a) somewhat more long-term and b) relate more to possible changes in thinking, valuing and acting in various work situations than to interpretation and making sense of change programme activities and messages. We admit that this aspect is hard to investigate, but it should be possible to detect clues about whether people can notice any differences around them or feel that new inputs have influenced their own thinking or values. An alternative is, of course, measurements before and after a programme, but it is difficult to separate the programme's impact from the myriad of other events that take place at the same time, in the organization and outside it. More importantly, it can be argued that one can't measure culture (Alvesson 2013). Culture is about meaning, not frequencies. Based on our study, we will raise serious doubts about the value of trying to measure culture. We therefore rely more on qualitative indicators of consequences of the change programme.

Each of the elements in our model is interpreted in some depth and so of course is the relationship between them. A practice – as materialized – may for example be in line with, moderately deviate from, give a specific twist to or contradict the intention. The intended and the picked-up meaning may cohere or diverge. There may, of course, also be ambiguity and inconsistencies (rather than clear divergence). It is important here to be open to the crucial role of the reception of the change programme by the large groups of people supposed to be affected.

The model does *not* indicate a linear line of reasoning – we do not assume a process involving a fixed set of separate steps that follow a particular logical order. We are just, at the moment, saying that, in order to understand organizational change projects, it is vital to seriously consider (perceived) background and context, intentions and strategy, design, practices (implementation and interaction), reception (interpretation) and outcomes. Empirical material referring to these elements can then be interpreted in different ways: intentions and context may, for example, be investigated in terms of being reinterpreted during the process and in retrospect by the people involved (cf. the idea of sense making, e.g. Weick 1995). Early strategy talk may differ markedly from later references to the initial strategy. Various elements may be loosely connected or even contradictory. We suggest that the investigative model of management represents a useful way of addressing the challenge of analysing extensive and complex empirical material since it is constructed around the activities and tasks of the organizational change efforts in this study. As discussed in Chapter 2, we think that there may be very good reasons to interpret elements or stages in processual terms rather than in terms of stages as indicated in the model (Jabri and Jabri 2022). We are interested in the ongoing constructions and reconstructions of what is happening in a particular phase, but also of the 'inputs' to the change project (perceived context, strategy, design, previous activities). But having some empirical material on the stated intentions before the change efforts are put into action is of considerable interest in understanding change work. Are original intentions important or not? Do these more or less clearly expressed intentions have a strong effect on what happens at later stages? Are intentions fixed or flexible? Are they coherent or not? Do they drift – consciously or unconsciously – or are they rethought in retrospect, so that initially expressed intentions are constructed in quite different ways at later stages? Considering questions like these is, arguably, of key significance for understanding organizational change projects. They encourage us to go beyond considering only retrospective constructions of intentions, even though we of course do not reject the importance of the latter.

The model is also relevant for understanding a much broader set of management and organizational themes than just organizational change. Arguably, any serious effort to understand what is happening when management initiatives or structures are put into operation – going beyond the black box that bypasses what is between input and output (independent and dependent variables) – calls for consideration of the six elements covered. For example, a leadership act, reward system or specific organizational (re)design is not understood properly without considering the ideas and intentions behind or preceding the act or arrangement, how it is implemented and received and what kind of outcomes, if any, seem to have been accomplished. We are not developing this theme of broader relevance here, but just pointing out the need for serious process studies to take into account a number of key elements and, optimally, to follow these closely in real time. We realize that time and access problems will make 'easier' types of studies – relying solely on measurements or retrospective interviews – more popular.

Method

The material for this study is the result of an extended and broad field study at TC. We initially approached the company after its creation as a subsidiary in autumn of Year 1 in order to gain access for the study of a variety of organizational issues in knowledge-intensive companies. We soon learned that TC was due to launch a cultural programme that aimed at facilitating its expansion as an independent company.

The transformation from being an internal software product development unit to becoming an independent subsidiary was considered by the new management to require substantial developments in many areas, of which one was the change from being perceived as an extremely technologically oriented unit to a company focused on business, customers and markets. In order to accomplish that transformation, management, together with external consultants, created a specific 'cultural change programme'. We thought that we were facing a rather unique opportunity to study a culture change programme more or less from its conception to its implementation and reception among employees.

In order to capture the change project as it progressed during the almost eighteen months, we had regular access to the company more or less all the time and could proceed with interviews and observations in parallel. This made it possible for us to collect in-depth longitudinal data as the change efforts unfolded rather than relying on snapshots or only retrospective accounts. Guided by the model, we did a large number of interviews with managers at several levels in both the (vertical) line and the (horizontal) project organizations. Senior executives; managerial staff from the support functions HR and Operations Department; and other employees, managers and subordinates were interviewed about 1) background and intentions, 2) ideas about specific change strategies and tactics, 3) how change actors and others worked practically with these, 4) perception of subordinates' responses and finally 5) long-term effects. We interviewed some of the most centrally involved managers and HR management on several occasions during the change process. All in all we interviewed twenty-five managers and thirty-five subordinates about their interpretations and responses, but also about how they perceived top management's intentions and generally assessed management initiatives based on the specific material. Interviews usually lasted for approximately an hour, or occasionally longer if the interviewee had more intimate contact with the culture change project. Interviews were all done predominantly at the headquarters, which also accommodated the main site, Titan in Scandinavia, but they were also carried out at Satellite in the UK. All interviews were taped and then mostly transcribed; in some cases the latter was done thematically based on the investigative model of management.

The observations were done at the company sites and consisted of us, the researchers, participating in a variety of different work meetings. The meetings were 1) smaller group meetings where primarily junior middle managers discussed work issues with their immediate group, usually consisting of ten to fifteen people; 2) several project meetings where employees (middle managers and project leaders) discussed project progression; 3) a few so-called employee seminars where senior middle managers reported the status of various projects to larger groups of employees; 4) a 'kick-off' meeting at Titan symbolically marking the start of Technocom as an independent company; 5) a management meeting where the culture change programme was first introduced to the majority of middle managers; 6) a workshop held by one middle manager in order to implement the cultural change and finally 7) a management meeting at Satellite where the culture change was to be implemented among managers. We thus covered the trajectory of the cultural programme, from the planning and designing stages to the implementation and reception stages. We were also invited to a meeting to discuss the results of the cultural change efforts a year after the implementation efforts. The observation at Satellite was of a preparatory workshop for managers aimed at establishing a common understanding that formed the basis for implementation among subordinates at that site. All in all we attended thirty meetings and workshops. All meetings and workshops were taped, and parts of them have also been transcribed.

We also collected and analysed a variety of company documents relevant to the cultural change process. Several consultancy reports as well as formal and informal documentation from meetings with consultants and between key actors in the design of the cultural change were useful in order to understand the rationale and arguments behind the cultural change programme. These reports and documentation also gave us an understanding of the chronology of key events. We had access to some of the formal correspondence between key individuals involved in the change process, which gave us further understanding of the progression of the cultural change efforts. Then we also gathered all the usual company information, such as company reports, annual reports, company newspapers and articles, and items in the mass media, in order to familiarize ourselves with the organization.

Our approach to the case is interpretative. We are interested in what is going on here, but even more so in addressing the question: what do people think they are up to? We explore issues around the dynamics of change – and the lack of it – through addressing not the 'objective' logic but the meanings, values, thinking and lines of action guided by these cognitive and emotional elements characterizing the organization and various groups in it. We approach these issues with a strong interest in how people construct and frequently make a mess of their realities. Compared to most interpretative researchers having a strong positive and neutral orientation, we recognize some ironies in the practices and misfortunes of management and organizational change projects. Some slight inspiration from post-structuralism matters here (Alvesson 2002; Alvesson and Sköldberg 2017), meaning that a somewhat playful attitude to an often messy and irrational world seems called for and that incoherencies and paradoxes should be taken seriously (without being exaggerated).

Note

1   The name of the company and the names of all persons from the case mentioned throughout the book have been made anonymous for reasons of confidentiality.

5 A cultural change project I

Background, objectives and design

In this and the following chapter we aim to elaborate on the cultural change programme according to the model of study presented in Chapter 4. The structure
of the two chapters will thus largely describe various steps in the cultural change
dynamic in order to, at least loosely, describe the emergence and formulation of
the ideas and frameworks of those managers initiating the cultural programme as
a planned change. We thus investigate how the managers (and others) perceived
the situation prior to the conception and initiatives of the cultural change programme; what (if anything) management wanted to achieve by initiating such
work; and how they worked with issues of design, implementation and interaction with the rest of the company. We also aim to show how the programme was
received by those supposedly targeted by it as well as whether the programme
may have resulted in any significant imprints on the organization. In the analysis
that follows, the design and implementation will be covered to a larger extent
than the other aspects of the process, since we will return more frequently and
extensively to the latter in the thematic chapters following the account of the
trajectory. The two chapters are thus organized as follows, following our model
for investigations:

I   Background;
II   Objectives: strategy formulation;
III Design;
IV   Implementation and interaction;
V   Reception and interpretation: immediate responses and thoughts about the
     messages and the process;
VI   Results and outcomes: more long-term responses (change of values/practices,
     picking up new concepts, observing changes that may be related to the cultural
     programme).

As noted, this is not an n-step model, in the sense of showing the linear progress
or clearly phase-divided nature of what is happening. It simply shows our observation points used to capture 'reality in flight'. We don't assume or expect there to be
any logical steps or directive force following from what is captured in the earlier
elements to the latter. Actually what 'goes on' in 'implementation' may be very

DOI: 10.4324/9781003474555-7

Table 5.1 The cultural change process and how we have tried to capture it

Spring	Summer	September	Autumn	December	December
Year 1	Year 1	Year 1	Year 1	Year 1	Year 1
TC is conceived	Excellence contacted (objectives)	TC starts (objectives)	Management workshops Titan (design)	Final Excellence draft (design)	HR people take charge (design)

January Year 2	February Year 2	Spring Year 2	June Year 2	Autumn Year 2	Spring Year 3
TC kick-off Titan	Management club Titan	Workshops Titan	Management workshop Satellite	Follow-up	Reflections in hindsight
(implementation)	(implementation)	(implementation)	(implementation/ interaction)	(implementation/interaction)	(results)

loosely related to strategy. But in order to understand what is happening, paying close attention to all the six elements seems appropriate. Covering all these aspects in depth is very rare in studies of change (Table 5.1).

We followed the project in real time between autumn Year 1 and autumn Year 2, relying on observations and interviews. We tried to access the background and first phase of the development of the firm and the programme through interviews and also did follow-up interviews where we tried to cover retrospectively what had unfolded.

In this chapter we will set out the intention, ideas and frameworks of the cultural change. In the next chapter we will show how these were put into operation in change-stimulating activities and how they were received by a number of individuals at the company.

Some key actors in our story

A number of individuals will appear throughout the story and give their views on some, or a spectrum of, the various issues around the change programme. Many of these people will surface only once or twice, while some will appear more frequently. In order to give a somewhat richer view of the key persons, we will briefly present them before embarking on the story. The most significant and frequently appearing people, apart from the consultant employed by GT, from the various departments, are:

• *John Howard*, newly appointed CEO and a former director within GT. Howard is a middle-aged former engineer, considered by many of the other engineers in the organization to be 'one of their own'. Howard knows and is a close friend of many of those participating in the formation of TC. He is also known for being interested in marketing and what some have described as the 'softer' sides of management, that is culture and personnel. At meetings Howard not infrequently comments about how people are late and that they will have to become more disciplined in terms of schedules and time.

- *Richard Allen*, newly appointed CTO and a former technical director within GT. Like John, Richard has a long history within GT and seems to know most of the people about to embark on the new venture. He is in his forties and describes himself as a person with a 'high profile' in the company, something that contributes to him getting a central role in the cultural change process. Compared to John, Richard gives a more 'business-like' impression, being fairly certain and seemingly clear in various performances and interviews. As will be seen later, Richard initially became intimately related with the cultural change project but then as it moved throughout the company became more distant and detached.

While John Howard and Richard Allen are top managers, the rest of our cast from the company are middle managers or HR professionals:

- *Tom Aldridge* is manager of the Operations Department (OT) and, in terms of age and history in GT, the most senior person among those involved. His long background in GT, including a few years abroad, perhaps gives him a distanced and mature view of the cultural change process. Tom was approached by John and Richard as a speaking partner in the design and planning of the cultural change, partly because of his experience of and background in the corporate culture and being a close ally of the two top managers.
- *Mary Duncan*, manager within the Human Resource Department (HR), in her early thirties, gives a very positive and highly energetic impression, at least when it comes to issues of culture, leadership and similar HR topics. Perhaps partly owing to her extrovert and inspirational style John approached her when the cultural change project was about to be launched to the whole organization, perhaps hoping that she would act as an inspiration to others.
- *Judy Hamilton* works in HR with Mary Duncan. Judy is not in a managerial position and also gives a more junior impression in relationship to the others. Working with Mary Duncan she became involved in the cultural change programme just prior to its launch to the organization in its entirety. Although she claims a great interest in this work, she does not feel very self-confident about it.
- *Tom Neville*, middle manager within a Technical Department (TD), is one of the managers targeted by the cultural programme. We picked him and his unit for careful study in the project and this is the reason why he is presented here. As an engineer he is regarded as being very skilled within his areas of competence, to the degree that he describes himself as being the 'technology guy' among some of his superiors. But he feels that this label no longer fits very

well, as he strives for more senior middle manager roles within the company, roles he feels he now deserves. Compared with some of his colleagues he appears to be positive about and interested in culture issues.

- *Clara Ridge* is the consultant from Excellence, the consultancy company that helped GT's top management with the cultural change project. Clara is a relatively young consultant interested in organizational culture. Her assignment to work with the cultural change programme can be regarded as a slight deviation from the regular work of Excellence, which is more oriented towards strategy and IT and the implementation of large projects, typically occupying a group of consultants over time.

Having introduced some of the key persons in the story we next turn to the culture change process. We begin with how people talk about the existing culture being part of the reason for embarking on a cultural change programme in the first place. This talk of culture seems to be the result of TC being a formerly internal unit required to serve other company departments.

I   Background – talk of an existing culture

When talking about the reasons for embarking on the cultural change programme, both managers and HR professionals and to some extent engineers emphasize three aspects that could be seen as internal drivers for change: a too strong or narrow technological orientation, a socially introvert organization and a low confidence in managerial leadership. These internal drivers are clearly related to external drivers, since they, and the two first aspects in particular, have been seen as barriers to the likelihood of accomplishing what they talk about as customer orientation, such as being able to deliver at the right time and at the right cost, as mentioned in Chapter 4.

A too strong technological orientation

Firstly, and most commonly, when employees talk about the existing culture they elevate the type of education and professional background people have by referring to them as engineers and technicians, presumably forming a technologically oriented culture. There is both a kind of positive acknowledgement of this, the opportunity of developing and using sophisticated knowledge, and a negative, focusing on the engineering and technological orientation as forming an arrogant, narrow-minded kind of thinking detached from the market and customers external to the organization.

One of the main architects of the cultural change programme, CTO Richard Allen, explained that within the former parent organization engineering was always the big issue:

The engineering culture within GT is applauded. They had twenty functions in their products that no one asked for while the customer aspect has been weak.

It has been too much 'the engineer' and too little marketing people. It has been very engineering led; everything has been done according to the engineers' ideas.

Allen also says that:

We (TC) were a technical resource unit that received a certain amount of money a year to spend in order to ensure that GT had the best and latest technology in their products. We had a very broad scope and worked on every possible technical feature, including features that no one asked for. As a technical resource unit we were able to resist when GT demanded various features for their products; we could say 'No, that is not consistent with our strategy.'

The 'applauded engineering culture' of GT times is seen as a problem. From being an orientation to be proud of it is now seen as an impediment for renewal and success. The problems raised by Allen are manifold, but interrelated. First is the lack of input from the market in the work of the engineers; second is the general deficit of marketing people; and third is the (quantitative) dominance of engineers. From being highly praised the celebration of engineering knowledge and orientation in the organization is now something that threatens the success, perhaps even the survival, of the company and should be corrected. The customer is thus an element that is drawn upon as an external force in order to depict the technological orientation as problematic.

It is tempting to nod approvingly at this kind of critique. It appeals to common sense and currently popular ideas. However, complaints about the lack of market orientation and engineers forgetting who they work – or should work – for, that is the customer, are fairly standard talk in contemporary business and it is tempting for people to echo what others are saying. It is not entirely easy to know what an engineering and technological orientation actually refers to. In this case people talk about how the technological orientation made engineers inclined to pursue their own narrow technological interests and less sensitive to the customers' wishes and needs. Of course, engineering myopia frustrating customers should be avoided, but engineering knowledge and commitment to product development must be a key competence in this business. The practice of using labels such as 'technological orientation' could perhaps be seen as serving to evoke its opposite, namely talk of business, customer and market orientation, signalling the speaker's progressiveness, and encourage some kind of move to considering marketing aspects to a somewhat greater or possibly significantly higher degree. Nevertheless, without saying yes, this seems to be an objective problem that must be fixed; we sidestep the issue and are more interested that there is some consensus about the desirability of a switch from a strong technology orientation to a stronger orientation towards customers, and investigate what is happening when TC management tries to accomplish such a reorientation.

Socially introvert orientations

Secondly, there is another line of talk about cultural background that has targeted what could be seen as the social aspect. In characterizing the culture, some have talked about the organization as introvert and asocial. There is little room for social small talk and other social activities. Communication among individuals is seen as mainly related to work. This is framed as a social deficit that needs to be remedied by a cultural programme. Aldridge explains:

> We are 90 per cent technicians and most are introvert. My impression is that if someone is sitting in the coffee room it is contingent upon an information meeting where you talk about technical problems. Then we have 'Friday coffee' but there are absolutely no mass gatherings.

Although not as common as characterizing the culture as having a one-sided, narrow-minded, technological orientation, many people characterize it as being introvert. People are generally not very socially oriented or skilled, it is said. This is seen as related to the heavy domination of engineers. The introvert orientation is viewed as a problem since it obstructs the emergence of a tightly knit and common culture characterized by shared values and positive orientations and also prevents more extrovert relations with the customers.

Low trust in management

Thirdly, some have emphasized a low confidence in management among employees as a problem. In spring Year 1, GT assigned a consulting company to survey leadership issues. According to the survey, managers in GT had low scores on leadership by not showing enough confidence in relation to subordinates. Aldridge says:

> The negative period [in GT prior to the creation of TC)] made people sceptical, suspicious and disappointed. We measured the confidence in management in Year 1 and it was quite low. The scepticism is still around, like 'How are we going to succeed this time when we didn't make it the last time?' The development of leaders is difficult. Technicians are not interested in being managers – they are more interested in solving technical problems – but as a manager you have to do administration. Then you may not have the time to develop yourself and that is sensitive for young people who think about their life careers. If you turn manager when you're 25 you may lose the first important years when you develop yourself and acquire knowledge.

The view on leadership is a bit varied, however, and some senior managers believe 'that people have confidence in our leaders' (Allen).

Although there is no consensus about a possible low degree of confidence, and a major architect behind the change programme does think that confidence is 'rather high', the impression remains that many might perceive the leadership in the organization in negative ways and that the issue of confidence is part of the problem calling for improvements.

In sum, the preceding statements indicate a rather introvert organization with a strong, somewhat one-dimensional, technological orientation, with a lack of focus on business and customers among large groups. In addition, subordinates seemed to have low trust in senior managers. The situation is partly a result of the heritage of being a technical unit within the larger corporation, GT. As we showed in Chapters 2 and 3, this kind of talk and sense of problems and hopes for a better organization in terms of values and orientations is fairly common and is almost standard in cultural diagnosis and planned organizational change projects (Sveningsson and Sörgärde 2023). Our interest is not in determining the 'objective' cultural situation of GT, but to try to capture some of the ideas and thinking, hopes and ambitions of managers in the company triggering a change project and see how this unfolds.

Although it was not directly expressed by our interviewees, we have the impression that senior people in TC think that a new company (subsidiary) calls for a distinct corporate culture and that something should be done to accomplish or manifest this. One may talk about an institutional expectation of any independent organization worth its salt needing to have – or at least to express – a set of presumably distinct values and orientations. Normative (one ought to have, in order to look good) and cognitive (this is the best way to operate) aspects guide people to follow in the footsteps of other organizations, or perhaps rather to imitate the media-reported impressions and stories about what these are doing (DiMaggio and Powell 1991; Meyer and Rowan 1977). The idea of a corporate culture can be seen as an organizational identity project – an effort to communicate something distinct about the company (Ashforth and Mael 1989). Ironically, this claim for distinctiveness and uniqueness is often similar among organizations, as organizations often imitate others in terms of the form (our 'corporate culture') and content ('market orientation', 'commitment') being used.

A too strong engineering orientation, lack of collaboration, the need to improve leadership and the expectation that it is necessary to express some version of distinct corporate culture form the background against which the cultural programme emerged and was formulated. Next we turn to the ideas behind the formulation, partly connected to the background just discussed.

II   Objectives: ideas behind and aims for a culture change project

As ideas of separating out TC from GT started to materialize during spring Year 1, those appointed as managers in the new company began to discuss what kind of organization might have a chance of surviving and prospering. The organization they foresaw constituted a radical contrast to what they viewed as the 'technologically biased' one. In order to accomplish an organizational change, they began to formulate a new culture for the new company, about six months before its actual birth. Thus, in spring and autumn Year 1, 'the management group defined where we are heading and what needs to be changed and reinforced; we had good basic material [with Excellence]' (Allen).

Senior management talked positively [about the new creation TC]. They allocated money at our disposal and we were facing a situation like 'What do we do
now as we basically have the same employees as we had six months ago, before
the separation? How can we create a new culture with everything that comes
with that?' You have to be customer oriented, you have to have self-confidence
and to be finished with your projects, and you need to have another pressure.

(Aldridge)

Besides sustaining the idea of the project as a solid management project, Aldridge
also includes additional driving forces for change by implying they have been weak
at teamwork, lacking customer orientation and self-confidence, missing deadlines
and lacking pressure to deliver in the organization. All this is seen here as indicating
shortcomings of the (previous and possibly also present) corporate culture.

Although the many problems discussed might justify a range of various issues,
for example organizational structure (working together), human resource management (self-confidence) and management control (e.g. about monitoring and
enforcing the keeping of deadlines), it nevertheless all comes down to matters of
'corporate culture'. In line with the view expressed by Allen, most organizational
issues are here gathered under the culture label. When asked about where the ideas
to work with the culture came from, Allen explains that:

It was our own idea. We realized that our role as an organization was changing.
Previously we worked on all the possible technical features. That's a luxury we
can't afford any longer. We are a business now; the customer is stronger and has
more say. They are not just colleagues, as earlier, when we could manage without a lot of documentation and directions. Now the customers sit in America and
you are forced to have everything written down, nice and tidy, with diagrams
and graphics as the basis for manuals. This made it clear for us in senior management that this is about an attitude change in the whole organization; everyone must understand that it's different today. We will still do good software but
the way we relate to the environment must change. The idea of a cultural change
programme was born in those discussions.

A consultant from a large consulting firm, Excellence, then becomes involved.
Allen continues:

We felt a bit lost in this so Excellence, who helped us with our business plan,
said that 'We have someone who is very capable. She could help you get started.'
So we hired Ridge. Then in spring Year 1 we thought a bit about how to create
some activities whereby we could change our culture to something that better
fits the new business.

Specifying the situation with customers having power seemingly made it clear to management that an 'attitude change' was needed, emphasizing that it had to reach every employee. Allen explains:

> One could call it customer orientation. It's a lot about making the customer *feel* pleased. That may sound a bit cynical but still it's a big difference between being pleased and feeling pleased and the most important thing for us is that the customer feels pleased. It's a matter of having good customer relations, something that hasn't been necessary for us to care about previously since we took our customers for granted, but now they can leave us. And this is about rather simple things like not sharing some problems with the customer; we need to work on establishing an image about how we are capable partners – things we haven't cared about in the past. Today the customer doesn't want to hear about our problems.

When elaborating on the attitude change, Allen turns to customers and image building; 'doing' customer orientation is here about making the customer pleased by complying with performance and avoiding discussing problems. 'Customer orientation' here seems to be a willingness to manipulate customers. When the customers were internal, one could openly discuss problems, but in relationship to external customers this should be minimized and problems hidden. We have in this case found frequent, even excessive, use of the vocabulary of customer and business orientation.

> We call it business orientation; you should think of what you do in terms of the business. Things you do should pay back. Previously we were measured on our technical progression but today it is more important to do things that work rather than do things that are advanced.

It thus seems that talking about the need to make money inevitably led to an uncomplimentary characterization of the former technological orientation. The formula appears to be: strong technological orientation = neglect of customers = bad business.

Allen, the main architect of the cultural programme, claims that the ideas of cultural change emerged within TC, referring to how it was the management group's insight that initiated the whole project, also positioning himself as responsible for the project (a high organizational profile). Allen identifies himself as the change agent, the 'initial force' (Latour 1986), and thus enacts what Weick and Quinn (1999: 373) characterize as 'prime mover' in planned change programmes.

We think two additional aspects are interesting here. One is the close to standardized set of fashionable terms and labels he – and others – are using in accounting for the background and key ideas of what is seen as internally based. The same set of words and ideas is familiar from the business press, consultancy talk and many other companies. There is, however, no explicit recognition of the following of (institutionalized) standards and recipes. Instead, there is a strong claim of internal grounding and contingencies on the specific situation of this firm.

The second interesting aspect is that the drivers behind the necessity to change the culture evoke a multitude of various organizational issues (articulated in sometimes broad and vague ways) that perhaps could be analytically treated as distinct organizational problem areas that might require a more differentiated set of organizational considerations in terms of how to deal with them, as suggested by many writers taking a more processual view on change (see Jabri and Jabri 2022). However, instead of dealing with the organizational complexity facing them, they group all 'problem identification' under the label 'corporate culture'.[1] Corporate culture appears to be a problem as well as the solution to a very broad set of themes. Although this was seen as the major issue to work with, the management group did not feel competent on culture issues and turned the 'cultural project' over to consultants, asking them to take a leading role in designing a particular cultural programme. We turn to the design issue next.

III   Designing a change project

Based on the 'problem identifications' discussed earlier, Howard and Allen agreed to work with a consultant company, Excellence Ltd, during summer and autumn Year 1 in order to form a new culture. Together they developed a preliminary design of a cultural change programme that was later adjusted and revised by HR before being launched to the entire company in Year 2. Next, we discuss this process as it progressed during autumn Year 1. As well as Excellence, TC top management also engaged two other consultancy companies. We briefly discuss the work of these consultancies in terms of its influence on the cultural design.

Designing 'target culture' with Excellence

Howard and Allen believed Excellence had the competence (being 'specialists on corporate culture', as Allen says) to design a major cultural programme that would reach every employee, although the firm was actually much more experienced in larger information and business systems change management. The consultant was to work with top managers in order to lay the ground for a 'culture' and 'value' programme that could be 'cascaded' throughout the organization by middle managers.[2] First the consultant was to execute a series of 'cultural' workshops with top executives, approximately eighty top and senior middle managers, during autumn Year 1 that would lead to a culture agenda; secondly, this agenda would form a basis for the design of a larger cultural programme that could be promoted to primarily junior middle managers responsible for its implementation. The initial workshops should thus be seen as preparatory sessions aimed at facilitating an intellectual inventory among top managers on their view of the present and, on that basis, designing a programme for the rest of the organization. Allen explains:

> Excellence is specialist on corporate culture and Ridge was to guide the senior management group. We divided senior management into a number of subgroups and made a SWOT analysis of the company based on attitudes and culture per-spectives. They showed considerable divergence, and Ridge and I tried to find the essentials in that material. The purpose was to find weaknesses that we could improve and strengths that we could exploit. We found a similar number of strengths and weaknesses and then we tried to identify a few of them. We really started by determining what major characteristics drive our business forward, so-called business drivers, and there were three.

From the role of the consultant as guide being initially downplayed, the signifi-cance increases as Allen describes how they worked together in trying to formulate the vital input to the cultural programme and in determining 'business drivers' and 'basic values', supposedly main themes in the design. Considering the remarkably diverse results from the SWOT analysis it is reasonable to assume a significant imprint from Allen and Ridge on the design of the cultural programme. Perhaps this was an outcome of a fairly free and arbitrary formulation of the key themes, rather than a rigorous analysis. Allen said:

> It was a bit fun that the three business drivers had the same initial letter as TC and I think we found these three letters through some rewriting in order to make them easy to remember. We used them as a guiding light and on the basis of the SWOT analysis we identified five basic values that we considered important for the success of the company. That we landed on five was just how it happened; we might as well have landed on six. It just happened that, as we went through the SWOT analysis with a variety of issues, those five values were identified.

The six values[3] were partly a result of the themes that had been considered dur-ing senior management workshops, a few of which received more attention than others. The most common of these was 'leadership behaviour'. Managers were displeased at being perceived by subordinates as 'not visible', 'not inspiring' and evoking 'low confidence'. In contrast, they agreed on the necessity of visible and inspiring leaders with clear visions. Leaders should provide direction, earn trust, engage in long-term strategy work and offer 'clear leadership'. In terms of actions, leaders needed to listen and improve two-way communication. The second topic was organization structure, seen as 'unclear' and 'centralized' in terms of 'tasks and responsibilities'. Managers agreed on the need to define responsibilities and improve delegation. Thirdly, it was suggested they needed a 'customer-focused' organization (not 'technology-focused'). It was vital to 'give the maximum num-ber of people the opportunity for face-to-face customer contact'. Managers also suggested making customer agreements available to employees. A fourth topic concerned improved working procedures, project work and product requirement specifications, etc. Issues five to eight were only addressed in one workshop each. Three concerned the establishment of a 'roadmap' for TC, improved communications and definitions of services and products. Finally, an eight issue dealt with the balance between customer focus and care of existing personnel, raising questions of education, salaries and TC as 'employer friendly'. Following the last workshop in November, Excellence (with Allen) made drafts for what came to be called the 'target culture', conceptualizing some of the preceding topics as 'basic values'.

Interestingly, at this point the original interest in weaknesses and strengths had disappeared and part of it had become integrated with the issues seen as important to work with. There were thus no clear indications on whether one needed to work with a specific basic value because the organization was perceived as weak on this, presumably needing drastic improvement, or whether one thought that this was a strong issue, which would imply maintenance and reinforcement rather than rethinking and change. One could here perhaps add that, if one thought the organization was weak on a particular value, this could infer not just attention and effort but also rethinking and learning, which would rely on an examination and challenging of assumptions and existing values, something not so easy to accomplish (Alvesson 2013). But this aspect does not seem to have been seriously considered in TC: working with culture is viewed as a relatively straightforward project, in need of some technical help from a consultant in terms of summarizing and analysing expressed judgements and then engineering a design, but not engaging in cultural learning at any deeper level. People seem to have assumed that they knew their culture, at least with some input from the consultants, who mainly seem to have gathered and summarized viewpoints expressed in interviews and not done any deeper analysis. This view of change processes expresses a form of understanding – a top management-idealistic subculture – of cultural change processes as initiated and driven by a straightforward, top management, well-planned design.

The first part of the drafts about the 'target culture' consisted of 'basic values' advanced as necessary in order to implement what Excellence called a 'winning culture' (see Figure 5.1).

This part of the target culture bears some resemblance to the idea of creating a cultural web, as discussed in Chapter 2. But rather than displaying statements of excellence in various areas as in Figure 5.1, the cultural web, as suggested in Whittington *et al.* (2020), was used more as a diagnostic device in order to display the interconnectedness between people's actual behaviour and governing assumptions. The approach with the cultural web was to take seriously the idea that behaviour and structural arrangements have some relations to (often historically anchored) deeply held assumptions, ideas and beliefs. Although there were some efforts in this direction in the implementation efforts, we will later see that any connection between people's behaviour and governing assumptions remained largely unclear and unexplored during the trajectory of the programme.

In the second part, the implementation, Excellence suggested a 'TC culture toolbox' specifying how to execute the 'target culture'. Part of the 'culture toolbox' was to be used by junior middle managers for discussions with their subordinates;

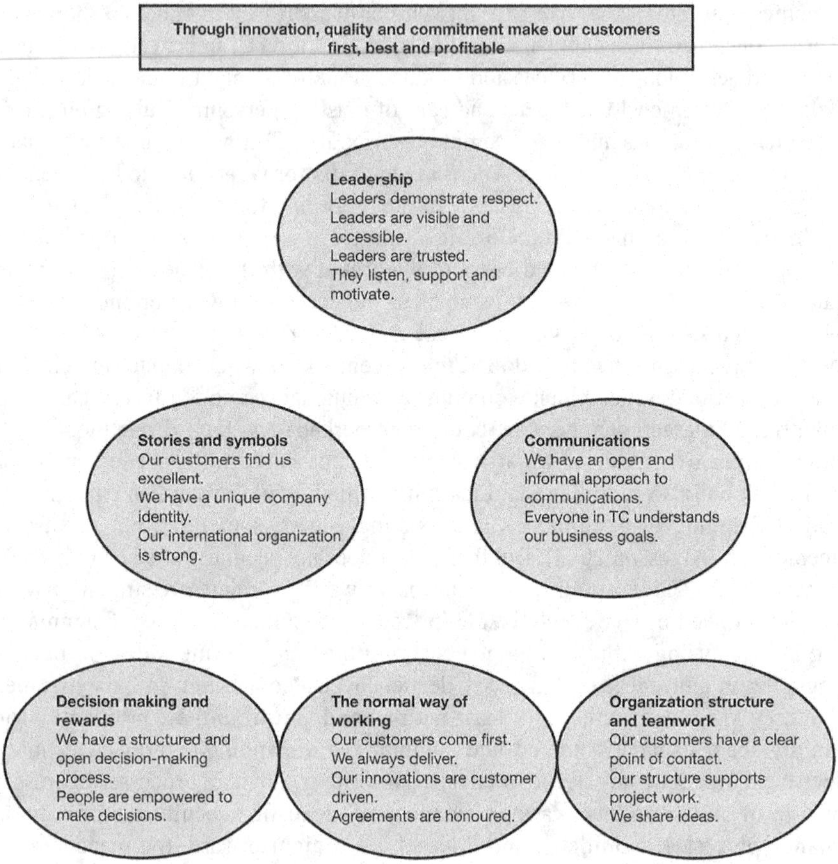

> Through innovation, quality and commitment make our customers first, best and profitable

Leadership
Leaders demonstrate respect.
Leaders are visible and accessible.
Leaders are trusted.
They listen, support and motivate.

Stories and symbols
Our customers find us excellent.
We have a unique company identity.
Our international organization is strong.

Communications
We have an open and informal approach to communications.
Everyone in TC understands our business goals.

Decision making and rewards
We have a structured and open decision-making process.
People are empowered to make decisions.

The normal way of working
Our customers come first.
We always deliver.
Our innovations are customer driven.
Agreements are honoured.

Organization structure and teamwork
Our customers have a clear point of contact.
Our structure supports project work.
We share ideas.

Figure 5.1 Draft of target culture

every employee was to be reached. For the culture toolbox, Excellence suggested a video showing Allen and other top managers explaining the TC 'culture' (the targeted culture is eliminated in this part of the material, a point we will return to in later chapters), the distribution of slides of mission, vision and business goals, an agenda for a two-hour meeting, templates for gathering feedback and actions from middle managers and engineers, instructions of how to do it, etc. Parallel to those specifications, there was also a time frame suggesting a 'kick-off briefing' for lower-level managers in December Year 1 and implementation during early Year 2, with feedback from meetings sent back to top management during the same months. Follow-up could be done parallel to implementation sessions.

In late Year 1, management also had to decide whether to continue with Excellence during the implementation. Excellence had developed a design for broader implementation and according to Allen it was important that every employee was involved in the dialogue on the target culture. Then Excellence was dropped prior to implementation:

> It is a bit sensitive if you want to accomplish a cultural change and where you need a buy-in from the organization. Someone from Excellence shouldn't really come and implement it, but rather your own people. It should show that senior management at the company stand behind the programme and that it's not an idea of a consultant but an idea of our own.
>
> (Allen)

Management also thought that the consultant was too costly. The final preparatory work for a cultural programme was now instead placed in the hands of HR, Mary Duncan and Judy Hamilton. Before continuing with the work of these two, we briefly discuss the less extensive work with the two other consultant companies, Blow and Eagle.

Design input from other consultancy firms

Like Excellence, Blow is a global management consultancy company. Although their task was not part of the preparation for the cultural change it nonetheless resulted in some suggestions taken up in the design of the programme.

The assignment to Blow included a request to develop 'communications strategies'. For this they interviewed employees, and these suggested the existence of 'internal rumours', lip service being paid to the importance of communication and that few bothered about 'administrative details', 'lack of goals and feedback', 'lack of information from management meetings' and that 'the information about and between projects does not work'. Other results showed that informal networks were important and that 'Management Team' meetings had an 'open and positive atmosphere', but that communication was 'unstructured' and lacking 'action points', minutes and common agreement about 'structures, systems and content'. From this Blow constructed two problems, 'the communication culture' and 'the information system and structure'. The former seemed 'informal with no clear roles and responsibilities and no communication routines'. Management was seen as 'invisible' and the culture 'informal, verbal and discussing', a 'technological student culture'. The study displayed a 'lack of confidence in the management', as 'management had short-term thinking and never gave any information in advance, which made people think that they were not trusted'. Blow concluded that the 'business situation' now had changed to the extent that a new communications culture was required. They advised 'a model for excellent communication' suggesting changes in strategy, structure, system and every dimension corresponding to the problem areas. The remedies were, however, generally rather abstract and the vocabulary used followed the usual standard business language and seemed to have left little specific imprint on the cultural project. What is perhaps most interesting is the significance of leadership and culture that emerged from their communication study. To some extent their problem identification is loosely similar to that made by

Excellence earlier, and the results from Blow seemingly confirm the work of Excellence and also the leadership surveys previously mentioned. It is notable perhaps that Blow didn't mention anything about the culture being excessively technologically oriented; they rather focused on excessive informality through the use of the student metaphor. This strengthens the feeling that the talk about being culturally biased does not necessarily reflect an objective reality or something agreed upon within the whole or a large part of the organization but is the expression of a particular perception or standpoint – or sectional interest.

Besides the preceding, Blow helped formulate vision and mission, the former expressed as 'The leading software provider for the electronics consumer market' and the latter 'Through innovation, quality and commitment make our customers first, best and profitable'. These emerged during autumn Year 1 and found their way into the Excellence drafts. Other suggestions that were incorporated were creating a website with news, a special 'Ask the CEO' button on the website, a newsletter from the CEO, all-employee meetings (to inform all employees about project status), website interviews with key people in the organization and a special management forum.

In sum, then, although the engagement with Blow was intended to focus primarily on communications, the work was apparently contagious in some respects. Next we turn to another assignment that also had some effects on the design of the cultural change programme, the work with Eagle.

By contrast to the other companies, Eagle was a small local company hired late in Year 1 for the purpose of giving junior middle managers and non-managerial employees an opportunity to discuss strengths and weaknesses. The primary weakness according to these employees' perceptions – or at least their questionnaire-filling responses – concerned leadership. Many suggested that managers need to be more visible, participate in daily work, act as leaders more than managers, form a culture, give clearer directions, etc. Other weaknesses were communication and information. There was a need, the investigation concluded, for clearer communication between sales and technical departments, better information on the web, cascading and transparency, and communication about strategies. Clear objectives and issues on customer orientation were also brought to light.

The problems raised are similar to those emphasized by Excellence and Blow. There are leadership, visibility and clarity issues, also seen earlier, and improved communication and information issues, which tend to be evoked in such sessions. There is also the issue of culture, although it is not specified. Leadership and management are therefore again made highly problematic. Especially interesting at one session perhaps was that when asked to state the vision and mission of the company very few of those present knew anything, and Duncan, who led the day, said that: '[Managers] don't yet understand the culture and values and what is expected from a manager.' She also suggested that managers were too operational and unable to distribute the 'right information' to subordinates. All this indicated the need to transform the organization: 'A company that delivers a vision and a mission that relate to the culture and values in combination with good leadership has an excellent chance to become successful fast.'

In the conclusions from the session, Duncan suggested that TC should prepare a leadership programme and transform what is called the 'management culture'. The course is interpreted much in terms of the preparations for a cultural change programme running parallel, and Duncan's conclusions are thus hardly surprising, but rather well aligned to the design of the culture programme, a programme she became involved with as Excellence was dropped. Next we return to this phase of the trajectory. We discuss the final preparations for the design of a cultural programme.

From Excellence to human resources – the final design

When Excellence (i.e. Clara Ridge) disappeared from the scene, the responsibility for fine-tuning and implementing (according to senior managers) the design was placed with Duncan and Hamilton, supported by Aldridge from Operations. Aldridge was thus now absorbed further into the project.

Duncan and Hamilton mainly used the Excellence material. In contrast to top managers, they looked upon and understood their role in the process – expressing an HR logic – very much in terms of packaging and delivering to middle managers what had already been accomplished by top managers and the consultant. Early in Year 2 they had a package outlining 'three drivers for business success' (also framed as 'our sources of competitive advantage'): 'outstanding customer relations', 'first-class technology' and 'strong teamwork'. These were backed up with five (as compared to six, as Excellence suggested) 'shared values' and supplementary material called a 'cultural change toolbox', comprising a brochure, various individual and group exercises and a CD with a video showing Howard setting out the new vision. The 'shared values' that form the 'winning culture' were:

1   '*Our way of working – commitment*, meaning commitment to the success of both customers and employees.'
2   '*Leadership – trust and inspiration*, meaning leaders who inspire others with their vision of our future and who earn trust through their knowledge and professionalism.'
3   '*Communications – sincerity*, meaning open sharing of information and open-minded attitudes to feedback.'
4   '*Decision making and rewards – empowerment*, meaning empowered with the right levels of responsibility and authority to take decisions and to demonstrate recognitions of achievement.'
5   '*Organization structure and teamwork – transparency*, meaning that it should be clear to our customers who they should contact, clear to each individual where they fit in and clear to everyone that teamwork is the foundation of Technocom's success.'

Each value statement was followed by examples of 'winning behaviours', in order to 'explain the essence of each value'. For instance, winning behaviours for commitment were:

- 'Our customers come first, and their current and future needs fuel our innovations.'
- 'We always deliver, and our customer agreements are met on time.'
- 'We are all customer oriented and familiar with our business activities.'
- 'We are proud of our technical expertise and we learn from experience.'
- 'We strive for high levels of job satisfaction.'
- 'We all contribute to Technocom's success.'

The three drivers are seen as the 'what' of the programme while the five 'shared values' constitute the 'how'. It is all related back to 'the marketplace' and 'business success', characterized as the 'why'. There is also a fourth component in this called 'in what way', concerning 'changed behaviours through the culture programme'.

> We arrived at these five basic values. We started with senior middle management and then we decided that in order to receive buy-in and maximum power from the organization everyone should be targeted by a workshop, everyone in the whole company. Connected to every value were some examples that clarified what was meant and what you wanted to achieve.
>
> (Allen)

An important part here is the involvement of middle managers: they should run workshops for subordinates, show the video and do cultural toolbox work. According to Allen:

> We have culture seminars run at unit level. Everyone should be targeted. We had them in the senior management group and now it is time to push them down to the departments. Every manager is to implement a culture workshop in his unit and come forward with suggestions of things that we should stop doing, start doing and continue doing. This will be reported back up through the organization.

The cultural toolbox suggested that workshops should begin with the video of Howard and Allen setting the agenda and legitimating the session. Managers should then present the vision, mission and objective (there were overheads in the toolbox for this activity). Next, they should turn to the drivers (technology, customer and team), followed by an exercise where all the employees have a chance to discuss their own group drivers, that is, how a particular group is functioning in terms of 'outstanding customer relations', 'first-class platform technology' and 'strong teamwork'. A central part of the toolbox was a particular set of templates that junior middle managers and engineers were to work with during the work-shops and later send back to HR. The templates were a way of documenting the workshops and possibly following the progress of implementation. One template was used in the exercise mentioned. The box then suggested a presentation of the 'shared values', with the exercise that followed focusing on a 'winning behaviour' within each of the five values (template two was called 'the unit winning behav-iours'). The purpose here was to see what constitutes winning behaviour within the values (empowerment, leadership, etc.).

A third exercise suggested that employees ask themselves how they personally employ a winning behaviour. This led to the theme of how they could change their behaviour in order to better demonstrate the 'winning behaviour' (template three was labelled 'individual winning behaviour'). In the fourth exercise they were to identify what behaviour on the organizational level could be seen as winning and which wasn't. In order to facilitate this there was a template with three options, 'stop' (coloured in red), 'start' (green) and 'continue' (yellow), for each of the dimensions. 'Stop' meant identifying behaviour that didn't support the new culture. Each dimension of the target culture was thus designed to be discussed on three levels, the unit, the individual and the corporate, the analysis focusing on identify-ing actions on each level and for every dimension.

The manager leading each workshop was then supposed to collect the analysis and return documentation to HR. Duncan said that the whole package was built on everyone being exposed to the exercises in order to be able to change the minds and behaviours of the employees:

> Managers will implement workshops with their units and discuss 'How can we live up to these values?', 'How will we as a team change our behaviour?' and 'How can I as an individual act in accordance with these values?' The whole culture toolbox is based upon you knowing our vision, mission and goal. The results from the workshops are then brought together and we have a big meet-ing in April where this is presented. Then we will see what has emerged at an organizational level, what behaviours we should stop, begin, start.

The expectation of new ways of knowing and behaving is explicit, suggesting a straightforward attempt at cultural engineering. The examples in the design explic-itly formulate the values which are supposed to guide how people should be and how they should act. On the other hand, the input is quite broad and vague, with considerable scope for how people can revise and improve work. Allen explains:

> There were two purposes. The first purpose was to distribute top executives' and senior management's idea about what is the appropriate, the right, view of the corporate culture we should strive for. The second purpose was to enable these units, enable employees, to stop for a moment, look at themselves and their group in a mirror and try to identify things that need to be done in order to come close to the corporate culture we want to strive for.

The workshops were thus seen as highly significant in distributing the ideas of top management and implementing the new culture, when the design left the drawing board and was put into 'reality tests'. We turn to this in the next chapter.

Summary

We have accounted for the background, the thinking behind the cultural change programme and the activities to bring a strong knowledge input to it, as well as the analysis preceding it and the design in terms of content and process.

Compared to what is common, it seems that a fairly high level of ambition and strong efforts to guarantee the success of the programme characterized the planning and design work. Top executives and some senior middle managers initiated the project and seem to have been highly involved. A large number of people provided input to it. A consultant from an internationally leading consultancy firm was involved. People from HR are connected to the design and implementation. In addition, people from two other consultancies contributed with knowledge input on the strengths and weaknesses of the company. As we will see later, another consultant monitored the suggested design and assessed it as good.

Although we have indicated that those involved in the process so far looked upon the process in different ways – based on different cultural backgrounds – one could say that the managerial planning and design are well aligned to many recommendations within the planned, rationalistic and linear approaches to organizational change. The stages through which the culture is to be implemented fit well with the planning approach where formulations of organizational change are based on perceived problems and the subsequent formulations of a new vision, mission and overall values. HR manager Duncan's talk about the significance of vision and mission in order to accomplish success easily comes to mind in this respect. There are some connections to and similarities to later OD approaches but we can also see that it is strongly top manager driven, which could restrain employees from feeling empowered and open to participate in and take ownership of the change process, the latter being highly significant in OD (Cummings *et al.* 2020). The change programme also exhibits characteristics of being of an episodic kind (Sveningsson and Sörgärde 2023) because of several more or less tacit assumptions in the managerial planning and design activities: a linear assumption of movement in time, progressive assumptions in terms of movement of the organization from one 'lesser state to a better state', and a goal assumption in terms of a movement towards an end goal. At the same time, the issues addressed are hardly of the kind that can be controlled simply from above and be solved once and for all.

The change programme is difficult to categorize in terms of the models for change presented in textbooks. Following the images of managing change presented by Palmer *et al.* (2022) there are ingredients of director – navigator images associated with top-down change management, but also a lot of space for people in the organization to interpret 'target culture', connect values and behaviours and decide upon what to do more specifically. This would downplay the role of senior managers, seeing them as more loosely shaping what goes on in only weakly predictable ways. Perhaps the image of interpreter comes closest, if one should be pressed to view the TC events within the framework of Palmer *et al.* (2022), reviewed in Chapter 2.

The impression given so far perhaps indicates that this is an ambitious, well-anchored, carefully grounded and – as far as possible – rationally designed and quality-checked change project. On the other hand, it is fairly broadly understood that cultural change projects are not easy to carry out. So what happens in the subsequent stages of TC's change programme? The impatient reader does not have to wait long for some answers.

Notes

1 This might, of course, indicate a more sophisticated, 'anthropological' understanding of culture as an interpretative perspective of culture by which everything – leadership, organizational structure, technology and administrative systems – includes a cultural dimension. Culture is then seen as a metaphor for organization, drawing attention to the cultural meaning aspect of virtually every phenomenon from products and budgets to the understanding of competitors and customers (Smircich 1983a). Accordingly, one cannot, in contrast to a (more) functionalist framework, single out something as 'outside culture' (Alvesson 2013). Culture is not everything, but everything that is part of a social context includes a cultural aspect or dimension of socially shared and expressed meaning. Our impression is that this is not what most managers have in mind when they tend to give corporate culture a very broad meaning and sometimes summarize all kinds of organizational 'soft' issues under the culture label.

2 We refer to middle managers as those managers being in between top executives (sometimes top managers) and the other employees, mainly engineers. Sometimes we refer to middle managers as either senior or junior depending on their hierarchical position. A senior middle position consists of responsibility for one or several departments. Junior managers are responsible for a work group or several smaller work groups within a department.

3 The initial cultural design actually consisted of six values rather than the five mentioned by Allen. The HR people dropped one later in the process.

6 A cultural change project II

Implementation, reception and outcomes

Having followed all the preparations of the cultural change programme, it is time to see what happens when the designed set of activities and various resources for organizational development meet the managers and employees they are supposed to make more responsive to customer needs, more skilled and willing to do team-work and, in the case of the managers, better leaders. We start by looking at specific practices associated with the programme and then move on to how various partici-pants interpreted the content and practices of the culture change programme, before addressing outcomes, as indicated by responses some months after the scheduled activities.

IV   Implementation and interaction

The implementation process of the culture programme began at a kick-off for the whole company, moved on to the management forum and was then located in the hands of primarily middle managers. Next we briefly elaborate on these three instances, starting with the kick-off.

The kick-off

The purpose of this, as explained to us before the meeting, is to present TC as an independent company with its own customers, market and economy, and to present the new target culture and the cultural programme. We are also informed that it is an important opportunity for managers to engage in inspiring and encouraging 'pep talk' to employees, thus preparing for the challenges ahead. Similar meetings are simultaneously held at other sites.

When CEO John Howard comes onto the stage there are still many people enter-ing the room and there is also some whispering and small talk as he comments on people being late. He says: 'I hoped when I arrived at work this morning that eve-rybody would have a watch with them.' He then continues:

> This is really the official kick-off meeting. The reason for having this now and not at the beginning is so that we, I mean, when you start a new company you

DOI: 10.4324/9781003474555-8

don't really know where you have the market and customers, especially in the business that we are, when we are now breaking new ground. . . . I will start by giving you some general information, and then we have the culture programme, which is also quite important. It should be fun to get to that.

Howard proceeds with customer and marketing issues, says that the financial results are mainly on target and then refers to TC's competence and its relation to what customers want, the progress of the market and competitors. He then states: 'Our objective is of course to be profitable and have a sustained profitability and customer satisfaction, and it is important for us to realize that we are working in a business environment.'

He then mentions that the financial markets predict their success and that it seems as if they are in control. Before handing over to another speaker he very briefly mentions culture and says that they will have:

inspiring management through the culture and values. Without inspiring management we cannot have fun. We talk to managers and point out the direction and that we should work in an inspiring way and get everyone to move in that direction. It is very important that we share the values. If we have the same values it will be easier for us to work together.

After some briefing by the CFO and the marketing director, Allen (the CTO) proceeds with strategy issues such as the need to define 'how you are' in order to develop an appropriate strategy and competitive advantage. Then HR manager Duncan joins Allen on the stage, briefly presenting the culture programme, after which Duncan asks a rhetorical question: 'Why do we need a strong company culture?' Allen says:

The basic reason is of course business success. Business success is the objective of the entire organization. To gain that we have identified three cornerstones: how we interact with customers, how we develop technology and products, and we also have the way we work together. We have to show them [customers] one face. Of course that is to some extent utopia because we are all individuals and we all have different roles. [But] there should be some basic element that we all share to make the customers recognize us.

After some standard talk about communication he elaborates on the five values and ends by passing over to Duncan:

It's important that everybody gets involved and that we get everybody's view on this, so the next step is to get this big ball rolling, and Mary Duncan is going to tell us a little bit more about how that is going to happen. Thank you.

Duncan says that the culture programme will be presented to all managers at a management forum and will be followed by workshops for the employees where they will have an opportunity to discuss the programme through various exercises. There is whispering in the audience during the presentation. People seem a bit astounded by the culture talk. Then Duncan abruptly rounds off by saying: 'Step four is our new Technocom winning culture. OK, thank you very much for your attention.' Some applaud while the whispering continues. Howard comes back onto the stage and talks about how the culture programme consists of different elements:

> It should all fit together. Someone made a jigsaw puzzle so I can show you that everything fits together. Hopefully all the other topics we have covered today will also fit together, all our plans, strategies, business, and the most important thing is that we, the people here, work together and that we can share this. That is the key to success. And that we can have fun. We will have fun today and we will work a lot on that today, but this is something which can drive you when you go to work every day: that you feel that when going to work it will be a fun day. We are now into the question session and actually we have worked in lots of the time that we lost at the beginning.

Howard emphasizes 'fun' as crucial. However, the connection to the culture jigsaw is uncertain and perhaps it is his way of trying to strengthen enthusiasm and commitment from those present. The few questions from employees are, we think, answered by managers surprisingly vaguely, by help of standard vocabulary rather than something that connects specifically to the organization. On our way out after the kick-off we run into Mary Duncan, who half-apologizes that the culture stuff was not given sufficient space and time and that it was not more properly presented. She (as well as some other managers we talked to before the event) had expected the kick-off to be more of an inspiring pep talk about the culture change for the employees, and that the jigsaw would have been clarified to make it clearer to the employees. She seemed disappointed, as though it had not turned out the way she wanted.

The management forum

As mentioned, TC's management, following a suggestion from Blow, also formed a 'management forum' where managers could meet regularly and discuss various management issues as well as the progress of the cultural change programme.

This was the first meeting, for around fifty managers supposedly responsible for the implementation of the cultural workshops. At the time the meeting was scheduled to begin, many people had not yet shown up. Howard asked Aldridge whether everyone knew the correct time. Aldridge assured him that they did. Howard got upset and said to Duncan (who was in charge of the event): 'I damn well hate when people can't keep the time right' and 'It's very typical for this company not to follow scheduled times', obviously upset by what he perhaps saw as not showing respect for the practices that they were about to embark upon. Duncan, Hamilton and Aldridge walked around the centre of the stage so as to show themselves as busy rather than idle. The researcher approached Aldridge, who said that it was common not to respect time schedules. This was an old cultural practice they now had to abandon, he said.

The meeting started, some ten minutes late, with a constrained welcome by Howard, explaining that management forum meetings would be held from now on. He assured them that it would constitute a kind of 'round table', where managers at various levels could discuss issues relating to the overall situation of the company. He stressed that every manager should give priority to future meetings and that it was quite unacceptable to be late. The introduction by Howard was formal, correct and a bit forced, lacking the engagement and stronger feeling he had shown when upset about latecomers. Nevertheless, everyone was turned towards him and they seemed to listen politely to what he had to say. Then Allen took over, explaining about the new cultural programme. They were now in a different situation as compared to the historical situation of the company as an internal unit, he said. Showing more engagement than Howard, he explained how the cultural programme was a way of securing success, seemingly anxious to convince everyone that either they changed culture or they would encounter problems. Allen here echoed a principal tenet of much contemporary pop-management writing on change in organizations: change or die! (Dealy and Thomas 2005) (See figure 6.1). Howard's and Allen's talks lasted about five minutes each. Then Duncan presented the new culture by showing the jigsaw of the 'values' forming the 'target culture', after which she turned to the video.

The values presentation went rapidly, not dissimilarly to that at the kick-off. The video showed Howard and Allen talking about the cultural change, trying to specify the shared values and their presumed relevance for the company. The video showed them in dark suits, formally and correctly discussing the values as something a bit beyond their everyday reality. Although the two were located in the company building, these were not living pictures from the organization. The ambition might have been to try to make clear and give some life to complicated concepts but the result seemed formal and sterile, lacking life and reality. Perhaps partly owing to the early hour that the video was recorded:

We really laughed at it because the video was produced at the worst possible occasion, a Thursday afternoon, and I was terribly tired. Maybe it's not that visible. Howard was filmed at 7.30 on a Friday morning and he was as tired as I was. So we were both completely tired when the producer filmed us. I had three cups of coffee and cold water in the face before it. Wood, my personnel manager, said, 'Damn, you look tired.'

(Allen)

The video lasted for ten minutes, after which Duncan explained the implementation process. She introduced the cultural toolbox and said that managers should use that as a key implementation tool. In some sense, then, the meeting marked the

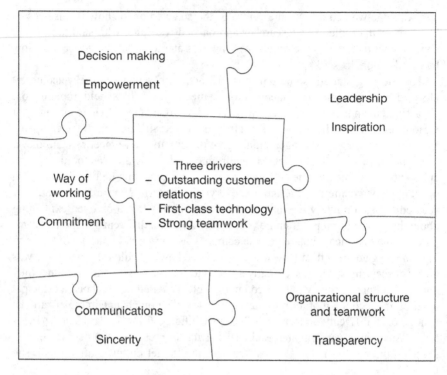

Figure 6.1 Jigsaw puzzle

introduction of the cultural programme to middle managers, or to the 'implement-ers', as formulated by Hamilton at the time. The new culture was here delivered as an object on the transition to the next successive stage – the middle managers – by a mix of request and command from senior management (Tsoukas 2005).

As the toolbox was distributed, Hamilton explained how the material was sup-posed to work. Every middle manager was supposed to have a workshop with his or her subordinates according to the procedure elaborated in the toolbox. She then went on to say that after workshops with their subordinates they should send in the results to HR, who would return with feedback. No serious questions were raised during her presentation, and Duncan and Hamilton concluded by saying that if anyone had problems they should contact them.

The cultural programme was, in contrast to what happened at the kick-off, presented first as the primary issue. Nevertheless the engagement behind it remained similar to that of the kick-off, and in the coffee break after the presenta-tion of the cultural toolbox people talked in sceptical terms about their own role and opportunity to contribute to the cultural change programme. This suggests that many felt a bit distant from managerial cultural activities, the latter being seen as a managerial project with no particular relevance for regular work activi-ties. In the weeks following the meeting, some of the middle managers expressed scepticism about the performance by Duncan and Hamilton, some indicated that they considered the issues concerned as 'soft' and others considered them as of lesser importance.

A workshop

The next and arguably the most important step in the programme was the workshops by primarily junior middle managers, supposedly leading to impacts on the engineers on 'the floor'. The major objective was to identify gaps between ideals and actual functioning:

> We made an analysis all the way down the company so that every employee should participate in a workshop. An action plan was created in every unit. A gap analysis was made. They analysed how they actually worked and compared that to the values and then concluded on what needed to be changed. It's like analysing 'What are we good at?' and 'What needs to be changed?' We then collected everything and compiled all the action plans. The top management group reviewed all of them and saw what was done, and we thought it all looked pretty good.
>
> (Allen)

In order to create a sense of the dynamics of the workshop, we have chosen to present a few representative excerpts mixed with our comments. We feel that these are typical of what emerged during the session.

Prior to the workshop the manager in charge of the occasion, Tom Neville, said that he might not be prepared enough, explaining that he felt uncertain about leading it:

> I came home late last night [because of a business trip] and haven't really been looking through these things [the cultural toolbox] as I should. There are plenty of words and concepts here that are difficult to work with and define. I have used some material I got at a business course at the university. Perhaps I can ask you to intervene on some occasions at the workshop as well, in order to support the work.

He showed the slides he intended to use, partly copied from a textbook that displayed a model of corporate culture. In that version, culture was understood as a blend of various connected elements (norms, significant actors, rules, objectives, informal organization). Together with the cultural toolbox and the talk from top management at the kick-off and management forum, that model formed his input in the workshop. In some other cases, middle managers had asked for and received such support from HR, although the latter only reluctantly participated, since their understanding was that middle managers should 'own' the culture programme at this stage. HR had delivered 'the culture' and it was now the task of middle managers to implement it.

Neville's group, consisting of about ten people, met in a small conference room, inviting a certain intimacy. As the engineers entered they acknowledged each other with a 'Hello' and then engaged in small talk, typically about work tasks. As Neville began about why they were having the workshop, there was silence. Neville talked slowly and cautiously in a low voice, taking unusually long pauses between words, displaying his usual 'poker face' and revealing very little emotion. He cautiously said that they would watch a video and talk about the vision, mission, drivers and values. It was difficult not to get the impression that Neville's cautious manner was an expression of uncertainty about the theme of his presentation and how people might react to it. It was obvious to everyone present that he was talking about things a bit beyond his regular tasks.

On one occasion Neville said: 'The goal of the organization is often seen from the owner's perspective but it can be seen from that of other interests as well.' He proceeded to discuss the Technocom goal: 'sustaining profitability through customer satisfaction'. Keane, a subordinate, asked: 'Sustaining? Why not just profitability through . . . ?' 'I don't know why', Neville said. Barnes, another subordinate, asked if Neville knew about the objectives of other organizations. Neville didn't and seemed at that point uncertain about how to proceed. He looked at the researcher observing the event and asked if he had any other objectives 'in his back pocket'. The response was that 'sustain' is very common in goals, and other statements like this one, referring to the long-term investment that companies want to signal.

On another occasion Neville stated the new TC mission formulation as: 'Through innovation, quality and commitment make our customers first, best and profitable.' Then Barnes asked: 'But if we have two or three customers that buy the same thing?' Neville assisted: 'Can everybody be the first?' People laughed, and Barnes said that customers could be best and profitable, but not first. Neville gave no answer and asked what 'best' means. Others joined the discussion. One participant pointed out that, if they found customers that didn't target the same product, they could be best and first. Another said, in regard to functionality, that TC could be the 'first' product to deliver the 'best' functionality regarding price and performance; it would be up to the customers to use it: 'It would be a possibility to be the first and best.' Neville supported that: 'The customers are different', he said, and continued with: 'TC delivers the possibility to be the first and best.' People looked at each other, bewildered, and seemingly remained sceptical about Neville's interpretation.

The excerpts illustrate the dynamics during the workshop. The participants were generally restrained and seemingly displayed moderate interest in the concepts of the cultural box. There were no real protests or objections to either the design of the meeting or the drivers or values. When objecting, or rather joking, it concerned logical errors about customers 'first'. Hence, in general people were quiet and seemed compliant. They were present at the workshop and talked a bit about how they could contribute to the success of the company. However, the concepts in the cultural programme seemed to have limited meaning to them. The only time the discussion unfolded a bit was when they refrained from sticking to the vocabulary in the cultural toolbox. The workshop thus tended to become a rather instrumental performance where the themes of the cultural box were followed as something that you had to go through without evoking any greater enthusiasm or engagement.

Nevertheless, as they finished Neville concluded: 'I think we spent useful time on this and I think it is a good sign that we were not able to rush through this in ten minutes, but really discussed it. That's good.'

Then it was all over; indeed there were no further culture programme activities in the group. If we take a quick look at the values underpinning OD, as discussed in Chapter 2, it seems as if the work at this particular group (and others that were reported to us) did not produce much commitment, participation and ownership of the specific change programme.

The Satellite encounter

Parallel to the workshops at the main site, Allen and Duncan, together with a colleague, Anderson, from the HR department, ran a preparatory workshop for managers at Satellite, a unit of TC, in order to inform them about the cultural change material and also to train them for their own workshops. At the workshop, in which about eighty people participated, many of the problems raised in the workshops at the main site seemed to emerge again. The mission statement for example met with substantial scepticism, and many questions were raised about the formulations and possible meaning of the values and drivers that were part of the cultural toolbox, especially perhaps about who the customer really is. At the workshop, Duncan's colleague Anderson started by saying that the idea with the workshop was 'to create a common language where we can get the tools to move forward', also mentioning 'shared values' and 'having the same words and using the same words in all parts of the organization', after which he continued with:

> The mission is to be the leading software provider for the consumer market. The key words here are 'leading' and 'consumer'. Leading means that we have the ambition to be a big baby, to be one of the largest. We're not going for a niche position. 'Consumer' means that the business that we are aiming at is high-volume business, not niche products. It's the products that the average person buys, manufactured in high volumes. John Howard would say that if you are the leading manufacturer you have a high market share and you drive the market. The mission is through innovation, quality and commitment make our customers first, best and profitable. What you read from this is that innovation, quality and commitment are cornerstones in how we deal with customers. The first, best and profitable is what we believe is important for the customer.

This statement evoked a rather confused discussion about definitions of the customer. First among the participants to question Anderson was Weller, site manager at Satellite, who said: 'We talk about the consumer market but our market really is the business-to-business market. Our customers deal with the consumer market.'

ANDERSON: Yes, the consumer market is our customers' market, so it's not our market.
WELLER: So the focus from our point of view is much more the business-to-business type sales.
ANDERSON: Absolutely. If we look at our business, it's not a consumer business, you're right. We're trying to compensate for that by having contacts with our customers' customers – the operators.

The confusion around who is actually the customer of TC remained after the effort to clarify it. On another occasion the HR manager at Satellite, Alison, presented her picture of the culture at Satellite, saying that they were engineering led, which evoked a heated debate among managers that further complicated the definition of the customer:

STEVENS: That is Alison's perception [of the culture]. I believe that we're customer orientated, we are customer focused, and we have been that all the way through our history. We've always been strong both internally to our customers and externally customer focused. I think we are customer focused and I think it is strong.
WALKER: I struggle with that, Stevens. Because I don't think nowadays we're close enough to the customer.
WELLER: What do you mean by the customers?
WALKER: External customers, to be honest. I mean, the internal customer, I think 'Yeah, fine, we're all fairly responsible in the way we treat people that we deal with', but externally I think we are miles away from the customer and have been for quite a few years now, so I struggle with that.
WELLER: I don't agree with that.
CLARK: I suppose it depends on your point of view.
ALLEN: But maybe you mean different things by customers. My interpretation is that when you say customer you mean the end user.
STEVENS: I think I do.
RICHARDS: But who is our end user? In the case of our closest customers, they are our end users, aren't they?
STEVENS: Yeah.
CLARK: Absolutely. We are a business-to-business organization.
STEVENS: We are customer focused but obviously we need to improve.
KELLY: There is some confusion about who the customer is.
STUART: Sure, the whole organization needs to know who the customers are. Is it the end user? The operators? The people we're actually selling to?
WELLER: The people that are actually paying the invoices we send – the businessto-business interface. It's not Joe Public on the street; that's *their* customer effectively.

FRANK: I think there's confusion in some people's minds.

CLARK: As I see it, we've got a customer focus for internal and external customers. A lot of people go out and talk to the customers and they actually, their focus, you know, [is to] satisfy their customers' needs, so depending where you are, what level you are, you have a focus on customer needs.

PETERSON: I think internally we do have customer focus but I think it's this interaction with our external customers that seems to be lacking.

Neither the degree nor the meaning of customer orientation nor who the customer is seemed very well clarified. The clarification effort of trying to talk about internal and external customers, respectively, seemed to solve little, and neither did the introduction of the concept of end user. Neither Allen nor Duncan nor anyone else from the main site was able to explain how to understand the concept of the customer, a main element in the cultural change concept.

Another theme of confusion at this workshop referred to the mission statement. About being number one, Weller, the site manager, began with: 'And the point about the first – our main competitor, Dotcom, wasn't first with the standard software product A.'

ANDERSON: No.

WELLER: But they're making substantial money.

ANDERSON: Yeah.

WELLER: We need to keep that reality in mind.

ANDERSON: Yeah, we do. They have a different strategy and they go for best. They try for first.

WELLER: They try for first.

ANDERSON: What is interesting is that when you meet people from Dotcom they have this priority too, but they constantly fail in this one. They were extremely upset that we got there first, that we beat them on standard software product B. Dotcom's success is based on many factors; one is that they have excellent logistics and materials management. They put manufacturing high up on their agenda and that never was the case here; they are better at understanding what is 'in' and trendy in applications. But I think you're right. They are putting more effort into best whereas we may be cutting a few corners to be first.

WELLER: I don't disagree. I'm just getting back to the reality that being first doesn't guarantee you success.

ANDERSON: No, that's very clear.

TAYLOR: There's a difference in culture between GT and Dotcom. GT is clearly engineering led.

ANDERSON: Absolutely.

TAYLOR: GT has tended to focus itself towards best, looking for innovative engineering, whereas Dotcom has been marketing and customer focused.

ANDERSON: Yeah, you're probably right.

DAVIES: I'm sure many hours, days and weeks have been spent on it [the mission statement] but I have an issue with being first. We should make sure that our customers are business-to-business. When a customer walks through the door he's got a date in mind. If we can hit that date, whether it's first or not, he makes that decision, but we should just ensure that we hit their project dates. I think first is slightly misleading.

ANDERSON: Good point. It's in your own time, rather than first.

DAVIES: I'm afraid first is slightly misleading.

ALLEN: To be quite honest, this is a copy of a CEO statement so it comes from the corporate mission statement.

WELLER: If it really means that we put our customers first.

DAVIES: People will read [customers first] as somebody launches a software product with a function first on the market. That's how people read it. But we have said that Dotcom has been laden with functions that we have offered earlier and still made cash, loads of money, so it doesn't matter. What matters is when a customer walks through the door and says 'I want your software by that date', if we can say 'Yes, you can have it by that date' or 'You can have it four weeks earlier', that's when we get the business.

EVANS: I think we should interpret that as the customer comes first with the product.

ANDERSON: I think we're spending a lot of time on this. I enjoy the discussion but I think we may need to move on.

The exchange at Satellite differed from that at the workshop at the main site, as people were more engaged in trying to relate to the mission statement. However, as with the dynamics at the workshop at Titan, they had difficulties in reaching some form of common understanding or commitment to the formulations in the change programme. The representatives of top management from Titan also seemed unable to guide the managers at Satellite in a consistent direction. The discussion thus ended rather abruptly and there still seemed to be a lot of uncertainty about the meaning of the customer being first as well as who the customer is. As seen from the perspective of the aim of creating a common language one could hardly say they had succeeded. Perhaps there were some significant cultural issues inherent in these processes. One could for example say that airing various understandings of the customer (or consumer) was important and could be an input to further discussions and ultimate clarifications of this vital theme. As such it could be highly valuable. A workshop leading to the expression of the diversity of meanings and ambiguities was, however, quite a different thing from one clarifying and strengthening key values such as establishing vision and mission.

Connecting to our discussion in Chapter 5 about the presumed value of talk about technological orientation, we can note how TC's successful competitor, Dotcom, is presented in various ways: 'Dotcom has been laden with functions that we have offered earlier and still made cash' (Davies); 'Dotcom has been marketing and customer focused' (Taylor); 'they have excellent logistics and materials management. They put manufacturing high up on their agenda' (Anderson). These statements are not directly incoherent, but illustrate that simple dichotomies such as 'technology oriented vs customer oriented' say very little and may lead to the establishment of a dubious or even misleading contradiction. But it seems very difficult to avoid.

Problems of implementation

Among the implementation activities the workshops were emphasized as being most important. A lot of responsibility for the change efforts was thus put on middle managers, and the HR people Duncan and Hamilton even hesitated to participate in them. However, the implementation through workshops entailed serious difficulties, and we will return to how various individuals responded to the workshops in the next section. Moreover, several managers did not appear to have run the prescribed workshops, some on the basis that they disagreed with management on their importance.

> There are some parts of the organization that say 'I will not present this in my unit because I don't see the value of it. I want a discussion with you and my boss before I proceed.' This is because they have been rather pressed and they say that this is not really their everyday reality. I understand their reactions because this is not their everyday reality.
>
> (Rogers, middle manager)

Follow-up work was limited: 'In that respect it is insufficient. We haven't followed up. But to what extent are we really supposed to police and control things?' (Hamilton). We can thus see how a variety of managerial efforts seemingly fail to create what many writers of planned change talks about as a 'sense of urgency' for the changes among the employees and how the efforts also seemingly fail to develop an engaging direction for the future that is easily communicated. Authors on change emphasize that communication in change processes should support a clear understanding of the reason for change (Kotter 2014, 2018; Palmer *et al.* 2022).

We will return to these themes, but before that continue with those who were exposed to the cultural programme. We turn to the question of how those targeted for the cultural change programme responded to its messages as well as its settings for communicating experiences and opinions around these.

V Reception and interpretation

The culture programme received a mixed reception among employees and lower-level managers. A few talked about the ideas as all right and to some extent important while others saw them as a way for management to control and manipulate.

Some employees talked about the targeted culture as being forced upon people:

> It feels as if they are trying to force upon us a culture, and you are not used to companies working like that normally. It's like in this company we have this

culture and this is the way it is. But culture diffuses among the employees. It is not top-down governed, but it feels like managers are enforcing this upon you.

(Lewis, engineer)

This is a paper product that theoretically could have been very good, if it had worked. But it is still a paper product. Someone has just said 'This is the way we will have it.' But people don't work like this in their daily work, so it is still a paper product. Then you can always shove it down the throat of the employees if you want.

(Price, middle manager)

Given the fairly loose design of the change project and the absence of any enforcement or monitoring of specific behaviours or operations (apart from the workshop), this feeling of the targeted culture being forced upon people probably reflected frustration with the organization and management in general more than experiences of the specific change project.

The large majority did not seem to react with any sentiments at all regarding the change programme, as they thought that the change programme was almost unrelated to what happened in the organization and therefore of little significance.

A middle manager, Scott, explained that the programme might be seen as unclear: 'People say "nice paper, fun ideas". I can side with this but where do I see this in reality?'

Another manager, Wilson, said that the content was good, but that the programme was far too weakly and partially implemented:

The cultural programme has a certain relevance. I think it's a good initiative; it's something that we need. But we are not there today and I am sceptical about the way it has been distributed. It was something that was presented at a management forum and we received this box. It was said that middle managers should run workshops, and I think that is insufficient, because not every manager participated.

The quotations represent a few typical spontaneous responses from middle managers and engineers. They were interviewed in connection with the implementation activities discussed earlier, that is after the kick-off, the management forum and, perhaps most importantly, the workshops. Many people talked about the programme as a 'paper product' from above with no links to what people, in particular managers, were actually doing. This view was partly supported by one engineer who said that the culture programme was 'of no use if managers talk about acting without actually doing it'. Most interviewees referred to the culture programme having weak or no connection to the everyday activities of the employees. It was about 'talk and paper', with a shortage of action.

People claimed that top and senior middle managers did not behave according to the cultural values, rendering the programme less valuable, something that was forced upon employees with top managers remaining outside, trying to control rather than being in it themselves. Most seemed to agree that the programme in itself expressed good principles and ideals, but that the way in which the values were presented and, in particular, contrasted with the experiences of the organization seemingly undermined the aims. We can thus see the following meanings ascribed to the programme:

- managerial hypocrisy;
- paper product;
- ideal quite far away.

The meanings overlap, but represent different understandings, where the view of it as a good ideal, but difficult to realize, is fairly positive, while the paper product view is somewhat negative and the hypocrisy view is strongly negative.

Next, we turn to a discussion of the possible long-term results of the programme.

VI   Results

Results here are not about bottom-line effects – these can never simply be correlated with specific interventions such as the change programme in a complex world – but concern possible effects on thinking, feeling, valuing and possibly acting. How have those involved come to view the outcomes of various activities? Is the change programme seen as having made any impact? When discussing the issue of results people had some difficulty in specifying what had really been achieved as well as whether there had been any documentation of the process. The results seem weak, perhaps even non-existent.

Uncertainty and lack of follow-up

According to Allen, the workshops were followed up: 'Every workshop that was implemented resulted in an action plan consisting of a number of issues, and middle managers followed them up so that they were implemented.' However, when asked if the top management group, of which he is a member, followed up the results of the action plans he said that they had not been able to do that satisfactorily. He talked about some form of review but was largely unable to present any knowledge of results from the workshops.

Still, Allen claimed that the management group was informed about the development and that they knew about the situation in the company:

A valuable thing with the cultural programme was the feedback that we received. We in the top management group could see all the action plans from groups compiled in a good way. So we saw what people were proud about, what they were frustrated about, where we were insufficient. This gave us a very good picture of the situation in the company.

He also claimed that the idea behind the change programme was to provide inspiration to rethinking rather than to accomplish something specific:

> This was thought essentially to be an impulse to the organization, an eye-opener. Of course you shut your eyes after a while. It's probably the case that it has been forgotten among us all. It's nothing that I think about now.

From starting with fairly strong statements about the valuable documentation of the workshops, Allen modified his position during the interview, ending up being more uncertain and modest about any specific results. Hamilton is also uncertain about what the workshops led to:

> If you look at the main site some things about insufficient meeting culture came out and also something about lack of coordination between units, from what I remember. [*Question*: Do you have any indications on what specific impacts the programme made?] No. Not very much, I'm afraid.

However, the problem Hamilton emphasized was known prior to the changes, even though it is possible that it was further clarified and addressed. Aldridge says: 'Generally it is rather easy to formulate actions, but to implement them and do follow-ups and measure them, that's far, far away. That's much more difficult, so there I see insufficiencies.'

The programme lost momentum along its trajectory. It started relatively ambitiously, but later steps got less attention and energy.

Lost momentum

As indicated earlier, the trajectory of the cultural programme lost its momentum along the way. Allen tried to explain how this could have happened:

> Howard was responsible; he was the CEO and had never delegated this. Hypothetically he could have delegated this and said 'Now I want you to take charge of this', but that never happened. The process dropped off; things come to nothing all the time without any apparent reason or thought; it just halted. When something just comes to nothing it is because no one does anything about it, not because you decide that things should come to nothing. It was not an intended action; it just sank into the background. Then I had paternity leave last autumn and had absolutely no time for these things.

One middle manager, Reid, talked about the result of the programme in much the same way as Allen:

> It came to nothing. The impression is that it came to nothing. It started well as we created a new company and we should have a common spirit and it's important to find out that spirit. To do that we were supposed to have some exercises

at departmental level in order to find out what was good and what was bad. Then managers were supposed to send the result back to the personnel department. I did my workshop but never sent back the results. Maybe it's my fault that it came to nothing but I never heard anything else. People complain about invisible management, cultural programme or not. There's been complaining about that since I started and nothing has really happened.

We have here the interesting paradox that the cultural change programme has produced what it was intended to do something about: lack of trust in management and a view of leadership as absent. It reinforces an impression it was supposed to counteract. We will come back to this in the final chapter.

About the outcomes of the projects, Neville said: 'I don't know but I suppose they wanted to build a new language in some way.' He was sympathetic to the intention, but had difficulties in connecting the value talk with everyday work:

[*Question*: The thought was to start using a new vocabulary?] Yes, I think so. I use it, I try, but it doesn't always fit into the daily work. But I try to use it occasionally. But perhaps it's a certain vagueness that contributes to you not having energy enough to drive these questions.

Another middle manager, Trevor, never thought he was supposed to actively implement the cultural change after the workshop, believing that the programme had petered out. When asked about whether there were any additional efforts besides the workshop, he said: 'Not as I understood it. I understood that something new was supposed to come out of this, about how we were supposed to act. [*Question*: Did you receive any feedback?] No, not directly. Not really.' He, like many others, seemed to view work culture as something that others initiate and instruct low-level managers to work with on a stimulus – response basis. On the question of any impacts he said: 'My impression is that reality hit us and the programme never had the time to make any impacts.'

One engineer, Parker, responded somewhat more positively to what the culture programme resulted in: 'Some things do work better today but it is difficult to know the reason for that. Indeed, it's impossible to know the reason.' But he also said that:

It was this workshop that we attended. Then we had a follow-up task that more or less came to nothing. It depends on whether you took charge of it or not. Then I haven't seen anything that came out of this initiative.

Even though some middle managers seemed favourable to the cultural programme few were able to specify any impact. It seems that it was unclear whether the culture programme should trigger ideas and actions based on the interest and initiative of the various managers after the workshops or whether they should just do them and then work with culture again when they got new inputs from management – instructions and instruments – for doing so. Most seemed to favour the second interpretation. But if they believed in the first option, they did not exhibit very much initiative and drive around culture work.

When we talked to the employees a year after the implementation process, they merely remembered certain parts of it. Nobody suggested it had made any difference.

Several interviewees said that they did not recall the key terms and values at the centre of the cultural change programme: 'It's been such a long time that I don't even remember the meaning of the concepts in the programme' (Turner, middle manager). 'I'm very bad at this. To be honest, I don't really know what they mean' (Cook, engineer).

This lack of outcome in the form of a clear memory of the content of the change programme is not necessarily associated with a negative view of the subject matter:

> I must say that you often have occasions like that and then you just forget about it all. We spent one day discussing what was good and bad and what we ought to change. We had a lot of suggestions but they came to nothing. Perhaps that is a sign that they weren't that important. I can't really remember if we did something after that, that is, some form of change that was connected to it [the programme].
>
> (Brooks, engineer)

> The programme was in connection with the start of TC but I don't think it has had any specific impacts.
>
> (Wilson, engineer)

The results of the cultural programme in terms of its organizational impact thus seem quite modest, if not entirely non-existent. We don't expect it to be possible to detect any simple cause – effect relationship in this area – efforts to measure culture's effects on performance are close to meaningless owing to the complexities involved (Alvesson 2013). But one can try to track whether the ideas, vocabularies, general feeling, rethinking, refocused attention, etc. seem to characterize the people targeted for, and encouraged to participate in, a change programme. There were very few signs of such effects in our case.

Even though some of the most closely involved managers tried to point to something concrete and positive coming out of the programme, they had difficulties in specifying what that could be. They talked about having received information about the situation in the company, and about what seemed to annoy people and what pleased them, including something about an unproductive meeting culture. This can, of course, have some value. And we can't rule out the possibility of people being a bit more conscious of shortcomings in how meetings are run, which may make these a bit more effective in some cases.

What is also interesting here is the effort from Allen to try to downplay the aims of the programme, pointing to how the cultural work should be understood as primarily an 'eye-opener'. This is a more modest – and possibly more realistic – objective as compared to what was stated at the beginning of the project, perhaps an adjustment to the perceived results (or lack thereof). This has been observed in other cases of organizational change. It is difficult to sustain engagement even among enthusiasts strongly in favour of change efforts as 'the realities of managing large-scale change hit home' (Dawson 2003: 160). Often enthusiasm wanes and the high profiling of change agent work is replaced by line tasks. It is not uncommon among managers to interpret this waning of change enthusiasm as a signal to abandon further change work. We will come back to this issue in the final chapter.

The middle managers also had difficulties in trying to specify the results of the programme, and some even had trouble remembering the programme. While a few talked about how the vocabulary might have had some impact, most said that the programme never reached people; many said that it just vanished in the sand. The engineers also seemed to have trouble recalling the programme and its content.

Summary – and questions

The cultural change programme seemed to accomplish very little. The efforts to make people focus on the key values targeted do not seem to have created any lasting impression and most people seem to have confined work with culture to specific ritualistic events when they were asked to do so. The activities and talk in the programme do not align well (or at all) to the substance of change as experienced by most people, something that normally produces not only frustration but also sometimes cynicism around change work (Bommer *et al.* 2005; Jabri and Jabri 2022; Reichers *et al.* 1997). In the majority of cases, managers and others did not seem able, interested or to have the time to work with the cultural themes on an ongoing basis. Very few of the original objectives appear to have been accomplished and as indicated by the examples in this chapter there are several reasons for this.

However, the programme may have had unanticipated and unintended consequences in the sense that it produced or rather reproduced and strengthened certain meanings, ideas and expectations characterizing the organization, including the view of top and senior middle managers as being invisible.

We can thus put within parentheses the ideas and objectives of the architects of the change programme and instead ask ourselves: what is happening here? What kind of communication of meanings and symbolism is taking place? How do the people involved – in different ways – contribute to the accomplishment of a shared organizational universe, or perhaps to a split and fragmented one? These questions partly mean a departure from a managerialist point of view and are well worth pursuing. Before going into these questions – which we will address in Chapters 10 and 11 – we will turn in Chapters 7 to 9 to addressing what went wrong in the change efforts and discuss how it happened that this large, internationally known company, aided by a consultant from a global, leading consultancy firm, engaging in a change project based on knowledge input also from two other consultancies and quality confirmed by still another consultant, monitoring the design – could fail so clearly in its efforts.

Part 3

Crucial issues in cultural change work

7 'It is not so damn easy'

Lack of consistency and expressiveness in cultural change work

Having described the change programme and how it was received, we now turn to how the people who worked with it viewed the process and the outcomes. We thus try to understand how people reasoned – to get the story from the actors' point of view. What from the outside may be seen as a rather peculiar way of working may thus appear to be more reasonable and make sense. We also use their accounts in order to produce some ideas about what went wrong – as indeed a lot of things did. This chapter reports reflections and comments from people involved in the process. These are typically post-project and reflexive – they look back and are produced based on hindsight. Partly based on this, we add our own analysis. We discuss the problems and failures of the change work and the process in terms of the absence of material offering 'cultural thickness', for example intensity and high-poweredness of symbolic meanings.

Immobilized engagement – on the difficulties in getting the process moving

A key idea in the change programme was to provide an occasion for people to address vital issues and encourage a flow of clarification and change work across the organization. According to top and many senior middle managers it was primarily the junior middle managers and their subordinates who were supposed to be 'culture carriers' and engage in and implement the new culture, based on ideals that were widely shared:

> The idea was to transfer a new way of thinking down the organization and also to encourage suggestions from below. The idea was to create a kind of wave within the company like 'Yes, we understand that this is a challenge and that this is business that we shall commit ourselves to.' The idea was that the individual should become the bearer of it [the programme]. The aim was to get the objectives of the company and the individual to be coherent, that you as an employee identify yourself with the company and receive something back, like challenging tasks, good salary and satisfying work conditions. But it is not so damn easy.
> (Aldridge)

DOI: 10.4324/9781003474555-10

We agree – and not much engagement, interest and identification with the company mission were produced. Junior managers seemed to expect that top executives and some senior middle managers would carry the cultural change. Neither senior nor junior middle managers were viewed as acting as role models in terms of embodying and enacting the claimed values. There was little engaged activity promoting the cultural change project in terms of pushing, persuading, reminding, preaching, reporting and making schedules for various acts and activities in line with the cherished values.

> We had our kick-offs as we became an independent company, and managers said 'We have a new corporate culture', but they didn't tell us what it was about so it all came to nothing. There was no substance to it. They talked extensively but without substance, and you didn't get any the wiser about it. They created some sort of ideal image that we don't have. We have a very long way to go there. It feels like they are not really working according to it but that it is some kind of show for the people.
>
> (Price, middle manager)

An engineer mentions negative attitudes to culture issues in the organization:

> At GT one can say that corporate culture issues have an extremely low status among the technicians, because as long as I have been working at GT every organizational change has meant that they only take the deck of cards and resort among the existing managers. This is done every year and there's no longterm strategy that guides the organizational change.
>
> (Cook, engineer)

The engineers sensed that managers did not take it seriously, that the new culture represented a utopia and that organizational changes were repeated yearly but mainly through letting managers shift position. The idea of creating a 'wave' of cultural engagement collapsed partly because the vocabulary accompanying the project was vague and efforts to clarify it mostly failed. As managers' interest and engagement were limited and the project for most appeared utopian with no clear connection to daily practice, the presumed surge seemingly never took off. There were plenty of deviations from what is suggested in the change literature. For example, managers did not function as (positive) role models, there was no clear rationale for why the company should embark on change, and there was not much anchoring of new approaches in existing beliefs and assumptions. But, as mentioned, this is the overall picture. Let us go more deeply into the situation and point out a number of key dimensions we think may shed some light on the misfortunes of TC in their efforts to improve themselves.

Key dimensions behind the problems I: coordination and prioritization

Some of the problems of the cultural change efforts seem related to lack of organization in terms of sufficiently clear and consistent roles and responsibilities as well as inexperience and lack of knowledge.

Problems of coordination – who is responsible and for what?

The managers involved in the project gave the impression that it was a bit frag-mented and half-hearted. For example, there was confusion about the responsibili-ties of those involved: 'To be perfectly honest, we didn't have any strategy. I've never worked with corporate culture before. I only felt like "Yes, this is really exciting", and I still say that. But it's incredibly difficult, really' (Hamilton, HR). Hamilton also said:

> If we could go back in time we would have worked differently. Howard pressed us. He said that the programme needed to be put into effect in the spring or too much time would have passed after the start of the company. . . . I didn't have all the information myself at the time of its launch; we just received the order 'This is what you should do.'

The comments indicate lack of reflection behind the coordination of the work: there are references to being ordered, time pressure, no strategy and neither knowl-edge nor experience. Judy Hamilton actually confessed that 'We should not have executed the programme the way we did.' Instead she feels that they should have continued working with the consultant 'in order to avoid the panic situation that we ended up in a year ago', but this was seen as too costly:

> Now we just took her material as it was formulated. I've never met her, although I know she was at some of the meetings talking about culture. But we should have talked to her and asked how she worked and how she reasoned about this and what the reactions were to this, all in order to implement it better.

There seem to have been several problems regarding responsibilities, and a year after the kick-off there were still many uncertainties. Those involved downplay their own effort and responsibility:

> No, I really didn't have any responsibility for it. I just facilitated somehow. It was John Howard and Allen who were its initiators and Duncan its implementer. Then they used me more as mentor and sounding board. Step one was that the ideas from below were presented to the senior management and now it's up to them to come back.
>
> (Aldridge)

Hamilton also minimized her own responsibility and talked about her own effort as some sort of 'post office worker', although she also blamed herself for not having done enough:

> Our task was really not to think so much about whether the basic values were what we really needed. [*Question*: You were supposed to gather what was avail-able?] Yes, and package it and implement it. Well, we weren't supposed to

implement it by ourselves but rather to give managers, who were supposed to implement it, a start package in which we explained what it was all about.

Key people then at least retrospectively disassociated themselves from the programme. This is in line with the restrained engagement of middle managers and engineers, as already seen. It is slightly ironic that the people supposed to be central in a change programme in which 'commitment' was one of the key words did not exhibit a great deal of commitment to the change activities. Change authors emphasize powerful coalitions driving change initiatives and active leadership, but in TC we can note how the lack of drive and powerful acting from those involved seem rather striking. On the other hand, when things don't go so well, people frequently downplay their involvement in and commitment to an activity or a project, for both psychological and political reasons. Parts of the disassociation are probably sense making in retrospect.

Another aspect of the coordination problem was connected to poor work processes, slow responses and limited pushing of managers:

The aim was that, apart from making people go through the workshop, we wanted to start some thinking. It sounds rather woolly but actually managers were supposed to document their workshops and send the results back to us. But then we ended up in stagnation and I met managers who asked me 'What really happened with the culture?' At such times I wonder 'Well, it just became an HR thing', which it quite easily becomes. You really should bounce this back to the managers and say that they are the ones who should be the cultural bearers, independently of what they think of these values. Another thing is that when they had reported in their actions from the workshop we should have followed that up faster. That's an excuse, of course.

(Hamilton)

Many of the managers involved in the programme were uncertain about their own as well as other managers' form of involvement and responsibility in the project. The uncertainties around tasks and responsibilities were partly attributed to top managers' problems of coordinating work, but there was also an element of self-blame. One can also note here the relatively narrow time gap between finalizing the design and embarking on the implementation activities that Hamilton referred to when talking about HR being pressed by Howard. This left little room for creative improvisation or reflectively translating the cultural vocabulary to local organizational conditions.

Other priorities taking precedence of the coordination problems seem related to many other issues, related to everyday work, taking precedence when the implementation of the culture programme began:

When we started the cultural programme many had clean desks, a new organization and a new management. Even if we had the old projects and people, there were new circumstances. What has happened since is that people's desks have been filled with daily problems and people don't have the resources to work with other issues. People work overtime and are constantly in crisis meetings in order to fix operative issues. You end up in a world where this week's performance becomes the most important thing, or making a delivery to a customer. Issues around communicating well, identifying organizational problems and developing managers get less prioritized. It's difficult to find the balance between the hard and the soft worlds, and the culture programme was soft. The workshops were not implemented in every unit either and not every manager was behind these ideas. You fall back into the old tracks and think that the new track is the way we always worked and nothing new really. It is easy to have such an attitude.

(Aldridge)

It appears as if some of the most sceptical engineers were partly right: there seems to have been a lack of communicated strategy and consistent organizational ideals where top and staff managers could exhibit support and facilitate the work of middle managers and their subordinates when there were efforts to go ahead with the culture work. In contrast, the work was described as inconsistent and fragmented; many people seemed involved but few had the time and support (or gave priority) to take the culture programme more seriously. This went for the entire spectrum of possible carriers and pushers for cultural change: top managers, HR people in charge of the practical work, senior and junior middle-level managers and the rest of the employees.

One could assume that a more ambitious change project would involve a powerful initiative followed by ongoing activities involving the mobilization of a multitude of actors calling upon each other as cultural change facilitators and workers: top and senior middle managers as role models engaged in pushing, encouraging and following up their subordinates; the junior middle managers communicating expectations up – as well as downwards – for clarification and enactment of values; engineers taking the opportunity of raising issues which they found unsatisfactory; and HR people facilitating the processes, reminding top managers of this work and trying to encourage them to keep attentive and mobilize at least some degree of persistence. The case shows shortcomings in all respects. It offers good insights on the problems of getting people involved in these kinds of enterprises. We will come back to this.

Key dimensions behind the problems II: on symbolism, emotionality and expressiveness

In addition to problems of coordination and the lack of experience in working with change projects (of this type) it seems that the efforts were characterized by insufficient symbolic and expressive managerial and organizational support. This aspect of organizational change is acknowledged by some authors on change but is still under-studied. We will now explore it in detail.

An emotionally unconvincing project

The project did not seem to stir up much interest and enthusiasm and was insufficient in terms of expressing an engaging and challenging message: 'I think that our cultural programme was a bit tame and bland. It wasn't revolutionary enough. The changes that were suggested didn't reach all the way' (Aldridge).

The high degree of instrumentalism – an emphasis on carrying out steps – undermined both intellectual and emotional identification with the project. This orientation was reproduced by middle managers, who also identified merely half-heartedly with the project.

The distance between the people supposedly responsible for driving – or perhaps administering – the change project and the settings where change work was supposed to be carried out is worth mentioning here. Hamilton expressed ambivalence about whether the HR people should try to push for action:

> It needs to be built on managers' interest and I don't say voluntariness, but this thing of phoning people and saying 'I can see that you haven't implemented your culture' doesn't fit my personal way of working. But perhaps that was what was needed.

The interest from middle managers was insufficient, requiring more follow-up and control from the HR people, something they were unable or unwilling to provide. This approach illustrates a central element in a behaviouristic perspective to change in particular, namely that the presumed change agent, here the top management and HR officers, position themselves outside the setting where change is to be accomplished (Tsoukas 2005). Many change efforts fail when staff are unable to involve line managers early on in the change process as part of creating a powerful coalition. This connects to difficulties in mobilizing energy and commitment from middle managers.

The instrumental approach to culture change can here be noted in terms of the construction of the possible intervention of the HR people as a matter of people 'not having implemented their culture' and the focus on specific actions. Doing culture means going through a procedure or following a manual. A stronger emotional engagement would have involved not just working with a predefined set of steps, but also exhibiting signs of and propagating the possible key values in a variety of situations. The HR people as well as the various managers seem to have been characterized by this quite constrained attitude to the culture programme.

Poor symbolic performance

This lack of energy and interest in the change work can be seen as related to the poor performance in those events and actions where the programme was being communicated.

This is supported by the reception and interpretation of the culture work, as discussed in Chapter 5. Many agreed with the importance of a new culture (although raising questions about the content in terms of its incomprehensibility) but then characterized the programme as a 'paper product', with superiors not acting as 'role models' and the culture as 'words without any particular sense and meaning', and in particular it seemed that the new culture was lacking reference in terms of how people and especially managers acted. Moreover, as seen previously from the kick-off, the management forum and the workshop, there was weak engagement and/or forms of instrumentalism, avoidance and neglect. A few things were striking about the presentation at the kick-off. One was the one-dimensional tone used by most of the managers as they neither raised nor lowered their voices at any particular moment in order to emphasize certain points or to arouse any feelings of excitement or any sense of urgency (Kotter 2018). (Mary Duncan was to some extent an exception.) The presentation was formal and proper and the jokes largely unsuccessful. If understood as an opportunity for an inspiring, persuasive and charismatic leadership, the kick-off could hardly be characterized as successful. The project simply did not appear to be particularly convincing.

This form of low-inspiring and low-convincing performance was continued by some of the middle managers in the workshops. Neville showed considerable uncertainty when carrying out the exercises, relying heavily on textbook material. Such material – quite the opposite of experienced organizational reality – is not easy to identify with. The issue that triggered the most intensive responses (as was the case at the managerial workshop at Satellite) was the logically fragile claim in the mission statement that every customer could be first. Perhaps this was a moment when the 'real' culture became manifest, engineers engaged in logical and sceptical thinking – and missed the very point of a value statement (which is not about formal logic). We can here also consider part of the discussion under results where one interviewee characterized cultural work as mainly consisting of filling in various forms with no real meaning to them. Many people hardly remember the programme and are very uncertain about how to respond to questions about its possible individual and/or organizational impact. All this suggests that there was a serious underestimation by top managers and corporate staff of what is needed in cultural change work just to create some interest and willingness to take these issues seriously.

Discussion – a challenge that vanished

Based on the interviews with engineers and managers it seems that the following aspects are crucial for understanding what went wrong:

- There was a moderate – and fluctuating – degree of engagement from senior managers and implementers, who introduced themes and advocated values without following them up or engaging in action in line with them.
- The formulations of the target culture were seen as utopian with no connection to existing reality.
- The project ambitions were vague and the means for accomplishing them were limited.

- Many of the persons involved seemed to lack sufficient experience and competence in working with cultural change.

The cultural change work was characterized by a certain ritualistic – rather than engaged and focused – instrumentalism. People did culture work as part of bureaucratic requirements and managerial requests and orders more than as part of a social movement. Listening to interviewees and seeing actors in operation gave the impression of a widely distributed lack of feeling for the deeper significance of culture as being about meanings and related to the experiences and consciousness of employees.

From a design point of view the project consisted of several dimensions that could be seen as important in working with cultural change. There was a target (wished for culture) which was supposed to create some form of inspirational stretch or tension, indicating values seen as crucial as guidelines in work, according to reasonably ambitious internal discussions and investigations by consultants. There was a cultural toolbox, including videos in which top executives emphasized and legitimized the culture change. There was a cascading process, emphasizing the importance of making every employee acquainted with the content and process. There were also the workshops, potentially held by primarily junior middle managers and involving almost every employee. However, when people talked about the process in hindsight, they did not complain about the idea of working with culture issues or the ideas expressed, but gave a direct critique against a far too weak design and the implementation of it – more paper than practice, more talk than real change. They were also sceptical about how the work was executed by the managers involved, in terms of the lack of both consistency and engagement (and perhaps identification) with the process.

Considering the comments about prioritization already noted, one could perhaps argue that with more time and less competition from pressured regular work tasks the situation might have looked different. So it is, of course, with 'extraordinary' or 'episodic' and long-term initiatives generally – they lose the battle for time and attention to what is seen as urgent and needs to be fixed in the short run (Sveningsson and Sörgärde 2023). The trajectory illustrates how the idea of cultural change as a 'quick fix' falls rather flat, since the centrally involved people did not seem to reflect much upon what they were involved in. The culture programme was insufficient to even modestly counteract short-term priorities and to inspire some ongoing interest in working with values and raise the perspective of the organizational participants. The culture work was marginalized and squeezed out almost entirely. It is perhaps surprising and not so common that the cultural challenge vanished in the context of immobilized engagement, given all the preparations and grounding in consultancy reports and, in particular, workshops involving as many as eighty managers and questionnaires directed to everyone in the firm. Given complaints about for example unsatisfactory leadership and other organizational problems, why didn't engineers and middle managers take the opportunity to use this event, where suggestions were encouraged, to try to influence things? We can here also point to many other knowledge-intensive firms, where people on different levels are actively and often with enthusiasm involved in working with organizational culture (Alvesson 1995; Kunda 1992; Thurlow and Helms-Mills 2015). One could here say that some organizations have developed a 'culture-affirmative' organizational culture, where people broadly see the value of culture and explicitly participate in culture shaping through communication and other practices. But TC did not belong to this category. The 'organizational culture' is rather one of 'anti-culture' – talk of values, etc. is poorly understood and seen negatively by many ('talk and paper'). The willingness and ability to organize from below – clearly encouraged and legitimized by the change programme – never materialized, reflecting deeper organizational patterns. This inability and lack of interest in local initiatives was certainly not only a matter of failures in the change work, but had deeper roots.

We have discussed the cultural work as fragmented and how there was a lack of expressive symbolism arousing and triggering people. Managers seemingly remained at an instrumental level – carrying out instructions, and unable to reach the hearts and minds of the employees. The cultural change work exhibited a form of architectural engineering with a significant shortage of flesh and blood, bearing the imprint of what Alvesson (2013) describes as 'a grand technocratic project' and Palmer *et al.* (2022) conceptualize as a director image of managing change. As we will discuss, these are not uncommon when corporations try to work with planned cultural changes. Dawson (2003: 168) suggests that, considering the contemporary climate of 'change fatigue' among many organizational members, it might be counterproductive to talk about the need for grand revolutionary changes: 'For many, change work is familiar territory and is more likely to promote cynicism and frustration than anticipation and euphoria.' There is little evidence from studies of organizational change that ambitious change efforts automatically capture the hearts and minds of people.

We suggest that the technocratic character of the project partly accounted for the problems many employees had in identifying with the content of the cultural framework and the implementation work. The cultural model contained items which people had difficulties relating to, especially the targets of the programme: the junior middle managers and the engineers, but also partly the HR people working as implementers and some of the senior middle managers. The culture frameworks could in this case be seen as devoid of 'deep' meaning. What was lacking was stories, actions from managers and others, examples, locally grounded vocabulary that was anchored in corporate history (of the parent company or of the businesses that preceded TC, as it was a recently founded subsidiary) and practice. In other words, it is vital to work with cultural elements and expressions that communicate messages and ideals that 'stick', that appeal not only to a 'this-sounds-good logic' but also to the hearts and minds of people and that connect to their lived experiences. There was no 'cultural thickness', for example intensity and high-poweredness of symbolic meanings behind the key vocabulary used. Translation to local vocabularies and circumstances, thus trying to make the large-scale programme seem important, was mostly lacking in this case.

Dawson (2003: 175) does not explicitly elaborate on the value of cultural thickness but suggests in general that there 'is nothing so impracticable as a packaged, prescriptive, linear change initiative'. We agree, but can add that it is not only impracticable but also unconvincing and non-engaging in terms of the hearts and minds of people. N-steps models are, as stated in Chapter 2, very popular – but also far from unproblematic (Sveningsson and Sörgärde 2023).

We suggest that the culture work suffered from what may be labelled 'symbolic anorexia'. This was presumably partly a reflection of the 'real' organizational culture and partly an outcome of the lack of competence, time, energy, fantasy and improvisational creativity of the managers, HR professionals and consultants involved.

Summary

In this chapter we have discussed the cultural work at TC as rather fragmented and instrumental. There was a significant shortage of strong intellectual and emotional/affective engagement from several of those centrally involved in designing and implementing the programme, but also from other actors unable to use the occasion to introduce and work with ideas, beliefs and values that could be seen as vital for improving the workplace. The cultural change programme thus exhibited traces of a technocratic orientation and did not provide a fertile starting point for working with the kind of expressiveness that culture projects typically call for.

We are not claiming that the change project would have succeeded if more engagement and persuasion had characterized the efforts. As this study, together with many others, shows, cultural change is difficult indeed. We are just indicating some important aspects contributing to the unfortunate outcome of our case. But there is much more than stronger 'input' to and engagement in a project that is important, as we shall see in the following chapters. Next, we turn to how the project unfolded among the participants taking part in the trajectory.

8 Disconnected work

Cultural change efforts decoupled

In this chapter we investigate how the change programme unfolded among the various participants on its trajectory. Considering the amount of preparation work and the seemingly well-engineered design previously discussed, one could perhaps expect the various participants to have been sufficiently well oriented about the trajectory and its aims. However, this cannot be taken for granted but needs to be investigated by following the movements of the actors and the kind of associations they established when facing the demands of the change programme (Latour 2005). In this chapter we thus trace the participants' views on how the programme unfolded more deeply than in the previous chapter. In particular we address links and transitions in the change work. We interpret the trajectory as a kind of continuous baton-changing in a relay race. We think that this metaphor has a broad relevance for understanding the management of change efforts. As stated, models of the n-step type, where the progression through a number of well-defined steps is supposed to lead to a high likelihood of success, enjoy tremendous popularity, and there is a great deal of trust in them (Palmer *et al.* 2022). Given this, an examination of the views, relationships and interactions – and lack thereof – between different actors more or less involved in various steps seems indicated.

In this chapter we investigate the problems of non-connections, reconnections and disconnections between primarily the consultant, the HR people, the middle managers (primarily junior) and the originators in top management (CEO and CTO).[1] We note a lot of contradictions and inconsistencies leading to a view that radically breaks with the ideas of continuity and consistency that were most central in the (drawing board) design.

The broader, and more theoretical, objective of this chapter is to illuminate the (limited) collaboration and interaction between actors – managers, consultants, HR professionals – in change projects, in particular problems with division of labour and a 'partitioning' of culture work.

From Excellence to HR – a first phase of loose connections

Previously we described how the HR people obtained the design of the cultural change programme from Excellence as a way of taking the baton and carrying it

DOI: 10.4324/9781003474555-11

towards the next phase, thus seemingly continuing and completing the consultant Clara Ridge's initial work. However, the HR people knew little about any cultural change project until late in the process. When she first saw a draft, HR manager Duncan thought that 'It was one-sided because she [Ridge] had only focused on the senior managers. We felt that it wasn't right to base a cultural programme and basic values solely on the view of senior managers.' Talking about how she had to complement Ridge's work, she said:

> If you want an impact it is very important that a cultural programme perme-
> ates and represents the whole organization and that's why we did the business
> orientation workshop at the end of Year 1. There we let employees define our
> strengths and weaknesses. One could say that the consultant did Part 1and then
> I had to take over and pursue Part 2, and then we put the two parts together.

Duncan suggests that her interventions connected to the work of the consultant and that she took over the baton in the trajectory as things needed upgrading. However, the drafts made by Excellence were more or less used as they had been constructed by Ridge in the distribution and packaging work. The one-day workshop mentioned by Duncan was rather something that moved in its own orbit parallel to the trajectory of the cultural work.

It is interesting how Duncan disconnects from the consultancy part (of which she is critical) in the design work, considering that it was the consultancy draft that Hamilton and Duncan took over and proceeded with in the packaging and implementation phases. However, the comment was made a year after the cultural launch, and some negative evaluations had surfaced, so the critical distancing from the consultant's ideas should perhaps be seen in that light.

Nevertheless, there were some concerns about the involvement of Excellence when a draft of the design of the cultural change programme emerged late in Year 1, and these concerns finally led to the dropping of Excellence:

> We had two alternatives. We could use Ridge in the implementation, but we
> thought that one million kronor was too much. She would have to visit every
> site and a lot of costs would be added. As Howard and we felt that the quality
> she had delivered was below what we had expected we didn't really feel it was
> perfect. . . . The first part of the programme had also been very costly. We took
> the decision, as we had the basic values, to pursue this from within, in contrast
> to using an external consultant. It felt fine to issue these messages from within.

It is particularly interesting here that despite some doubt about the quality of the material produced by Excellence the TC managers used it as the major intellectual input into the building of a new culture. The decision to disconnect from Excellence was based on the aim of showing the change as a company initiative:

> It should be clear that senior management back this, that it is not an idea of
> consultants but an idea of our own. We never dropped Ridge but rather agreed

that we take it from here. Her competence to run workshops was not higher than that of our own HR department. Her skill was to be able to see a company as a whole, to see these critical values and together with John and me identify these values that we needed in our business.

(Allen, CTO)

Discontinuing the work with Excellence is presented as natural. However, there were also other considerations: the insufficient quality and high costs of the consultant's work. There were, however, questions about whether the TC people could manage the implementation themselves:

We were not sure whether to proceed with Excellence or not. It was difficult to know how to act and proceed in a situation like that. We needed and were searching for a language that seemed relevant for those working here, a cultural vocabulary that people could recognize.

(Aldridge)

This view is partly supported by the interpretation that the task was reduced to passing on the message. Hamilton says that this work was about the straightforward delivering of the material to the managers who would implement the 'start package'. But there is also a view implying that this was not so simple:

It probably would have been best if Ridge had been able to participate a bit longer so that we could have achieved some form of overlap. We were in contact with her several times, but she seemed incredibly occupied, so it didn't result in more than her sending us her documents. We just took them and made compilations from them.

Hamilton further explains that: 'We should have proceeded with Ridge instead of just taking part of her material and using it.' Duncan is more inclined to emphasize the complexity of the work when she said the HR people had to decide upon the values to be communicated.

Nevertheless, the HR people received the material without any particular specifications for its use, although they had to come up with something in time for the kick-off in early Year 2. The comment suggests that they received something almost out of a 'clear blue sky' and, even though Duncan tries to reconstruct some form of continuity and logic when talking about the two parts of the programme, they could also be seen as very loosely coupled and the HR people could be seen as having merely vague notions of what to achieve. Even though Allen stresses that the disconnection of Excellence was natural and logical, Hamilton seems equally convinced that it would have been much better had they continued to use the consultant and avoided her fairly abrupt cut-off and the resulting discontinuity of the work. It is often suggested in writings about organizational change that the use of consultants can be valuable in successful change work, to the extent that they provide expert knowledge that empowers and significantly facilitates managers' change work (Cummings *et al.*

2020). Consultants also mean additional and focused labour. When looked at from a distance and on a more general level, the consultants in the case of TC could be seen as having provided the change agents with an appropriate cultural framework for executing change. However, looked at more closely and listening to those involved, it becomes clear that matters of how to interpret and relate to the material were considerably complex and difficult. To pass on the baton successfully is thus very much a matter of interpretations of the meaning of the baton by those involved in the change process. Nevertheless, the HR people received the material very late in the process and had to make something out of it; one thing was to make the material a bit more comprehensible.

Complex concepts and circumstances

The HR people thought that the values as stated by the consultant were:

> difficult to understand. They were difficult concepts that overlapped. I missed a simple version and had difficulties in understanding how this was related to myself, how I could position myself in those terms. I had difficulties in taking a view on the material because I thought that it included very big concepts and, no, I did not feel comfortable with them.
>
> (Duncan)

Hamilton also says it all 'went too fast' and that competence in the change was lacking. Duncan similarly says that:

> We had a workgroup and Aldridge, Allen, me and Judy felt that no one of us had any experience in pursuing questions like this. We had confidence in Ridge initially. She had created this material and done a lot of work that had cost us an enormous amount of money, so it was difficult for us to question this. We only had our gut feeling to base our judgement upon. Then we met this consultant who worked with issues of corporate culture and he thought that the material didn't look too bad and we used him as a sounding board. He also gave us some advice on how to manage the material in the implementation phase.

Here Duncan reinforces the notion that the amount of energy and resources that had been invested in the project made it difficult for them not to proceed with the packaging and implementation efforts by using internal resources. (This seems to be an example of the 'sunk costs' syndrome.) One had at least to try to take over the baton and continue the trajectory despite many uncertainties in the project and lack of competence. Bad timing added to the problems:

> The difficulty with this programme was to start working with the values before the organization had been formed and before anyone knew where we were heading, how we were supposed to be organized or what our customer portfolio would look like. We did the programme very early in the establishing of TC. If

we were doing it today we would have another view of where we were going. Now we have customers that provide certain values. It was too early to define values the way we did. The reason we did the 'business orientation workshop' was that people were totally confused and had no idea at all about how we would make money, what we should sell or how we would sell our kind of services. At that time the values were already created; it was very early; people hardly knew what they were supposed to work with. Senior management could have waited and let the organization and the senior management establish itself so that the managers would know more about the strategies and objectives.

It would seem that the culture project as such was disconnected from several other organizational dimensions. The comment reinforces the feeling that managers were indeed entering deep and unknown terrain. It was difficult for the HR officers to adjust, improvise and translate the material to organizational conditions.

In contrast to the neat and linear process as described in Chapter 4, the preceding statements suggest a process far from being well planned and designed, but rather loose, disconnected and forced. The change of baton from the consultants to the managers at HR was far from clear-cut in terms of both how and what (the meaning and significance of the content/vocabulary).

From HR to middle managers – a second phase of loose connections

In spite of the confusions and near panic created by the disconnection of Excellence and the time pressure, the programme was, as described in Chapter 6, launched at a company kick-off, a management forum at Titan and a management workshop at Satellite. These occasions were supposed to constitute forums for the change of baton from HR to middle managers. As previously discussed, these occasions were not particularly strong in emphasizing and explaining the cultural change programme, which did not emerge as the central issue in any of them. At the kick-off, issues of culture were introduced briefly and the impression was that the ideas about culture were still to be developed. It is unlikely that the attending managers felt that they were taking over the culture baton and were expected to become cultural carriers or change agents in any ambitious way. At the management meeting a couple of weeks later, the culture issues received more attention but even there the presentation lasted for less time than planned and was restricted to stating the vocabulary noted in Chapter 4 and distributing the culture toolbox. At Satellite the attending managers from the main site had difficulties convincingly stating the company mission and the idea of customer orientation, hardly creating the impression of an integrated change of baton in a fine-tuned trajectory. Perhaps the most obvious way of changing the baton over to middle managers at Titan was by the use of the cultural toolbox. Owing to the lack of substantial (non-formal) contribution from top managers beyond this, the culture materials seemed a bit 'out of context' and, although some of the attending top managers stressed that the issues were important, others seemed sceptical (at both Titan and Satellite). Indeed, one of the middle managers at Titan said at the coffee break that this kind of activity rather than facilitating work would obstruct technical and more important tasks, indicating that he would neglect to conduct workshops for his subordinates.

We can identify three problems here. There were uncertainties among many managers about the following:

- The what of the corporate culture: what is the meaning of the values?
- Who is supposed to do what in this process?
- Why is this important?

As described in Chapter 6, the workshops often did not function very well. Some middle managers proceeding with implementation reiterated the distanced approach that characterized top managers involved in planning and designing. Moreover, the material produced from the workshops was only partly documented and not analysed systematically. The often self-critical Judy Hamilton explained the weak documentation as follows:

> We should have worked a lot more with the managers. There are a lot of things that we should have done differently. It would have been easier to work with these issues if those of us from HR had attended the workshops, even as just silent observers and listening to the discussions there. But we really just received the basic values like that, and I think it was six at the beginning although we dropped one. I think that five values are too many for people to manage, and then there were three drivers on top of that.

The self-critique about lack of support to managers may be compared to the reluctance to be involved expressed at the time of the workshops, where the HR managers distanced themselves and emphasized the central role of primarily the junior middle managers.

Self-critique was also expressed about the lack of follow-up, but raised doubt about whether they should act as police: 'We haven't followed up. But to what extent are we really supposed to police and control things?' Apparently there were no significant attempts at systematizing the results and reconnecting to middle managers in terms of feedback. The process thus seems to have halted after the workshops took place. Neither Duncan nor Hamilton reconnected to the project as middle managers disconnected. Middle managers (those who attended the workshop, completed the documentation and sent it back to HR) sent the baton back to HR, where it seemingly was stored, at least according to Allen:

> You only have a certain amount of energy and time for these kinds of renewal activities and that time was engaged by another change programme [launched after the culture change programme]. When no one asks anything about it nothing happens. We stopped talking about the cultural programme at the Monday meetings. [*Question*: Who was responsible for the cultural programme when it

disappeared?] Howard was responsible all the time and he never delegated it although the implementation was the task of HR.

It appears as if the CEO was seen by others as the director in charge (to use the image of managing change suggested by Palmer *et al.* 2022), while he seemingly believed that others somehow would run the show. Accordingly, the programme vanished on account of lost momentum. Nevertheless, in Year 3 some claimed it was still alive (although it did not seem to be lively):

> [*Question*: So the cultural programme is still alive? You are still working on it?] Yes, we are. But I don't do very much now. We talked today about how we should work with the culture in general in the future. We still have to compile the results from the workshops. [*Question*: So by working you mean compiling the results?] Yes, that really sounds like something special but, yes, that's right. That is what we are about to focus upon now.
>
> (Hamilton)

What is most interesting here is the extremely instrumental way in which Hamilton referred to the programme. Cultural work is something that you do on certain occasions, when you are ordered to do a specific task or assignment. Somebody hands over the baton and you do something with it, hand it over to somebody else and then do not consider it much more before you receive it the next time. (Or you just drop the baton.) To use another analogy, working with culture is similar to filling in the tax forms.

Discussion – disconnected change of baton reflecting bureaucracy

When the HR people took over the baton from the consultant they 'received' something they knew little about and had difficulties identifying with. They were unable to clarify the meaning of the 'new culture' with the help of the one handing over the baton, the consultant. The relay race with its neat and pure continuity implied in Chapters 5 and 6 breaks down on account of the disconnection between key persons. Some authors of change suggest that those driving change efforts should constantly revise and modify plans in the light of problems and specific challenges encountered. This calls for continuous reflection, improvisation and local adjustments. A precondition is that the company refrains from doing too much in too little time. For example, a company that at first failed to initiate TQM revised their initial strategies by using an external consultant to communicate the ideas behind TQM in order to overcome barriers to implementation (Dawson 2003). These forms of local translations and adjustments were not present in TC, and a consequence was disparity of meaning and the experiencing of uncertainties.

There was also a significant disconnection in the change of baton from the HR people to the middle managers. An interesting paradox was the decision to disconnect the consultant and let HR pack and communicate the cultural change programme as it would look peculiar and untrustworthy to let a consultant present the company's values, followed by the recognition of the HR people that they had very limited understanding of the company's values. Realizing that they were unfamiliar with what was claimed to be the company's culture (or target culture), and feeling low confidence and credibility as presenters of culture, made them feel that it would have been much better if the consultant had been central, although as invisible as possible, in this part of the project. One can imagine a kind of optimal situation where the HR people are on stage reading the messages about what the company – which they represent – is supposed to believe in and value, supported by the consultant. She is simultaneously the director and prompter of the play, increasing the likelihood that the presenters 'get it right', but without being visible to the audience, which is led to believe that this is a corporate rather than a consultancy project. 'Authenticity' does not appear to be a key characteristic of the situation.

It can be added here that the HR people were also probably not really credible as representatives of the core groups of the firm. This was an organization dominated by engineers, and many seemed to see HR and HR projects as somewhat peripheral. The HR people then had the thankless task of delivering messages about the organizational culture that they did not understand to a group of people who saw them as non-credible in terms of representing key values around work and business. The only comfort was that what they saw as the nearest alternative – the consultant – would have been seen as even more non-credible.

As seen from Chapter 4, working with culture and using culture as a management control tactic or technique are typically seen as an alternative to bureaucracy. Control is exercised by values and norms rather than rules and formal hierarchy (Fleming and Sturdy 2009; Ouchi 1980; Ray 1986). Bureaucracy is characterized by division of labour – vertically and horizontally – including the separation of conception and execution, instrumentality, a limited focus, a strict chain of command, and a focus on following rules and delivering specific behaviours. The idea of focusing on culture is typically to encourage wholeness, integration, a wider commitment, the reliance on values and norms for control, etc. Against the division of labour of bureaucracy there are the shared values and ideas of organizational culture. It to some degree counteracts or supplements bureaucracy.

The strong degree of disconnectedness between the various levels and groups in the culture change programme bears the strong imprint of bureaucracy. Top managers and the consultant did the thinking; the HR people and middle managers were supposed to carry out the work with little understanding of the thinking behind the words they were expected to work with. There was very little integration or communication between the thinkers and the doers: the HR people were hardly involved in the planning and did not seem to have any say about who should be involved in the implementation. When the top managers 'dumped' the project in the hands of the HR people, there seemed to be strict boundaries between the latter and the former as well as with the consultant. The compliance of the HR people seemed partly to be grounded in their assumptions that 'enormous sums' had been invested and that they therefore had to proceed with it without raising any doubts or trying to get an overview or a stronger input through participation by top managers or consultants in the implementation of the target culture. In the absence of a deeper understanding and commitment the HR people took a cautious position, reducing themselves to the position of 'post office workers' supplying the input to the culture-shaping events.

The negative side of bureaucracy became even more apparent at the next stage, when the middle managers were supposed to work with culture. They tended to follow instructions – or in some cases resisted doing so – through the exercises in the workshop without much understanding of what was behind this or the purpose of it. The idea that they should be active and reflective and act as carriers of change did not seem to occur to them. Instead, there was a strong barrier to the conceptions, ambitions and sense of totality in terms of thinking through what they were doing and taking the initiative for reducing the gap between ideals and behaviour. The intentions and reactions of others in the chain seemed to receive limited attention. We can see here how bureaucratic structures and their effects on all involved quite effectively counteracted the cultural change work. It is also important to relate the outcome here to the problem of doing too many things in too short a time, common in many organizations.

We can thus point to two levels of structural problem undermining the change efforts. One was how the work was organized or rather not organized: where top managers, consultants, HR people and middle managers were disconnected and where the various steps in the handing over of vital tasks in the change project weakened its potential power. A second level was the underlying bureaucratic structure and the kind of cultural orientations that it produced, making it very difficult for the people involved to transcend the division between those who think and plan and those who execute, without much thinking.

A note on functional stupidity

The portrayal of people involved in the case is perhaps not too flattering and we may wonder if they were not so competent or very unlucky as the organizing went wrong. Some of these confess some mistakes and sources of embarrassment. As we will come back to, their misfortunes are not clearly outside the normal and many of the problems we have pointed at belong to business more or less as usual for many organizations, although not revealed by more superficial studies. One aspect of all this is what Alvesson and Spicer (2016) call 'functional stupidity'. This means seemingly sensible thinking within narrow, taken for granted assumptions and limited ability or interest in considering what makes sense from a broader perspective and lead to valuable outcomes at the end of the day.

In many cases functional stupidity means inclinations to stop thinking independently and simply follow orders, bureaucracy and expert advice. It often causes common sense, critical reasoning and the use of judgement to fail. Functional stupidity means that people think 'correctly' within a very narrow framework, type doing what is correct according to job description, a specific professional ideology or the fashion or follow instructions without much wider thought. Staying within a narrow identity, ideology and interest spectrum and following its imperatives without any broader reflections or critical reasoning is the core of functional stupidity.

People often have limited interest, energy or capacity to think outside and above immediate job demands. There is an inclination to reduce ones' scope of thinking and focus only on the narrow, technical aspects of the job. Functional stupidity is present when managers and employees are encouraged to do the job correctly, but without reflecting on the purpose of the wider context. One often assumes that arrangements and procedures are rational and that senior people and experts know best. Doing things right is more encouraged than careful thinking trying to doing the right things and take initiatives.

Sometimes functional stupidity represents an organized attempt to stop people from thinking seriously about what they do at work, as managers and others may want a docile work force simply doing what they are told to do and not creating problems through insisting on thinking for themselves and raise difficult questions, upsetting those much into hierarchy and other elements of the social order. They may believe if people simply do what they are told, things will be turn out well. But often functional stupidity simply emerges from below or from the complexity of contemporary organizations, including division of labour.

Relay race and hand over the baton thinking can be seen as closely related to functional stupidity. The latter both leads to such thinking and is an effect of work organized by it, with strict division of labour and limited capacity or interest in transcending it. People are then not so capable or willing to try to understand broader patterns, check their meanings with others, outside one's small unit or group and seriously consider what is the end result of all the work. What does it actually lead to, if anything? may be a difficult and worrying question. It is easier to stick one's own small work box and tick off tasks.

Sometimes people prefer to work within their own narrow horizon and refrain from efforts to take a helicopter view. The preference for functional stupidity and remain in a narrow thought-world is often strong.

In our case most people acted reasonably although narrowly rational in line with box thinking, contingent upon hierarchy and division of labour. This was obvious for middle level managers and HRM people. Top management also stayed within a sort of box, a strategic architect position and mindset, assuming that there work was more or less ready when having developed a plan and sparked it off. They did not realize the old wisdom: 'A plan is perfect until the first contact with reality.' Forgetting about the need to realize that plans far from always work according to the plan exemplifies a common form of functional stupidity in the executive suit. It is vital to have some sense of what goes on outside one's own small cognitive box and have some not too superficial indicators of reality 'out there'. Of course this is easier said than done, time and overview are limited and many people are eager to report good news and cover up problems they assume top managers prefer not to be told of. Positive reporting often dominates and badly informed views of the change project as fairly successful seem to have been common among senior management and people reporting to them.

Summary and comment

In this chapter we have looked at the trajectory of the cultural programme as a relay race. The changing of the baton may be a key element in the problem of getting any results. The process seems to have suffered from discontinuities between actors supposed to be central at various stages and the weakening of commitment, focus and an understanding of what the cultural change should be about. When new actors got the baton they did not seem to know sufficiently what to do with it, where it came from, what it should be used for and exactly by whom it should be used.

We have focused on the disconnection of the consultants, the connection of the HR managers, the disconnection of the latter, the connection of the middle managers, and finally the disconnection of the middle managers and the inability of the HR managers (or top management) to reconnect to the programme. Parallel to this we have also shown how top management, after the initial phase, mainly seemed to have relied on delegation and thought that the intentions would be more or less automatically realized through people following the designed procedure.

On one level, the apparent problems confirm many normative authors' convictions that top or senior managers must be involved and actively encourage or even demand middle managers to lead change in their units rather than to drive change through corporate staff- and consultant-led programmes (e.g. Beer 2017; Heracleous and Langham 1996; Kotter 1996/2012). But this is perhaps too simplistic. The case shows how the difficulties of translation of messages make the various restarts taking place when an actor enters the picture in the next phase of the project quite open and unpredictable, that is, when it comes to meanings and the carrying out of routine tasks. Top and senior managers being active and putting pressure on middle managers would perhaps help, but what people do with the material they receive is as important as the force or energy they are exposed to (Latour 1986). And there is often resistance or radical revisions of ideas by groups targeted for change. Change should be seen as constantly performed through actors actively reproducing it through additional force. There is no energy in the trajectory that somehow keeps it alive if it is not fuelled by a 'fresh relay' (Latour 2005: 38). It is thus not only – or perhaps even mainly – a matter of top and senior actors being highly involved and pushing. Even more significant are the acts of broader groups: the extent to which others become enlisted and share something with each other. Their actively making sense of what is going on and what they could do in this context is crucial and this is not the simple effect of managerial push.

Orientations and behaviours indicated by the relay race metaphor are quite common in change work. In many cases, the change of the baton is perhaps less unfortunate than in our case, but it is very possible that the difficulties indicated by our study are quite common. Our case raises questions about whether the n-step image and way of organizing change work is as positive as regularly portrayed. Perhaps what is needed and would have been beneficial is more overlap between elements (a reduction of planning/implementation divisions), placing various actors in a broader context, and broader and interactive sense making and interpretation of what has happened, what is going on and what will happen. Some idea of phases or milestones and ingredients is presumably necessary, but, as already stated, step thinking has its drawbacks and risks.

Note

1   As explained in Chapter 5, the process of developing a cultural change originated during spring Year 1. The Excellence consultant, Ridge, took charge of the development during autumn Year 1 in order to develop a design for a cultural change. As Excellence was disconnected in December Year 1 the design was placed in the hands of the HR people. They were assigned the task of formulating a culture change programme to be presented to the organization in January and February.

9 Hyperculture

In this chapter we further investigate the ideas and expressions of the cultural change programme. We frame it as a hyperculture – a collection of positive-sounding statements about values that is often decoupled from the everyday-life thinking and practices in organizations. We also briefly address 'real' or experienced organizational culture – emergent culture as implicitly expressed in a variety of work situations – and compare the two.

The term 'hyperculture' is inspired by certain postmodernists using the term 'hyperreality'. They emphasize representations or simulations of reality which are communicated and attain interest and thereby, in a sense, become more real than the phenomena they are supposed to mirror (e.g. Baudrillard 1981/1995; Boorstin 1961). Representations in the media, including advertising, take the upper hand and matter, socially, more than other kinds of realities. The brand is more real than the object it is supposed to aid the identification of. Persuasive images are attractive, pedagogical and aesthetic, and are easy and positive to focus, meaning that hyperreality sometimes becomes more significant than other phenomena. This centrality of representations may be valid mainly for some groups and then only part of the time but sometimes they may be more significant and taken seriously more broadly. There is a general trend in this direction. Some occupational groups – communicators, consultants, marketing people, branding 'experts', educators, staff, managers, politicians, government officials, pop-management writers – may to a large degree have less of a reality contact and mostly be engaged in plans, policies, PowerPoint presentations, media reports and more idealized talk about activities and organizations (Alvesson 2022). Occasions such as meetings and representations following their own logics and conventions on how to report about phenomena may be more significant for these groups of people than any clear feeling for the reality 'out there'. Sometimes it is even possible to trace a certain 'operational phobia' or anxiety, an unwillingness to get intimate to the concrete core and real practice of an organization. This distancing is sometimes also legitimated with that of 'development projects' and 'strategic questions' which are highly significant. It is also important to avoid intervening in what other people – the concrete and core business – are engaged in (Sveningsson and Alvesson 2015). There are thus many reasons for people to avoid 'reality' and concentrate on representations, projects and ideas detached from, and sometimes even

DOI: 10.4324/9781003474555-12

decoupled from reality. (This is facilitated by uncertainties about what is exactly reality – plans and images are in a sense also part of the reality and for many managers and consultants PowerPoints may be much more 'real' than any possible reality 'out there' in the R&D department or factory.)

Employing the term 'hyperculture', we address the formulated culture and the activities to express, reinforce and/or change it in terms of its highly packaged and thereby very tangible nature and ceremonial talk and as a somewhat surreal fantasy, with a remote connection to everyday practices, meanings and experiences. We also emphasize its manufactured and aesthetic nature.

A 'hyperculture' is not unreal. It is rather an easily identifiable narrative of corporate culture, portraying culture as clear, strong, homogeneous and convincing. It is typically either ambiguous in relationship to or detached from the 'real' organizational culture – the latter referring to complex and often fragmented organizational life. A hyperculture is also about specific acts and activities in which culture is focused. It is typically composed of a set of positive-sounding stated values circulating in the business press, in consultants' standard vocabularies and in many companies' mission and value statements. We will further explore the concept after we have looked at the work at TC from this angle and then connect to some relevant theoretical literature. We begin exploring hyperculture by investigating it as a package and a manufactured product, after which we discuss its ceremonial aspects and, finally, consider it as fantasy.

Culture as an unpacked package

The kind of culture addressed in the cultural change programme has a very distinct and materially anchored character in the sense that it is written down and is the focus of very distinct activities. At TC the 'realness' of the culture in this sense is illustrated not only by it frequently being thought of as a package but also by its very material character as a parcel, including the equipment to be used for the reinforcement and/or change of culture. 'Package' is, in our case, not just a metaphor.

As shown in the earlier chapters, for some centrally involved people the tangibility of the culture work was very strong. When the preparations for the design were handed over to the HR people Hamilton referred to the task in these terms:

> Package it, or rather package it and implement it. Well, we weren't supposed to implement it by ourselves but rather to give managers, who were supposed to implement it, a start package in which we explained what it was all about.

Culture is like a parcel, and the supposed cultural change experts appear mainly like post office workers, seeing to it that the parcels reach those to whom they are addressed.

The HR people were more or less to assemble the parts of the cultural toolbox into something that looked like a well-coordinated and tightly knit package. This contributed to the reification of the 'culture' and to the view that 'we, in HR, had to take the package and bring it to shore'.

The post office work was scheduled by the kick-off and management meetings, making delivery times tight. The time pressure was also evident in the recordings of the two tired top managers in the video, part of the package to be sent to employees.

At the management meeting the delivery of the parcel was effected as the cultural toolbox was handed over to people. People took the toolbox and generally seemed a bit lost. Duncan and Hamilton were running around seeing to it that everyone had received their toolbox, making sure that no one left without 'the new culture'.

The overall image and specific vocabulary are worth noting here in some detail: 'package', 'parcel', 'distributed', 'delivery', 'landed here', 'bring it to shore'. There is a high level of consistency, recommended by some authors as important in order to produce coherence and direction and shared understanding (see Palmer *et al.* 2022). We are, however, not sure that the vocabulary of post-delivery is the most suitable to the creating of cultural change. One would perhaps assume that this coherent vocabulary would lead to efficient post office work, but this was not the case. Somehow the reports delivered by the managers after the workshops were never delivered to the right address.

The new culture is, at least on the level of the espoused, thus quite distinct, specific, concentrated, simple and thing-like, as indicated by the formulated values and the produced material. Culture as a parcel including a toolbox and a manual and a few labels is thus quite the opposite of culture as pictured by scholars of organizational culture. These portray culture as partly tacit and implicit, associated with a set of meanings and understandings that are manifested in different situations guiding thinking, emotions and actions (Alvesson 2013; Geertz 1973). Culture is complex, messy and difficult to understand and grasp. It is the opposite of a parcel or a thing. We will come back to this, but here restrict our account to contrast the hyper-qualities in the programme with what we see as a view of culture grounded in meanings and experiences.

The parcel and post office metaphors suggest a quite severe dose of management wishful thinking, common in many planning approaches of how to accomplish change. The logic here assumes that things will work automatically as long as the post office works according to the design. It seems to be believed that the appeal of the cultural values expressed will do much of the trick. Middle managers will take the suggestions to heart, understand the importance of them and try to implement the managerial expressions and ideals.

Sometimes managers are criticized for focusing only on the formulation part in trying to create cultural changes, neglecting the implementation phase. In this case, however, a link between these two parts is advanced, with the agents of the post office, HR people, delivering the formulation to the implementers. Still, of course, this expresses an assumption that the cultural toolbox is self-explanatory, the vocabulary speaks for itself, there is no or little need of further clarification and the recipients of the material will refrain from returning it to the sender (at least with too many demands for clarification). It also assumes that the managers easily understand and identify with the values expressed by the vocabulary. For the implementers, the middle managers, it is presumably merely a matter of unpacking in order to let the new culture install itself like any other software program. Indeed, the cultural toolbox almost becomes the new culture. It comes close to a parody on corporate culture.

A particularly interesting aspect related to the post office image is the considerations around using HR instead of the consultants when presenting the cultural values. We turn to this aspect next.

Culture as manufactured

Even though we, for pedagogical reasons, occasionally express ourselves straightforwardly, our basic position is social constructionist in the sense that people do not meet a fixed, given reality but 'do something with' it, for example construct meanings. We are not claiming that hyperculture is 'false' in relationship to 'true' culture.

There are, however, different kinds of constructions. This is clear when we consider the task of the senior managers and the consultants in our story. To produce a version of culture that is supposed to be used in order to represent and improve an organization in public settings is an activity different from efforts to make sense of, interpret and communicate one's everyday experiences in less exposed and formally engineered contexts – even though both activities are matters of constructions.

In the context of hyperculture we talk about manufacturing a representation of (projected or targeted) organizational culture – in opposition to other, informal, everyday life-based construction efforts. In manufacturing organizational culture there is the restriction of producing something that is short and accessible and sounds good. There are clear production rules and constraints for people in the hyperculture business – consultants, executives and HR staff.[1]

A big problem in the work with the 'new culture' in our case was that the material – from workshops with managers, etc. – was quite diverse, so getting it down into five values seemed quite arbitrary. The logic behind the outcome ('the culture') was less the material indicating the values, meanings and reasoning than the more or less tacit product expectation – and institutionalized norm – that it should end with about five values capturing quite a lot. This apparently called for some fairly brutal interventions and arbitrary moves in sorting and combining input to culture from various workshops. The idea of manufacturing hyperculture – rather than just 'discovering' it – seems indicated.

An interesting paradox is that the culture is something that is invented to a large degree by the consultant, but to show that the 'culture' refers to the values of the firm the consultant must be disconnected and be replaced by the HR people. Their problem is that they do not really know what the terms signalling the 'culture' stand for. They assume that the consultant does, but this can be doubted. She could probably define the terms, but possibly not relate these to the meanings, experiences, values and beliefs of the people at TC.

Nevertheless, through this arrangement a kind of catch-22 situation is produced. The person who is thought to be able to present and explain 'our values' is excluded from doing so because of not being 'one of us' and thus a poor representative of 'our culture'. The persons who are, by top management at least, seen as legitimate representatives of 'our culture' can't present it, at least not without much uncertainty and doubt, because they do not know what 'our culture' is.

The values are thus disconnected from those supposedly holding and/or wanting to promote them. This disconnectedness and the artificial nature of 'our values' really being a consultancy product with an uncertain relation to 'us' can be seen as a key characteristic of a hyperculture. The continuing loose and ambiguous relation between the culture and those supposed to be carrying or led by it reinforces the impression.

We think it is common for firms to rely heavily on consultants and HR staff who are often not able to attain a deeper understanding of culture and face expectations of producing something that appears easy and accessible and sounds good – and is thus often deceptive. We think that a lot of ignorance or poor understanding and questionable representations are typical for 'culture experts' working with hyperculture. Limited competence as well as time constraints and customer demands all matter here. We will show in Chapter 10 that this was at least the case in TC's change programme.

It is important here to underscore the institutionalized nature of 'corporate culture'. Broadly shared expectations and norms for the formulation of cultural values put strong imprints on it.

Culture talk as ceremony and ritual

An interesting aspect of the cultural work is that it is mainly restricted to a few situations where it is explicitly addressed. During these events there is much talk about culture, although with only a minor bearing on any organizational reality outside these settings, according to many middle managers and employees.

One engineer said that what is important in cultural change is that management should 'not just talk about how we should behave because that does not work; they have to behave differently in order to make us behave differently' (Dunbar). Another said similarly that words about how things should work are insufficient in trying to change the behaviour of employees:

> If someone orders me to raise my motivation it will not help at all. If I, on the other hand, see that something is actually happening and things are really moving, you see people who are doing something and not just talking, that's another thing.
>
> (Holmes)

The statements suggest that those presumably driving the change also need to behave in accordance with the new values, to 'walk the talk' as is commonly suggested by authors of organizational change. But, according to many interviewees, the values were perceived as remaining at the level of ceremonial talk, restricted to certain situations where everybody seems to celebrate these values. It seems more important to carry out the performances scheduled in the cultural programme rather than work substantially with the cultural values related to the everyday reality of employees, as considered vital by most authors of change (Cummings *et al.* 2020).

Many people remembered that there had been culture meetings and a programme in circulation in the company but, at the same time, they were scarcely aware of its particular content nor did they have any particular knowledge about whether it may have mattered in any respect. 'At the bigger meetings, they have someone who is responsible for the culture and they come on the stage and say something but then it sort of becomes unimportant' (Henley, engineer). Corporate members then saw performances such as the kick-off, the management forum and the workshops as being primarily ceremonial in a negative way. Ceremonies can, of course, also be positive, inspirational and pride enhancing. Dawson (2003) discusses a manufacturing company using 'roadshow meetings' where staff were encouraged to discuss operations and express concerns about a quality programme. In another case, that of a bank, a forum or 'one-day event' functioned as a way of communicating intentions of change in an inspiring manner. However, absence of observations and in-depth interviews about what actually happened during these events and how those involved related to these makes it difficult to assess the possible positive features and outcomes. In TC similar occasions were weak in terms of any substantial cognitive, affective or behavioural impacts on employees. Corporate culture – or at least work on it – appears as an aside.

Culture work seemingly circulated between specific, orchestrated events and at (ideal) levels beyond the everyday lives of most employees, including managers. It remained a senior management-driven set of events with which few employees identified themselves. One may talk of empty rather than rich and expressive ceremonialism. CTO Allen, for example, said about the values that 'It is nothing that I think about on a daily basis. However, the five basic values are still valid. We even show them to some of our customers and we also show them to newly recruited people.' The values then appear as a signpost, functioning as a flag, waved at specific extraordinary events. The marketed culture represents something a few of the managers involved would want to see rather than something realized (we return to this aspect further in Chapter 10). Culture – and here of course we mean hyperculture – is something that you refer to when you want to give a good impression to those who are not really familiar with the organization. You may salute it, but not necessarily pay much attention to it.

Culture as grandiose fantasies about the future

Interestingly, a few managers talked about the new culture as already being in place, that is, not as a target culture. Given the perceived distance between the presented and experienced values of most employees this appears as a fantasy about being a grandiose organization. The rhetorical appeal of hyperculture thus catches some people, but – and this is a feature of hyperculture – only in specific situations when it is in focus. It is a temporary seduction rather than a conviction held consistently.

In the drafts of the target culture created by TC top managers in collaboration with the consultant and reproduced by the HR people there was a certain mixing of descriptive and normative elements. Descriptive here refers to top management's claims to have captured what existed. In some of the presentations, the kick-off and management forum, this mixing of managerial ambitions and descriptions of the existing situation was further pronounced. Going back first to the draft it indicated the shared values reflecting existing reality. For example, commitment was seen as our way of working, leadership was described as characterized by trust and inspiration, communication was placed on a par with sincerity, decision making was characterized by empowerment and finally the organization structure was clear and guiding people in their teamwork. If we also turn back to the 'explanation of the essence' of commitment as presented in Chapter 5, the mixing of ambitions and descriptions may become even more apparent. For example, there was talk about: 'Our customers come first; their current and future needs fuel our innovations', 'We always deliver; our customer agreements are met on time', 'We are all customer oriented and familiar with our business activities', 'We are proud of our technical expertise and we learn from experience', etc.

Commitment is thus described as a 'shared value' in the organization, that is, the way people at TC are working, and this means that customers come first, that we always deliver, etc. This could be understood as not explicitly suggesting aims but rather claiming to describe existing and actual conditions.[2] As we have seen, the great majority of the employees did not support the claims that this was the case. However, for those producing and presenting hyperculture there is a blending or oscillation between ideals and what most people (including probably themselves, if encouraged to critical reflection) believe exists.

Since the shared values are symbolically displayed as a jigsaw consisting of a few pieces that fit nicely together there is a strong suggestion of harmony and fit between central organizational elements describing the existing organization. The draft creates an odd feeling. The description is labelled 'winning culture' and it presents the 'targets' or what could perhaps be described as wishful managerial thinking of the ideal organization as something of an existing reality. At the kick-off, CEO Howard commented on this jigsaw when stating that:

> It should all fit together. Someone made a jigsaw puzzle so I can show you that everything fits together. Hopefully all the other topics we have covered today will also fit together, all our plans, strategies, business, and the most important thing is that we, the people here, work together and that we can share this. That is the key to success.

It seems that Howard is not only presenting aims but also stating how they in fact are working, turning the managerial wishes into existing reality. The feeling of talking about something in the future as already being in place is also expressed by HR manager Duncan:

> Part 1 [of the cultural programme] was when the consultant met every manager globally in workshops and defined what they wanted to retain from the old unit and what they did not want to retain. We took these results and complemented

them by asking the employees what they wanted so it was not just a managerial matter. What emerged from this was the five basic values and three drivers: five jigsaw parts as our basic values, and in the middle of those we have defined our three drivers, i.e. the heart of our business, that which makes us a bit unique as compared to our competitors, that which characterizes our business. It's about having outstanding customer relations; we have to have good relations with our customers. Our success builds on our customers' success. Then it's our first-class software technology, that we have a fantastic software technology, and then we have strong teamwork, that we work a lot in teams – that is important for us. This is really what constitutes TC. These three parts are the cornerstones of our business: our employees in terms of teamwork; our technology: what we sell; and that we have good relations. The three drivers must live in balance with the shared values. It's them together that make our target culture.

This quotation is fascinating in a number of ways. The culture ideas are said to be the heart of our business, something that perhaps distinguishes us from our competitors, and what characterizes our business. Here we find the essence of the company followed by an uncertain idea about what may distinguish it from its competitors (perhaps 'a bit'). Then follows what is probably standard stuff in a large number of contemporary business organizations: customer relations, technology and teamwork. Here the technology is indicated to be the best: it is both 'first-class' and 'fantastic', while customer relations are 'outstanding' or 'good' and teamwork is 'strong' and 'important for us'. Then it is all put together in the 'target culture'. The account then moves from where we are now to what is targeted, without any apparent awareness of the need for distinction and clarity about the heart of our business and what we hope to become. There is a kind of projected 'us', transcending any sense of realism, as the current situation, as understood by most employees, is broadly seen as quite far from an ideal situation, with a tricky corporate situation and a problematic heritage.

   This kind of mixing of claims of what exists and ambitious targets (ideals) underscores the idea of a hyperculture. It is neither a serious effort to capture analytically what exists in terms of values, meanings and orientations, nor a clear ideal (ideology) stimulating improvements, based on clearly recognized imperfections. It conflates ideals and what exists with 'target culture' – used to signal ideals and values which are clearly not realized, but which are important to strive for and embrace. Reasoning around target culture – in opposition to hyperculture – realizes (at least some of) the imperfections of current reality and focuses on the gap.[3] For top managers and consultants eager to confirm the target position in delivering positive news and developing and maintaining an appealing picture of a fine organization, there is an inclination to go for what sounds very good:

To be honest, I think that when TC was created the new CEO thought: 'Well, now we have a chance to start a company totally anew and now we are going to make a real role model company.' Then he hired a consultant supposed to participate with the CEO and his leadership team in order to produce a corporate culture which they presented as: 'This is the ideal and this is what we stand for and this is what we are going to work towards.' But then the daily reality hits and it turns out to be a paper product – a paper product that theoretically could have been very good, if it had worked. But it is still a paper product. Someone has just said 'This is the way we will have it.' But people don't work like this in their daily work.

(Hamilton)

It is an idealized claim to 'culture', much better – more appealing, simple, straight-forward, aesthetic – than the presumably less appetizing cultural orientations 'really' characterizing the firm, that is attractive to top management. They prefer 'hyperculture' rather than something more complicated and less aesthetic. We will address this – based on an interpretation of our empirical material rather than the TC people's claims about their 'culture' – in Chapter 10.

Conclusions

In this chapter we have demonstrated the significance of different ways of mobilizing language and other popular expressions in change efforts (Brown *et al.* 2009). More specifically we introduced and developed the concept of hyperculture, argu-ably a key issue in understanding a lot of work with managing culture and working with organizational change. We have addressed how the TC change programme can be understood in terms of this concept.

Hyperculture is a set of claims about culture, which is real in the sense that there are specific documents, a video recording, a specific vocabulary and a set of activities. The representations claiming to capture culture are clearly there. Hyperculture may even be said to be more 'real' than the values and meanings expressed in everyday practices. The latter are not so clear, espoused and easily communicated as hyperculture. Hyperculture is often claimed to be unique for a specific organization, but tends to be institutionalized. This forms the 'uniqueness paradox' (Martin *et al.* 1983) – claims to be different are expressed in standard-ized ways. The appropriate values are to be found in management writings and the mass media, and turn up in many firms. They are often standard stuff, copied because they sound good, are easily recognizable, provide legitimacy and have an aesthetic appeal. Hyperculture overlaps 'target culture', but the latter is used to signal ideals, while hyperculture has a more uncertain status in relationship to what actually exists, and managers often confuse ideal and reality. This seems to be common for organizations' claims about their cultures – indicating a broad rel-evance of the concept of hyperculture.

We have in the chapter discussed the cultural work focusing on hyperculture in terms of:

- post office activities;
- manufacturing;
- imitation and conformism;

- ceremonial talk; and
- ideal fantasy creations.

Firstly, the post office activities pointed towards an interpretation of culture as possible to assemble and package. This package is just waiting to be opened and automatically installed, perhaps upgrading the existing culture. The idea here is that, when unpackaged, the new culture is self-explanatory and virtually living its own life.

Secondly, 'culture' is the production of this material that lends itself to packaging and post office-like activities. Manufacturing hyperculture calls for 'culture experts' boiling down a wide diversity of meanings, understandings, value claims and beliefs into something that is economic, sounds nice and is appealing. A challenge here is often to deny complexity and accept only a remote connection between various inputs to the culture definition and the end product.

Thirdly, the element of copying more or less standardized statements about culture is salient, reflecting the general tendency to isomorphism in organizations (DiMaggio and Powell 1991).

Fourthly, culture as ceremonial talk refers to how much of the work was experienced as empty rhetoric without any real substantial bearing on the experienced reality of both engineers and managers. The idea here is the ideal rhetoric living its own life as a form of hyperreality or, in this case, hyperculture.

Fifthly, cultural work portraying an ideal state can be described as a grandiose fantasy. This fantasy is sometimes blended with the existing reality as if the future ideal were already realized in the company. People seem to move unreflexively back and forth between what they see as an ideal world difficult to realize and their experience of what actually exists. To the extent that the future ideal state is taken or seen as the present real world, it certainly can be seen as a (primarily) managerial idealization of the existing reality with limited reality sense.

Culture in this sense – that is, hyperculture – appears as a cut-out representation that is loosely related or even quite unrelated to the complex and mixed meanings, ideas and orientations characterizing organizational everyday life – what most serious students of culture would refer to as organizational culture. But the purpose of the hyperculture is perhaps not to capture what goes on or what can realistically be accomplished; it is rather appreciated and used for its aesthetic appeal and its elegance at the level of presentation. It is to be used for 'official' communication. This can also be seen in the business for quality management as well. Organizations usually adopt quality programmes for, as they say, improving intra-organizational participation, trust and communication. The problem with many of these programmes is that they remain at the level of the espoused in relation to reaching deeper cultural levels of meaning and beliefs. However, they do sustain image building and fantasies of identities of what the organization stands for. Dawson (2003: 149) states that: 'It is the rhetoric and bureaucracy of quality management which requires scrutiny and criticism, if companies and their employees are not to fall foul of a totally questionable method.' The purpose is to appear good – and this may make senior managers and consultants dealing with this fine-sounding

vocabulary also feel good about themselves and the fine organization they are leading (or advising) when talking about it in ceremonial situations. In this way hyperculture is a better phenomenon to address and focus upon than whatever goes on
out there in the everyday life of an organization, which is the social context for
complex, ambiguous and often far-from-ideal (from a managerial point of view)
cultural manifestations. A great problem is, however, that most employees, at least
in our case study, may experience organizational life as so contradictory to hyperculture that the latter creates frustration rather than satisfaction. In this sense hyperculture does not – as postmodernists like Baudrillard (1981) indicate – make a great
impression on most people and occupy their sense of reality; it only takes hold
with those heavily engaged in working with it. For many, it leads to irritation rather
than inspiration. Their outlook is quite different from that of those manufacturing, approving, distributing and buying into hyperculture – 'symbol workers' (top
managers, consultants, HR staff) at some distance from the majority of employees
whom one tries to reach.

We postpone generalizing from our case until the final chapter, but would like
to emphasize here that hyperculture is a general phenomenon, although we do not
claim that all organizations are 'doing hyperculture', nor that it leads to many negative reactions and confusions at TC. Indeed, the tendency of other organizations to
talk about culture as a fine-sounding set of values and ideals is a prerequisite for
using the expression 'hyperculture'. There is often some local variation, but the
publicly available standard for how management in organizations talk about their
uniqueness tends to guide consultants, senior management and HR people setting
up a corporate culture composed of five (plus or minus one) positive values. Hyperculture then is a matter of broadly shared and easily accessible espoused ideals, not
so much about what is really believed in.

Of course, the observations and ideas put forward here are not only relevant for
work on organizational culture change, but most likely relevant for understanding
management and change projects addressing a range of other issues (where culture
is perhaps only implicitly involved). Phenomenon such as TQM, agile ways of
working, knowledge management, digitalization, HRM policies, etc., often come
out, we imagine, as more real in technologies, programmes, plans and other representations than in the experiences and practices 'out there', amongst larger groups
of employees. Arguably, contemporary organizations have a lot of this 'hyperqual-
ity', although it is salient mainly for managers, consultants, staff and other people
preoccupied by a particular kind of symbolism.

Notes

1 There are, of course, also rules for others, including anthropologists and other culture
  researchers (like ourselves), on how to talk about culture, but these tend to be looser and
  are not constrained to a few stated values. The rule for qualitative researchers is to not
  reduce culture to a few characteristics. The rules for academics writing about culture are
  of less interest to us here.
2 Of course, claims of these being existing values do not rule out that there may be variations and imperfect realization of work practices based on the values. One could imagine

something in between ideals and what is realized – something believed in and partly realized. One could for example say that everybody seriously strives to increase the job satisfaction of the employees and that this is an ideal actually guiding managers and others without necessarily being realized fully. In the present case there is no clear indication that this is what people in TC have in mind – the fluctuation is between ideals (targets) and claims of what exists without much explanation or nuances.

3   Hyper- and target culture are similar in the sense that they express simplified, good-sounding, for semi-public consumption versions of 'culture', but differ in the sense that target culture refers to ideals and objectives, something to strive for, while hyperculture indicates a representation of what exists or is at least unclear about any possible discrepancy between the existing and the ideal (objectives).

Part 4

Getting into the substance of organizational change work

10 Working with culture versus culture working on change workers

A general question is whether people can control organizational culture or whether organizational culture is controlling people. Can we access and do something about the deeper aspects of culture? Or are these operating behind our backs? These are key questions around cultural change programmes far too infrequently raised. We think our case study provides good material for illuminating this.

Study of a change project of course tends to focus on an intended change and the process and outcomes of the change efforts within the explicitly targeted area. So far we have worked with such a focus, but now we redirect our attention somewhat and investigate certain *non-targeted* cultural manifestations that come across in the organizing processes in various change activities and responses to these. This means that we do *not* confine ourselves to the change people try to achieve in terms of reinforcing or changing value orientations in line with the target culture. Our approach means that the change activities are not considered in terms of how they consciously and instrumentally affect culture, but how they non-consciously and involuntarily *express* culture. We are here more interested in how a cultural perspective can illuminate organizational life rather than looking at the change efforts per se and the failures and successes of these. In other words, we try to study what the people in action can reveal – often unconsciously or involuntarily – about the organizational culture. As is often the case with organizational cultures, in TC it works behind the backs of people, through taken-for-granted orientations and unreflective ways of working (Alvesson 2013).

In this chapter we are still interested in the activities and processes around the change work, but we approach this more 'openly' and 'freely' than previously, and do not stick to the investigation model guiding this study as a whole. Here we relate the change programme to a broader organizational context. It is thus not seen as an instrument for change, controlled by managers, but as a non-conscious expression of organizational culture. Later in the chapter we explore how parts of this non-recognized culture are reproduced, thereby undermining and counteracting what the cultural change programme was said to accomplish.

DOI: 10.4324/9781003474555-14

Concepts of culture

In order to clarify the perhaps easily confusing use of the concepts of culture, we will make a distinction between three versions of culture – or rather 'culture':

1   Hyperculture, as explained in the previous chapter, that is brief and idealistic representations of corporate culture bearing the imprints of consultants and key managers involved in designing the programme.
2   Experiences of culture held by organizational members. This refers to what these members tend to think, feel and pay attention to when accounting for values and practices associated with corporate culture.
3   Organizational culture in an 'anthropological' sense. This is a more theoretical and researcher-driven view, where the idea is to describe and interpret the 'deeper' or tacit, perhaps non-conscious or non-registered, aspects of culture. This is a perspective on organizations which draws upon but goes beyond the ideas of organizational members. This is the view that we described in Chapter 3.

These three concepts can refer to empirical phenomena that are disconnected or overlapping to various degrees. Hyperculture may not contradict the experienced reality of most organizational members to the same degree as at TC, but some disconnections from and contradictions in relationship to experienced culture are typical characteristics of hyperculture. Anthropological culture may go hand in hand with the other two to various degrees, but normally there is a difference. The aims and logic behind hyperculture, the lived reality and the outcome of ethnographic work and cultural analysis tend to show some or considerable variation (see Table 10.1).

Some discrepancies are unavoidable and are characteristic of the inspirational and promotional purposes of hyperculture, but too profound contradictions lead to frustration and cynicism and/or change work where change agents have no control over the change work. The TC case illustrates this.

Table 10.1 Concepts of culture

Hyperculture	Explicit, for semi-public consumption, management-driven representation
Experienced corporate culture	Organizational members' ideas, values and sentiments about organizational cultural reality
Anthropological organizational culture	The culture researcher's 'thick description' of in-depth meanings, based on ethnographic work and cultural analysis

The change programme as an expression
of organizational culture

As many interviewees expressed the opinion that the culture change programme was a paper product remote from their everyday life and the real organizational practices, one could say that the cultural change programme tells us very little about organizational culture. It may tell us more about how consultants operate or how executives live in their own worlds, as seen in studies taking the experiences of employees more seriously (Dawson 2003; Preece *et al.* 1999). Arguably, this is a general phenomenon of considerable relevance for corporate management and change projects. What is being espoused thus says something about aspirations and ideals, but less about the shared meanings and values that actually inform people's thinking and actions and thus shape organizational practices. Still, how people worked with the cultural change programme can be seen as offering vital clues to organizational culture (Balogun *et al.* 2015; Van Marrewijk *et al.* 2010). Talk, events and actions as well as the reception and interpretations of those targeted for cultural change – mainly engineers and middle managers – can be seen as cultural manifestations, with effects on the shaping or rather reproduction of sets of established meanings and understandings, that is culture.

Organizing work: top management driven?

An interesting phenomenon that comes through strongly in the critical comments of the culture programme is the strong emphasis on top managerial behaviour. Cultural change for some people seemed to be entirely dependent on top management changing its behaviour. An engineer, Dunbar, was asked about the implementation of the shared values: 'The only way that a culture can change from above is when management acts differently and not only talks about acting differently – not by writing about it in a booklet.' It is easy to agree with the opinion that writing about things in a pamphlet will not lead to much, although some enthusiasts of organizational discourse – believing in the magic of language use – may dispute this. Our interest can then focus on managerial actions (or lack thereof). From most normative points of view, typically embracing managerialist understandings, where management acts and other people react, this appears self-evident.

We don't deny the relevance of such viewpoints, but think that considerable attention should be devoted to how other groups, for example middle managers and highly educated non-managerial employees, think and act (Todnem *et al.* 2018). It is far from self-evident that middle managers and engineers can't take the initiative to change, at least on the local level of projects and work within specific units. There are several studies of organizational change that suggest that changes, sometimes radical, emerged primarily as a result of local actions and spontaneous experimentation and learning from lower-level managers and employees 'on the floor' (Beer and Nohria 2000; Palmer *et al.* 2022). As discussed in Chapter 2, Dawson (2003) shows in a study of the introduction of TQM that the employees did not really understand the statistical side of the quality systems and instead of using sophisticated techniques invented simple numeric measures and group-oriented problem solving such as brainstorming. The statistical aspects of TQM were replaced by interpersonal skills, communications and group relations. There are of course sometimes casualties of change but employees are seldom just powerless victims of top management priorities and organizational structures. The large majority of the employees of TC were civil engineers, highly educated people from a large Swedish technical university. They were not underpaid immigrants or third world workers in a sweatshop under a harsh regime. But in our observations and in the interview accounts about the cultural change programme as a paper product unrelated to reality, very little came through of the engineers and the middle managers as resourceful and active subjects, contributing to the formation of an organizational reality through their values, beliefs, orientations and, partly based on these, actions. In the change project at TC, employees were passive and reactive. They constructed an organization in which culture was done by others – senior people – to the majority, who thought that they must wait and see what top management did before relating to ideas about values.

We find strong indications of this passivity and avoidance of agency. However, some nuances are notable here. For example, when asked whether cultural issues were a concern only for management, an engineer responded:

> No, they are not, but it's a matter for them to begin and words do not help in this case. You have to show how things should work in a way that helps. If someone orders me to raise my motivation it will not help at all. If I, on the other hand, see that something is actually happening and things are really moving, you see people who are doing something and not just talking, that's another thing.
>
> (Holmes)

Here top management is not seen as the only category responsible for organizational culture, but the rest of the organization is placed in a follower position. The basic orientation is one of wait and see. Only when top management clearly demonstrates something may one consider actively relating to this. We think it is possible to identify two prototypical interpretations of the cultural change programme:

- *Interpretation 1*: 'If they think they have created culture only because we put values on everyone's door, well, it will not help if you're not working actively with the concepts. I don't think you create culture like that. Culture is rather something you see when the different parts of the programme get support and establish themselves. No, I don't believe in talk and paper if nothing happens' (Turner, junior middle manager). This interpretation seems to dominate strongly among, primarily, TC junior middle managers and employees. People are sceptical, cautious and very reluctant to try to contribute with ideas and initiatives in the organizational culture area.

- *Interpretation 2*: 'The point is that you plant a seed and then it will work by itself' (Anderson, senior middle manager). This interpretation is less based on the top-down model of the organization and assumes that the cultural change programme is intended to work as a source of inspiration, to mobilize employees broadly in the form of taking responsibility for values, and in bridging the gap between values and behaviours. A positive interpretation would suggest that the stated values were fairly well grounded in broad discussions within the firm and that the workshops offered some support with and inspiration to working actively with these in terms of adjustments, improvisations and experiments at a local level.

That interpretation 2 seemed to be so uncommon in the firm gives us strong clues of organizational culture (and likely in many, if not most organizations). This can be said to be characterized by hierarchical and bureaucratic orientations. People take hierarchy and existing work structures as given. These can perhaps be changed by top management, but not by themselves, people assume. There are frequent complaints about bad management, invisible leadership, etc. But this is one-dimensionally ascribed to higher levels in the organization. Ideas and values promoting local initiative or down – up pressure – feedback, critique, suggestions, actions – to improve the frustrating situation seem to be absent, on the whole. Of course there are exceptions, for example, Neville's co-workers provided suggestions for what he should do.

In this organizational culture, where the assumptions and values mean that agency is ascribed to top and senior levels and reactivity to oneself (as a lower-level organizational member), at least when it comes to organizational issues, a change initiative relying on low-level participants as chief cultural carriers is not likely to succeed. One can compare this to Heracleous and Langham's (1996) findings from a consultancy company, discussed in Chapter 2, in which a governing assumption about human nature was that people were self-motivated and self-governing agents acting in an entrepreneurial manner in terms of taking local change initiatives. Since this assumption and its connection to behaviour and organizational practices were made visible in the change process the cultural change work could acknowledge that and thus make the changes more productive. In the TC case, with the absence of detailed pressure and pre-specification of what to do, and the general open design in terms of what the workshops should lead to, this kind of assumption was not absent in the change programme. There was a loosely indicated assumption of employees being able and willing to be active and reshape the organization. It did, however, surface only vaguely and incoherently and was not backed up by broader orientations. It lacked directive power in terms of seriously affecting the identities and orientations of lower-level middle managers and employees. As with many change programmes emphasizing participation, it included the paradoxical combination of being initiated and driven by top management while relying on people lower in the hierarchy to be activated and engaged (Musson and Duberley 2007). Of course, the former easily undermines the latter.

Bureaucracy

We can add to this point by considering what is being exhibited during the cultural change programme in relationship to bureaucracy. Contrary to what is commonly suggested in the business press, pop-management books and even in many social science texts, bureaucracy is still a common, perhaps the dominant, organizational form in one version or another (Alvesson and Thompson 2005; Monteiro and Adler 2022). This, of course, reflects the considerable advantages of the bureaucratic form. As indicated in Chapter 4, TC and its parent company were in many ways strongly characterized by the characteristics of bureaucracy: hierarchy, horizontal division of labour, disconnected work tasks, separation of conception (planning) and execution, a strong emphasis on procedures, etc. Of course, this picture needs to be nuanced. There was no detailed control of the engineers, who had operational authority over their own work. Rules and standards for how to work did not play a large role in the execution of labour processes – at TC most employees did knowledge-intensive work with a fairly high degree of discretion over their work. There was space for innovation, and in many everyday work situations engineers were more active and self-directive than they appeared in our case (Rennstam 2007). Still, the overall organizational form – in particular as it came through in the cultural change work – bore the imprint of professional bureaucracy.

As we pointed out in Chapter 5, the cultural orientations associated with this structural form were clearly manifested in the cultural change programme. There was the division between those who planned and those who executed. People saw their work mainly in terms of limited and constrained roles. These tended to be taken for granted: middle managers tended to wait for instructions on what to do. Vague suggestions – such as 'work with culture' – were resisted or led to a very limited response and then no further initiative. Individuals typically did their own tasks in the overall chain of labour and took little responsibility for or developed little interest in what happened before or after they had conducted their own piece of work. In the change project, those involved exhibited little engagement in the overall project work. People worked mainly alone and there was not much teamwork in the change programme. Individual managers were supposed to do their work on their own; there were no efforts to link up groups of people to support each other and work jointly on the culture theme. (Of course, they worked with subordinates, but not much with other people expected to lead workshops and cultural change.) There was also limited interaction between different levels. Middle managers did not take much initiative in finding out what was the purpose of all this and how various actors – from top management to lower levels – could interact in order to make something good happen. Middle managers were understood to be people who worked on the implementation of ideas decided by senior levels, not actors participating in organizing processes through initiative and thinking about strategic and long-term developmental possibilities. This 'passing-on-the-message' orientation was very different from what we refer to as everyday reframing – a more local and active way of working with cultural change (Alvesson 2013; Todnem *et al.* 2018).

The HR people and the managers appeared to work with culture mainly as tasks to be ticked off after they had been carried out – this was a work style that fitted into a bureaucratic form, where people carry out procedures irrespective of personal feelings about them. The problem is, of course, that for values to work people must believe in them. For managers leading workshops expressing values they do not adhere to may be counterproductive. And work with cultural change is perhaps not best done if treated as if you can do it in certain delimited situations and forget about it most of the time. Culture work needs to be 'non-bureaucratic', at least as long as it is not about values such as order, control and rule following. (Of course, some organizational changes are about realizing these ideals, but here the change work needs to deviate from a 'bureaucratic' style and use means such as horror stories about the dangers of lack of order, discipline, obedience to rules, etc.) But, as discussed in Chapter 2, most models within the planning approach apply some form of n-step logic and can thus be seen as more or less bureaucratic, perhaps a key reason why these models so often fail as guides to accomplish change according to objectives (Pettigrew 2012). The latter, especially cultural change, normally involves breaking away from an emphasis on formal rules. Organizational change usually involves encouraging creative, innovative and experimental activities (Balogun *et al.* 2015). This is not to say that a degree of bureaucracy should or could be avoided; some use of instructions, standards and rules is often necessary, but it should not be a major element in change work.

At the kick-off for TC, CEO John Howard emphasized that 'we will have fun', but the tone of the speech was formal and diplomatic – with the exception of an irritated remark about people being late. There was not much fun exhibited here. Instead the value of neutrality, reason and formality was being communicated. Rather than a 'fun' workplace, a bureaucratic one – typically constrained in terms of 'fun-ness' – is being expressed.

Remote managers claiming to 'be involved'

The change process also exhibited various indications of managers being invisible or distanced from lower-level employees. One example of this was that the top managers, after launching and presenting the project, did not seem to express much interest in it. The lack of follow-up could be read as a low priority being put on exercising visible leadership on an ongoing basis. Top managers communicated the importance and claims of commitment to a set of values, but the lack of persistence and variation in demonstrating this did not improve their credibility in the eyes of their subordinates. Another example was how middle managers were also viewed as quite distant. In a workshop we noted the following statements among subordinates discussing the leadership of Neville as part of a cultural exercise while he was absent for a short time:

> 'What is very good for Neville, I think, is that you talk to him on a regular basis', says Marsh, being the first to mention Neville's name, 'every second week or so, just five minutes to chit-chat, tell him what you are doing, what's

on your mind, so that he gets sort of in touch, so that he stays in touch. If he doesn't come to you, you should go to him, just to tell him what is going on, because sometimes he is very busy and I think it would be very good for him if you just steal five minutes from him every now and then.' 'If he can', Kerr says, 'he should dedicate one day in his calendar, one afternoon, to support, and talk with everybody.'

When Neville re-entered they all made 'shh' jokes and laughed. He said: 'Leadership and trust. I think from my point of view, what is very important is being involved without controlling.' His idea of leadership was more about support and less about expertise and problem solving. The others then told Neville what they had been talking about, stressing the idea that they had to tell Neville more about their problems and that Neville should be more involved in informal activities such as coffee breaks. Neville then summed up ways in which they could support each other.

Here Neville emphasized that he believed in being involved and giving a lot of support to people. But the personnel indicated that they saw him as heavily occupied by other activities and the valued support would call for some significant changes to be realized.

We seem to have here an example of the generally quite common discrepancy between the espoused, which sounds good, and the practices, which appear typically less positive (Argyris 1982). Even though events such as this encounter may encourage changes to reduce the distance, the overall picture of the change project seems to have been that senior managers preached involvement and visible leadership but then exhibited limited ongoing commitment to the very project supposed to lead to the realization of these ideals.

Scepticism about organizational and HR issues

Another example of how the change programme manifested cultural orientations rather different from the espoused ideals concerned how organizational changes were viewed as top managerial initiatives disconnected from the specific work of the employees:

> I think that most of the ideas in the cultural programme are right. I do think that we have a hell of a job to act in accordance with it. But I think that every step we take in order to reach it is good. But there has been a tired scepticism since the years when we were an internal unit within GT. There we went from golden times to not-so-golden times and had a leadership always telling us how fantastic everything was. There is tiredness in the organization like: 'Now top management thinks we are going to do this but what does it actually mean to me?'
>
> (Rogers, middle manager)

The understanding of organizational changes was then that these were often habitual, sloppy, short-sighted and useless, and that work with organizational issues was viewed as negative. A related experience was that change efforts were understood as HR issues, unrelated to the substantive issues and concerns of other people:

> Managers were supposed to document their workshops and send the results back to us. But then we ended up in some stagnation and I met managers who asked me 'What really happened with the culture?' At such times I think 'Well, it just became an HR thing.'
>
> (Hamilton)

Ideas and talk about organizational change were seen as unrelated to work and practice, but strongly connected with superficial ideas and with HR people and top managers ignorant of and perhaps not interested in 'substance'. To the extent that this negative value of work with organizational changes guided people, there was a negative framing of the cultural change programme from the start and an inclination to call for evidence that this was serious business before giving it a chance.

This negative framing was then reproduced and even reinforced through the experience that the culture project did not become more than an 'HR thing' (Legge 1995; Wang *et al.* 2022). One cultural consequence of the project then was the devaluation of this kind of work and thinking. Generally in corporations, there is some scepticism against 'HR things'. In many organizations where culture is viewed as the key thing, there is no association to HR (Alvesson 1995; Kunda 1992).

The change project as evoking existing task-related priorities

A key motive of the change effort was to encourage the employees to move away from a narrow technological focus in favour of considering wider concerns associated with the market and ways of working.

Among the top managers at TC there was one who was less favourably positioned towards the cultural programme and even used it 'negatively', that is, as a means of reinforcing a view that the existing technically oriented tasks were what should be the primary focus in the organization. This manager, Klaus Wolfe, suggested that one did not accomplish commitment, customer focus and other parts of a cultural change by the use of a planned cultural programme, instead suggesting that managers (and engineers) 'live culture'. Being in charge of very large projects, and deeply involved in technical development issues, with tough demands on subordinates, he influenced how some people saw the cultural change. About the cultural programme, Wolfe said:

> I don't believe for a second that you can come up with a programme and only talk about things; you must live it. If you don't live it as a manager you can do whatever programme you want. Maybe you will get some progress on the surface but at the end you will not move anything, not for a second.

Further, Wolfe criticized this in the management team, saying 'We must stop the management tralala [culture programme]' and that he was 'getting really upset about this cultural tralala'.

One manager at Satellite said about Wolfe: 'We have these ideas about culture and the cultural workshops but what Wolfe does is completely contrary to that. So there are two cultures. There's Howard's idealistic culture and there's Wolfe's culture.' Another manager at Satellite explained similarly: 'Wolfe doesn't buy into it. If he in theory agrees with it, he doesn't buy into it in practice, so it's a different . . . he runs a different culture.'

Although there were mixed views about Wolfe's style of management, many seemed to think his way of acting impressed people and had effects:

> He has been up here twice and he did a very good PR job on the people who were working on this project, because he does have breadth of knowledge and the way he says things means that engineers can associate with him more than with Howard. [*Question*: Why?] Because he takes decisions; he makes decisions. The way he says it the engineer can relate to it; he jumps up and around shouting; he definitely motivates people.

Engineers seemingly related to the demands and ideas of Wolfe's emphasis on the specific work tasks and the technical aspect of the work within the company. He thus to some extent undermined the change project and, although he was against its form rather than its substance (the values expressed), his focus on and celebration of the work tasks and his generally negative view of the cultural change project had some spill over consequences on the objectives of the change project.

It may appear that Wolfe's approach – with a strong focus on action and a powerful (even authoritarian) way of emphasizing his points – could easily be seen as superior to the one expressed by the cultural change programme, in particular as most people saw this as too much talk and paper. However, the value of reflection and trying to lift the focus from immediate accomplishments in existing projects should not be underestimated. Wolfe's focus on intra-organizational project work may also be seen as reinforcing the technological orientation of TC, which, as we saw in Chapter 5, according to top management and consultancy reports was too strong, at the expense of market and customer values.

Unintentional reinforcement of existing culture

The cultural change work seemingly accomplished a relatively weak impact, if it achieved any impact at all, in terms of changing what most people in TC perceived to be the existing culture. Did this mean that it had no effects? Not necessarily. It would seem as if the cultural change programme in unintended ways reinforced the existing organizational culture and to some extent counteracted the espoused objectives. In this section we elaborate upon this, perhaps for some change-minded people, paradoxical result. If we emphasize the 'deeper' aspects of culture – which are not necessarily what people in an organization recognize as culture – then it is difficult not to be caught and be guided by them (Alvesson 2013; Schein 1985). This is the case even if one believes that one is engaged in the business of changing culture.

In terms of our three concepts of culture, one could say that 'anthropological' organizational culture puts a strong imprint on and runs the show behind the backs of those trying to push for hyperculture. Non-conscious assumptions and meanings portrayed by this cultural understanding also influence the experiences and views of organizational members to 'wait and see' and towards disinclination to take the initiative (see Figure 10.1).

The overall objective of the change programme was to improve the organization. An important element of the culture concerned scepticism about organizational

Hyperculture

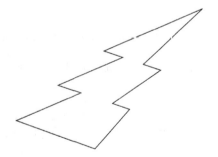

Experienced corporate culture

Counter-change force

Anthropological organizational culture

Figure 10.1 Levels of culture

issues and organizational 'knowledge'. As stated, broad groups of managers and employees viewed organizational initiatives and change efforts as superficial. Work with development of the organization, value talk and HR was viewed as soft, fluffy and of limited value and relevance. These meanings informed the reception of the change programme and contributed to its lack of success, but were also reinforced by experiences and meanings ascribed to the programme. The majority of the TC employees appear to have got their views confirmed and reinforced. The outcome of this was increasing scepticism against efforts to work with organizational issues and additional difficulties in doing so in a successful way. A down-valuing of organizational work meant decreased capacity to do so. In this way the change programme backfired. Experiences of earlier change programmes played a major role in accounting for the success or failure of subsequent ones (Palmer *et al.* 2022, Sveningsson and Sörgärde 2023).

Related to this was the view of managers as distant and invisible, and 'leadership' as generally weak. One idea behind the change programme was to improve leadership and reinforce the trust in managers. There were some discussions around leadership that may have led to increased understanding and perhaps feedback for development. In the case that we followed in detail, the exchange of views regarding Neville's espoused value of being involved and the subordinates' perception of him not being so was probably productive. Discussions like these are often valuable. However, given the frequent references to the change programme as a paper product and top and many senior middle managers as not doing anything visible in line with the espoused values, one effect of the change programme on organizational culture thus seemed to be to produce or reinforce meanings and assumptions around top management as detached from work and not very credible. We got the impression that many people seemed to think that top and many senior middle managers were superficial and inclined to wishful thinking and appeared to be out of touch with what went on in the organization at the level of production.

Other aspects of the reproduction of the existing ideas, meanings and beliefs may in more subtle ways have worked against the intentions and aims of the change project. As stated, the beliefs and orientations associated with a technocratic-instrumental and bureaucratic work style characterized the change project. This work went against objectives such as teamwork, commitment and customer orientation, all calling for a more social and flexible orientation to work, in which considerations wider than just focusing on one's own piece of work were vital. The relationship between intentions, actual cultural manifestations and cultural consequences was, however, probably weaker and more indirect here, as it was restricted to a small group. Even though it is questionable whether a bureaucracy-impregnated way of trying to accomplish change had any significant consequences in terms of organizational culture, one can note that the key group supposed to drive cultural change was guided by and reproduced orientations that were out of line with the direction of this change.

The non-emotional, non-expressive, asocial, constrained commitment signalled in some of the acts of top managers trying to communicate cultural values probably did not appear as very convincing, but may not have counteracted the intended ideals. These were not about creating the kind of original and colourful hoopla-hoopla culture of a sect-like nature that characterizes firms with 'very strong' corporate cultures and a special climate and style. (This surfaced to some extent in CEO Howard's talk of having 'fun'.) Nevertheless, when the cultural change activities showed managers with 'poker faces', these encouraged other orientations than those openly propagated by the change effort.

Our overall assessment is that, even though many of the elements of reproduction of the existing culture did not directly run against the cultural change programme, parts of these stood at odds with the change ideals and sometimes even tended towards the direction of reinforcing what it was supposed to change. It is difficult to assess the significance of this, but we can note that there was at least a non-negligible element of guiding thinking, feeling and values in another direction than the one espoused in the change project.

Conclusions

In this chapter we have addressed the general (re)production of cultural meaning in the change programme. This means that we are less interested in what was accomplished in terms of goal achievement (or failure) and more interested in the meaning creation outside, independent of and occasionally in contradiction to the change programme and its targeted values. We have asked what the events, actions and interpretations around cultural change activities tell us about the organization from an anthropological-cultural perspective.

Existing culture is here defined as the meanings, beliefs and values played out in various everyday situations, guiding organizational members in a variety of scenarios (see Chapter 3). This is a bit more specific and oriented towards everyday practice than what most people focusing on cultural change have in mind, in particular if they subscribe to a hyperculture view on culture. Hyperculture can, in principle, connect with and change these cultural manifestations. Values signalling explicit ideals rather than the values people live by may trigger moves closer to the former, making hyperculture less remote from the values, beliefs and meanings actually guiding people at work. But this does not seem to have been the case with the change programme we have studied. Most employees saw it as remote from how the organization worked and there were not many signs of reduced gaps.

A key feature of the organization, in the context here studied, seems to have been the passivity of most actors. People seldom referred to a 'we' or reasoned as if they themselves as members of collectives or as departmental managers put any imprints on the organization. Even a manager like Rogers referred to how 'it' was, not what he or others did. He even said that the 'project I am working does not act according to these values'. It can be noted that he did not say that 'we do not act according to these values'. His formulation indicated that the project lived a life of its own determined by something above the heads, minds and hearts of the project members. Of course, in a relatively large organization like TC one can't expect a group of engineers or a manager to have a significant impact on the entire organization. But one individual or group may influence the values, ideas and meanings being imprinted on the specific projects and other processes they were participating in. Culture is 'made' from below and locally as much as or more than from above. This of course fuels cultural variety within organizations. Ways of working are not just mechanical effects of overall corporate structures or cultures or top management decisions, but are to some extent created by the people directly involved. In our case, these were managers and engineers doing knowledge-intensive work, not workers on an assembly line. One could have expected them, in principle, to be sufficiently resourceful and motivated to raise their voices and try to influence the organization in various ways. But employees, even many middle managers, seemed to believe in managerialism in the sense that the important things came from top and more senior managers and the rest were followers. Bureaucracy and managerialism then were key features of organizational culture, and crucial in understanding the problems of getting the change programme moving beyond hyperculture.

The impression is of an organization characterized by fairly rigid boundaries between levels. These were not just structural features, but very much a matter of people having developed cultural orientations around doing predefined engineering work and limiting the work accordingly. Managers in most cases seemed to view themselves as foremen, administrators and project managers, with rather limited work domains. They seemed more inclined to complain about corporate culture and top management than see themselves as exercising influence in various directions and as potentially forming productive relations with top managers and, through this, being active producers of organizational reality. Again, this can be seen as characterizing a bureaucratic culture and managerialist thinking.

This culture was being manifested during the change work and formed a kind of organizational paradigmatic background (Van Marrewijk *et al.* 2010) which was not really addressed, and presumably not clearly recognized, by the people at TC. These orientations and in particular the passivity and limited area of responsibility of most employees counteracted the possibility of the cultural change programme being inspirational or creating a wave or a flow in the organization, as indicated to be the idea or hope of the architects of the programme. The combination of a weak change programme and, perhaps even more vital, a strong but unacknowledged orientation towards managerialist assumptions and bureaucratic inertia seem to have contributed to the limited effects of the programme.

Although the cultural change programme had limited effects, at least in terms of the stated objectives, it may have had other, unanticipated and unwanted, effects. We have the interesting paradox that the cultural change programme to a degree produced what it was intended to improve: lack of trust in management and a view of leadership as absent. It to some extent reinforced and fuelled the beliefs and orientations it was supposed to counteract: scepticism and negative assumptions. Low confidence in top and many senior middle managers seems to have been segmented rather than changed. The programme also led many people in the company to feel confirmed in their views about work on organizational issues being superficial – it was about talk and paper products. These were seen as 'HR things' rather than related to work practices. Organizational knowledge was soft and fluffy and led nowhere. Although we can only speculate on this, the other side of this is that technical knowledge appeared as even more real and valuable. Humanistic ideas around culture, values, participation and people issues lose against values such as those propagated by 'action men' such as Wolfe. It seems likely that the value hierarchy of an engineer-driven organizational culture was reinforced.

A major idea in this chapter is the distinction between three concepts of culture: hyperculture, experienced corporate culture and anthropological culture. We think it is vital to encourage researchers and practitioners interested in understanding and working with changes to consider the deeper aspects indicated by our third concept. Otherwise the risk is high of one-sided concentration on 'surface work', circling around hyperculture, while the cultural forces in operation are much more profound and do their powerful work undetected.

11 Working with change

In this chapter we extend the discussion of change work by addressing the sense making, work activities and identities of those involved. After some initial comments on the value of in-depth studies we discuss the problems of a technocratic approach to change. Another key feature is how non-recognized organizational culture working behind the backs of people plays a key role in the change efforts.

An exceptionally unfortunate and/or a typical case?

In this book we argue that, in order to assess change programmes, in-depth and micro-oriented studies are called for, and with a few good exceptions there is a certain shortage of such cases (Helms Mills 2003; Tsoukas and Chia 2002).[1] Quite often, in cases coming close to the 'ideal', there are varied views on what happened and what were the outcomes in terms of consequences and the value of these (e.g. Badham *et al.* 2003; Mackenzie *et al.* 2021; Reissner 2011). It seems fairly common with change initiatives that are started with energy and enthusiasm, but where the level of commitment soon drops and where sometimes the entire change project is dropped (Amundsen 2003; Jackall 1988). Many efforts to change organizational culture have been essentially unsuccessful (Ogbonna and Wilkinson 2003; Siehl 1985). There is thus no reason to assume that this case should be exceptional – it seems to fall within the spectrum of fairly typical or at least not very untypical cases.

But some readers may think that the case presented in this book is not a very interesting or relevant one, believing that it was unexceptionally badly conceptualized and/or executed and therefore of little interest. The reader wanting positive examples and assuming that organizational change efforts are often rational and lead to positive outcomes may feel disappointed – and think that there is little to learn from the case. However, we have a strong feeling that there is a tendency to overreport intentions, designs and good cases or to portray cases that are open to quite different interpretations in a positive light. Dawson (2003: 174) suggests for example that success stories 'are often *post hoc* rationalized accounts constructed to convey a preferred message to an intended audience'. This seems to be the case at least outside academic studies, but also, when academics try to provide principles and recipes on for example how to accomplish change, they tend to report highly

DOI: 10.4324/9781003474555-15

successful cases (although a few clearly failed cases with horror-story qualities are also popular) (e.g. Beer 2017; Beer and Nohria 2000). Of the cases of organizational culture change reviewed in Brown (1995) and Palmer *et al.* (2022), most addressed objectives, design and process up to implementation. So far everything looked good, but it is what happened then that is perhaps of most interest, assuming that we are interested in studying those involved in the process as mediators rather than just intermediaries (Latour 2005). In terms of good cases, one can assume that companies are more likely to let researchers and journalists in if they have something they perceive to be positive to show. They are, of course, more likely to communicate these themselves through various intended audiences. A vital part of management is to manage image; organizational culture is not just a matter of internal operations, but is also a major aspect of marketing and image building (Hatch and Schultz 2002). The business press typically focus on new CEOs and/or new initiatives in the early phase and have little patience to see what happens after a time, when possible effects may start to materialize. In addition, there is a tendency for top managers, consultants and others involved to perceive projects they have been responsible for and identify with in a positive light. As these are overrepresented in writings and presentations on changes, their self-serving bias may lead to ambiguous change efforts being not only presented but also understood in a positive way. In the current case, we can note that the managers responsible for the change programme were (or expressed themselves as) more positive about the programme than the majority of the people we talked to. The claims for success and failure are thus usually part of the political process of any organizational change (Jackall 1988; Pettigrew 2012).

That there are more positive cases in circulation in public than less successful ones does not mean that the latter are uncommon. As discussed in Chapter 2, it is suggested that more than two-thirds of most change initiatives fail in relation to what they set out to accomplish (Beer and Nohria 2000; Sorge and van Witteloostuijn 2004). Although this number may be contested (Hughes 2011; Tasler 2017) the fairly few careful studies conducted give the impression of more failed than successful change projects, although of course many are not so easy to categorize in terms of success and failure.

That our study portrays an organization having great problems in matching the rational and idealistic views of organizational change in management textbooks may tell us more about the shortcomings of the latter than the specific faults in the specific case. We think that there is a lot to learn from so-called failures, not least through the multitude of experiences of what presumably went wrong and where things were less or more problematic. This constitutes a rich source for the further understanding and managing of organizational change.

As stated at the beginning of this book, there is no reason to assume that TC should be inferior to other organizations in its (in)capacity or ambition to carry out these kinds of projects. TC is part of a very large, internationally leading firm, is seen as an attractive employer and hardly attracts or employs below-standard professionals or managers. In terms of the rationality and thoughtfulness of the design of the change programme, it should perhaps once more be pointed out that this was 1) grounded in a number of studies, workshops involving large groups of managers, and consultants' reports, and 2) relatively thoroughly checked and approved by other consultants. In this sense one could say that the change programme was quite ambitiously planned and even quality-checked. The general design does not deviate much from that of many other programmes. A few key values, a mission statement, talks by the CEO, workshops and some educational material typically developed and distributed by a mix of top management, consultants and HR staff seem to be close to standard in the cultural change business and organizational change in general (e.g. Kotter 2018; Ogbonna and Harris 1998).

Given the fairly good anchoring in investigations of experienced problems and opinions about current and desired conditions, one could have imagined that the change programme would engage managers and employees.

One of the authors presented the case to a group of managers in a workshop, who confirmed that this was not atypical. As one person said, 'It ends like this every bloody time!'

All this contributes to taking the case seriously. It is likely more common than unique, even if, of course, there are also more thorough and carefully executed and successful change projects.

We don't think, however, that what we can learn from it in terms of more generally and theoretically relevant conclusions is a matter of whether it was less well planned and/or executed than many other cases. All cases provide a basis for interpretations and discussions of broader significance. Whether a case is more or less successful than the average one has very little to do with how cases can be used for the production of insights about organizational change. In-depth and rich case studies provide great possibilities for learning, independent of whether the case is typical or atypical. In this case we think that 1) our careful following of the entire process and the specific actions – and inactions – of the people involved or uninvolved and 2) our broader interpretation of the targeted values in relationship to the unacknowledged organizational culture context in which this takes place offer interesting results.

On the re-engineering of engineering culture

Much of the knowledge created in this study concerns difficulties in the case project, but this can also be turned into something more 'positive' through emphasizing what it is important to pay attention to in change work. We'll start, however, with the 'negative' aspects.

Problems with a technocratic approach

To sum up from the previous chapters, we may say that a common thread in much of the organizational cultural change literature is trivialization. Culture is deprived of some of what makes it important in organizational life for the benefit of convenient handling (Alvesson 2013; Heracleous and Langham 1996). The assumption seems to be that culture to a large extent could be managed – or at least significantly improved – by the culture change programme. The design indicates a grand technocratic approach expressing a managerial tool view on culture, where people and the cultural toolbox are seen as simple transporters, or intermediaries, of the initial force of change (Latour 2005). This grand technocratic approach overlaps with what Palmer *et al.* (2022) refer to as director and navigator images of change: the manager is in control and is showing direction. As stated in previous chapters, there are also more humanistic, OD-type ingredients in the design, but these are less prominent, partly owing to the inability and unwillingness of many organizational members to act upon them. We will come back to this issue.

This approach, as indicated by our case, has the following problematic features:

* managerialism;
* big bites;
* quick fix;
* emphasis on planning and design work;
* limited expressiveness.

We have addressed these elements before, so a repetition and minor supplementation are sufficient here. Mainly we want to pull together, summarize and clearly show a common but problematic 'configuration' of cultural change work.

Managerialism refers to a strong emphasis on managers being in charge, possessing a superior overview, knowledge and authority (Alvesson and Willmott 2012). The manager and management knowledge are supposed to do the trick. With the correct decision, design and inputs from management, the followers as intermediaries will deliver the results (Latour 2005). In our case there is talk of cascading the changes down the hierarchical level through progressively involving more middle managers and employees in the proposed changes through the workshops and seminars. The cascade method is fairly common and often the preferred way to accomplish organizational change (Burke 2018). However, our case suggests that contextual features, such as the strong expectation that top managers would take the initiative and be central and in control throughout the project, made such a method less appropriate.

Big bites refer to the inclination to assume that complex and messy phenomena can be condensed into a few boxes and thus be dealt with. Issues like leadership, teamwork and customer orientation are immensely complex and difficult, but when transformed into a few words in hyperculture these qualities are lost and they emerge as ideals or characteristics to be dealt with.

Related to this is the belief in *quick fixes*. Of course, it is important not to ascribe too much naivety to managers and consultants here. Most realize that the issues at stake are difficult and call for long-term work. But still there is a strong adherence to the assumption that considerable progress – starting a wave – can be accomplished through rapid and limited interventions.

Another key characteristic of a grand technocratic approach is the *lack of emotionality and expressiveness*. A technocratic view downplays and marginalizes the organization as an emotional and social arena. The use of abstract words, neutral and uninspired verbal performances, and a lack of rich examples grounded in organizational history and practice ('stories') all contribute to 'thinness' in terms of expressiveness and emotional appeal.

A final key and more overall element is a strong *emphasis on planning and design*, while there are insufficient attention and resources devoted to process. This is not uncommon. Much writing within organizational change emphasizes the planning and designs aspects (see models of change in OD, Bradford and Burke, 2005; Cummings *et al.* 2020). There is also typically a lack of sensitivity in process work. This view of planning and design as the heavy and important part and the implementation process as straightforward and easy is at odds with an understanding of the unpredictability of meaning constructions. Our case supports the importance of sensitively following and working with the expectations and interpretations of those supposed to be influenced and/or stimulated.

This discussion of a bias in planning/design versus implementation/process is in itself, however, not unproblematic. One could argue that a thought model dividing up the work in planning and execution is misleading. Thinking very much in terms of steps may be problematic here. People also produce and reproduce an organization and express cultural meanings – of a changing or reproducing kind – when they plan for future change work. How they talk about, act and pay attention to themes in particular ways frames the cultural orientations of those who are present (Forester 2003). Rather than assuming a rigid distinction between planning and implementation it may be better to see the ongoing process and the open-ended ways of expressing and interacting as crucial. Even if people seemingly stick to prepared scripts – and in our case they did to a large extent – this is an expression of an interpretation of a plan or design rather than pure implementation. But even so they acted as mediators when transforming the programme to a marginal existence (Latour 2005). Another possibility could have been to broadly follow the script but do so in a livelier and engaged way, and adapt more to the situation through, for example, engaging in horizontal interaction in order to make sense of the cultural efforts and their accompanying material. Still another could be to improvise more, for example if the stated values did not seem to work.

As discussed in Chapter 2, the process approach, largely in contrast to a technocratic approach to change, acknowledges the importance of considering (middle) managerial meaning constructions in change processes. Some writers emphasize how meaning and managerial sense making generally are sustained by various forms of conversations in organizations. Conversations facilitate interpretations and the emergence of managerial intersubjectivity, and are usually regarded as supporting organizational change (Balogun and Johnson 2005; Barrett *et al.* 1995; Collins 2018; Ford and Ford 1995). In our case it seems as if such a form of sense-making practice was quite limited, both vertically and horizontally. In particular, conversations facilitating interpretations of the change efforts were limited after the design had been developed and decided upon by senior managers in agreement with the consultant. Of course, part of the problem here was the lack of effort from those who initiated the project to work with sense giving, to try to explain, convince and encourage other people to understand and grasp the ideas and objectives. Management can be seen as a matter of working with understanding (Sandberg and Targama 2007).

The organization of change work: beyond steps – and on to identities

Change work as passing on the baton

As seen in Chapter 8, interruptions, disconnections and discontinuities apparently characterized the trajectory, adding further to experiences of fragmentation and lack of consistency, determinacy and endurance among several of the persons involved. It seems as if those involved passed the project on to each other expecting the ideas to materialize automatically through the next person in line doing what was needed.

At one level, people seemed to share some understanding of who was to implement the ideas that had been produced. All adapted to their role in the chain, at least on a superficial level. But just scratching below the surface gives another picture. Here we find a disparity of meaning between the people participating and problems of translation, leading to the next set of actors involved seemingly understanding the project work and their own role quite differently from how others saw it. This can be understood in terms of a differentiated cultural background – subcultures – within the organization (Fine and Hallett 2014; Martin 2002; Stensaker *et al.* 2021; Van Maanen and Barley 1984; Young 1989). One can also emphasize the act of translating the change programme when a new subject encountered it (Latour 1986). Such acts of translation are guided by the cultural orientations of those supposed to work with and do something with an idea, an instruction or a work task, and in many situations cultural differentiation associated with division of labour and other conditions feeding into diversity means that people will effect the translation in ways others do not expect – in particular those who are at a considerable social and cultural distance (as top managers, consultants and staff were in the case of our study).

We can reconstruct the interpretative positions of the four major groups/actors involved in the change work – the strategic architects (top managers), the consultant, the facilitators (HR people) and the implementers (middle managers) – as follows. We will divide the last group into two categories: the positive/compliant group and the sceptics. It is worth noting that we examined several different groups of employees involved in the change efforts. Most studies of organizational change with a social and cultural orientation typically emphasize a single category, for example middle-managerial sense making (Balogun and Johnson 2004; Rouleau 2005) and/or the experiences of senior managers (Balogun *et al.* 2015) or shop floor employees (Dawson 2003). Considering a variety of different groups may give a richer and perhaps more nuanced picture of the complexities surrounding organizational change efforts.

We now turn to some accounts of the cultural change programme from the various participants' points of view, as reconstructed by us, formulated in slightly ironic ways:

- *Strategic architects.* For these people creating change is about careful planning based on qualified knowledge input through consultancy support and internal workshops. The decision about which cultural values to strive for is of utmost importance. It is also crucial to have a design for implementation. This process then has to be kicked off. Having done so, top management can rely on the HR people and the middle managers to implement it. The HR people are needed to make it credible that these are 'our' values, not just something invented by a consultant. Some following up may be needed to check that everything is going to plan. But if there is a lack of time to do so, it is not a great problem. Middle levels will make sure that change is produced. Strategic architects do not interfere with details and process. They plan, decide, give instructions and set the ball rolling. The strategic architect starts the wave.
- The *consultant* gets the task from the strategic architects to assist in developing a new culture. The consultant wants to make the client satisfied. She conducts seminars with the senior and middle managers and gets a large number of proposals concerning what should be suggested as guiding values. It is the managerial world and the interests of the client (top management) that are important – the rest of the organization is peripheral. Having worked with the CTO and developed a proposal, the consultant gets the message that the client will not be using her for the next stages. Being perhaps disappointed with this, the consultant is less willing to spend more time helping the client's HR people with what is now their task.
- *The facilitators.* Creating change, for the HR people, is ensuring that the intentions and objectives of top management are carried out by middle managers. These need some instructions and some material aiding them in their work. For the facilitators it is vital that the instructions are clear and that this material is available and used. It is less important that the HR people, concentrating on their limited part of the entire process, fully understand the content of the change process. It is outside their mandate to question whether there are alternative ways of organizing the change work, even though they are uncertain about their competence and might have benefited from further consultancy assistance. Instructions from top management and the imperatives of the large sum of money already invested in the design make compliance reasonable. As delivery persons – operating the post office – they should not interfere too much with the senders and receivers of the messages.
- *The compliant implementers.* From the position of middle managers (and to some extent their subordinates), creating cultural change is a strategic idea of top management that also seems to be very much an HR project. The implementers were instructed to spend half a day going through a set of exercises about culture. This session was somewhat hard to follow: stated values were

often seen as vague and difficult to grasp. The people participating sometimes had problems coming up with ideas and suggestions. A part of the exercise was to fill in answers to various questions. These were sent to HR. Not much more really happened. There was no direct response to this or further instructions on what to do. So the theme tended to be dropped. The implementers view themselves as information gatherers (more than implementers). What is done with the information is for senior management to decide. One does one's duties – and when the task is done it can be ticked off without too much further concern.

- *The non-implementers.* Creating cultural change is another idea of the people at the top of the organization, in close affiliation with consultants and HR people. The idea is, like previous examples of organizational 'change', loosely coupled to technical work and expresses the desire of new managers to do something about the organization. But time is limited and what is important is to do real work and deliver. The change programme will divert attention from more urgent tasks. The non-implementers find working with culture and organization soft and fluffy. This is another 'HR thing' – nothing important.

As can be seen, there is thus a divergence of meanings around who is central and who is going to do what. The picture that emerges here is quite complex and, in contrast to that of many authors adhering to a more interpretative approach to change (Balogun *et al.* 2015; Barrett *et al.* 1995; Rouleau 2005; Todnem *et al.* 2018), significantly more diverse in terms of various actors' sense making. The strategic architects rely on the facilitators and implementers to carry out the work. The implementers see the others as providing guidelines and providing instructions for further work. The facilitators wait for the other two groups to do more, feeling that they can do little to influence any group. The architects see the cultural change as an eye-opener and a wave – some initial triggers are supposed to do the trick here. The facilitators rely on the design and the technical equipment (cultural toolbox) to do it – and view the carrying out of instructions as the key element in cultural work. The implementers see cultural work as driven by the top management (perceived as more than just architects) and wait for further initiatives and guidelines and instructions after going through the first exercise and sending the information to HR. Nobody involved appeared to see him- or herself as a significant change agent: this job was ascribed to somebody else, but for most it seems to have been unclear who.

Following the change of baton metaphor somewhat further, one could say that the various baton carriers held various views of the meaning of the baton itself (i.e. what do these values mean?), and also of their and the others' role in carrying it. The middle managers ('the implementers') thought they had handed over the baton to others, while the others (HR or top management) did not realize this. It was somehow dropped in the process and not really picked up again. In this sense, people did not just stick to a poor image of change work; they also acted quite poorly based on it.

An alternative view: change work as a football game

An alternative image for the change work could be a football game. Here everybody is assumed to be engaged and active all the time. Participants have an overview of what goes on and are prepared to support others: with action, advice, encouragement and perhaps instructions. A football game is very different from a relay race, where people mainly are doing their part and are not supposed to interfere with the others. While there are clearly defined steps in a relay race, a football game can't be divided up in this way.

A major problem with change work in line with the football metaphor is that it implies much more engagement, time and resources than work implied by the relay race image. And in the real world, people's time and attention are taken up by endless tasks and commitments, although many of doubtful significance and relevance. There is much so-called pseudo-work, lengthy meetings, form-filling or training that do not lead to much actual core work (Alvesson and Spicer 2025; Nörmark and Fogh Jensen 2021; Sutton and Rao 2024). Nevertheless, time is limited and, in particular, senior managers must rely to a considerable degree on delegation. The football image does not imply that everybody should be equally involved all the time and devote most of their attention to the change programme. This is seldom possible. But mentally they need to be prepared to at least occasionally keep an eye on what is happening and be prepared, when needed, to become more actively involved, at least for a short period. Focusing on a limited, concentrated contribution and forgetting about what happens before or after leads to problems. For managers seeing themselves as producers of the game, making preparations, picking the team, developing a strategy, instructing players, having the kick-off and then leaving and hoping for a good end result is a very risky way of dealing with change management. In terms of allocation of time, perhaps less work on preparation and more time spent following the processes and having some ongoing dialogues, also with some people in 'core work' (and not just administering a change project) would have been a good idea, that is, more action and less decision rationality might have been beneficial (Brunsson 2019). For people supposed to work more on the detail of operational matters, some earlier involvement in reasoning, decision making, etc. might also appear necessary.

All this goes to some extent against popular ideas of delegation of tasks and step thinking in change management. At least our case warns against too much delegation – decoupling of the senior actors – and assuming that the following of clearly differentiated steps ensures progress.

Identities in change work

Ineffective change work is not just a matter of simple misunderstandings or lack of clarification of expectations (roles). It is an effect of 'mis-logics', that is, different logics – or ongoing sense-making projects (cf. Weick 1995) – not corresponding and the dynamic interaction creating breakdowns and unintended effects.

In our case, the actors involved seemed to shape their respective parts of the overall project guided by four key aspects, the combination of which formed a particular organizational logic:

1   the overall meaning of the project;
2   their own situated identities, for example how they defined themselves in this context;
3   ascriptions of positions to others (roles); and
4   their own models of how the organizational world looked and their own (limited) place in it.

1 Diverse and disconnected meanings of the programme

The various people supposed to be central in the cultural change work conceptualized this in quite different ways. For top managers, it was – at least in the later stages of the project and in retrospect – a wave and an eye-opener, HR people tended to view it as a parcel, and middle managers related to the change work as a tick-off task and in many cases, like their subordinates, viewed it as a sign of hypocrisy, as they saw divergence between the values preached and actual organizational practices.

For top managers, the cultural programme was seen as an inspiration to rethink the business, to create awareness of the corporate situation, to create a positive atmosphere and possibly to transform the organization. The CEO emphasized having fun and the CTO emphasized the ideal of creating a positive force, a wave.

This ambition backfired, and in the hands of HR the programme became rather a matter of distributing instructions and tools. The HR people described the project as 'landing on their table'.

Middle managers expected that top managers would carry the cultural change. Managers were not viewed as acting as role models in terms of embodying and enacting the claimed values. There was little committed activity promoting the cultural change project in terms of pushing, persuading, reminding, preaching, reporting or setting schedules for various acts and activities in line with the cherished values.

As the culture programme moved from top management and the consultant it went through a meaning translation from a wave and an eye-opener to a *parcel* – a package to be distributed and later collected. When it reached the middle managers as an input in the workshops it became translated into a *tick-off activity*, which also, amongst large groups, was seen as another indicator of top management *hypocrisy*. The last meaning may to some extent be an outcome of the earlier translation in the process and the resulting perceived disconnectedness between management talk and their actions.

2 and 3 Situated identities and view of others

People's actions were informed by the positions they were coming from, expressive of different identities and with these, related subcultural meanings. Sometimes

Table 11.1 Situated identity constructions of key actors

Category	Self-view	View/expectation of others
Top managers	Initiators	Drivers of change, hypocrites
Consultant	Change agent	Designer of programme
HR people	Post office workers	Implementation experts*
Middle managers (compliant)	Subordinates (instruction followers)	Culture carriers
Middle managers (non-compliant)	Engineers/project leaders working on vital tasks**	Culture carriers

Notes: * The view of top management. Middle managers probably saw HR as peripheral administrators.
** View of those resisting working with the cultural change programme.

this led to quite contrary assumptions of what people were supposed to do in relationship to others. The strategic architects assumed that they had done their job when they sparked off the change work, but were believed by their subordinates to be the people who would follow up what they reported and direct the process over time. The implementers saw themselves as ticking off activities, while the top actors viewed them as the key actors in an eye-opening wave. Table 11.1 gives an overview of the situated identities of the key actors and the identities (roles) ascribed to others.

There are clear discrepancies and misfits here. Generally the views of self and others do not align, and they account for unexpected translations of work tasks at various steps of the chain of work tasks. One could say that the inter-definitions of the actors (Callon 1986), for example the involvement of a series of actors by establishing their identities and the links between them, were ineffective. Expected roles were unclear and these contradicted the identities of people.

4 Models of the organizational world

The contradiction between bureaucracy and culture can be related to fundamentally different themes or modes of organizing. One can make a further parallel with Latour's (1986) two models here, as this is not just helpful for illuminating what is happening – local translations as part of the transformations – but also grasps problematical forms of local thinking about how the world functions. Generally in organizations, carrying out work often fits bureaucracy and the diffusion model – which is related to the grand technocratic approach to change, mentioned earlier in the chapter. This approach may be relevant in highly structured and predefined work. But in other cases, such as working with culture, the translation model captures the work and the difficulties much better. This kind of work is open-ended and 'meaning sensitive' – subtle interpretations and translations become crucial here.

This open and meaning-sensitive character of the work means that action becomes strongly influenced by the specific identities of those involved. The meanings of the various actors did not supplement each other – new translations were often out of tune with those conducted by others involved. It seems that all involved worked according to the principles of bureaucracy: separation of conception and execution and horizontal division of labour. In one sense this was built on shared meanings and the mobilization of a set of complementary identities. But, as stated, different actors viewed and associated with the programme differently. The different 'subcultures' of the HR people and the low-level employees intervened here, as is not uncommon in change projects (Balogun *et al.* 2015; Martin 2002; Martin and Meyerson 1988; Stensaker *et al.* 2021). The top managers largely failed to actively enlist middle managers and others potentially interested and engaged in terms of facilitating the development of roles and identities aligned with change efforts (Callon 1986). The top managers assumed that their initial force would be picked up and carried on in a cascade model down through the organization – the power of hierarchy and bureaucracy would imply diffusion and cultural change. But, for others, bureaucracy implied conducting narrowly defined, specific tasks carried out in an instrumental way. Acting on this model was one element in the transformation of the eye-opening wave to a parcel and a tick-off activity as well as in activities contributing to the perceived discrepancy between the talk-and-paper and 'real' changes. Bureaucracy-induced identities were not helpful here.

The organizational context of change work

The bureaucratic undoing of culture work

Elements of bureaucratic culture are thus a key aspect of the context of change work. We can see how a bureaucracy-paradigmatic framework in various subtle ways guides actors and obstructs their achievement of effective work processes and persuasive communication. The most salient examples are a strong orientation towards taking the vertical and horizontal division of labour seriously and the view of culture work as following prescribed procedures. We can connect here to the previous discussion of limited sense making and interpretative activities both vertically and horizontally. Most of the participating groups refrained from engaging in conversations or other activities that would help them to better understand the prescribed change efforts, which is vital according to most authors (Balogun *et al.* 2015; Barrett *et al.* 1995; Ford and Ford 1995).

We thus see a certain passivity on the part of all but the senior managers. This is indeed remarkable, given all the literature on organizational participation in most OD models of change and decision making in general and human motivation stressing aspects such as the 'need' to take responsibility, influencing the work situation (Cummings *et al.* 2020; McGregor 1960; Weisboard 1987). And one would perhaps assume that the list of values could spark some interest and engagement. Of course, in TC, qualities such as being active and taking the initiative were salient in a lot of individual engineering work (Rennstam 2007), but not in the somewhat broader aspect of work organization that was of concern in the change work. Aspects concerning human beings as oriented towards being co-constructors of reality also to some extent would lead one to assume a higher level of interest and agency. Francis and Sinclair (2003: 703), for example, refer to how subordinates in an industrial organization were able to create new understandings of the subject matters introduced by management and also to 'shape the interpretive frames of their immediate managers'. They also claim that 'all organizational actors had some ability to manage meanings'. It is hard not to agree with this, but in the case of the change work at TC many people did not do much to manage their meanings in a way that led to the shaping of the interpretative frames of their superiors. The baton metaphor illustrates the absence of this in vital respects.

We can of course interpret the responses or rather lack of strong responses in terms of resistance, as previously indicated (Knights and Vurdubakis 1994; Palmer *et al.* 2022; Ybema and Horvers 2017). The cultural change programme may be viewed as an example of management control and positive engagement in that it could lead to higher levels of commitment, demand and self-constraints. At the workshop we noted jokes about commitment meaning working harder and longer hours. The clearest example of resistance was produced by a senior manager, Wolfe, becoming quite agitated and demanding that 'the cultural tralala must be stopped'. And one could perhaps see not only those managers not setting up the workshops but also the lack of engagement in many cases plus the comments about nothing happening except talk in terms of resistance. We do not want to push this aspect too far. People generally supported the values highlighted in the change project (although many had problems understanding what they meant). We see uncertainty and confusion as more significant than resistance in our case.

Irrespective of how one assesses the degree of resistance, the way a bureaucracy forms an interpretative framework guiding people on how to think about, give meaning to and respond to various elements in the work is worth emphasizing. The generally relevant point here concerns the significance of how an organizational culture provides a framework which gives particular meanings to intentions, messages, roles, events and acts – meanings that can be quite removed from those assumed and espoused by the architects and facilitators and that can lead to unanticipated outcomes. The logic of a change project may be radically remade by the various people involved and, as this process may be undetected by change initiators and facilitators, the ideas informing these actors' actions may be quite different from what top managers expect.

Cultural change as an unintended expression and reproduction of organizational culture

A general insight in culture thinking is that people tend to be constrained by their cultural framework in their view of the world and their habitual ways of acting. It is very difficult to fully transcend or neglect culture, even though in contemporary society and business there is enough plurality of groups and ideas to avoid a fixed and constrained world view associated with an isolated society. Clearly a lot of the thinking and action in our case had an impact on the existing culture in respects rarely intended by the change-minded people involved in the project.

To repeat the major issues, the background of the project was a widespread perception of a narrow and self-indulgent technology orientation, socially introvert personnel and low trust in management. The aim was to try to do something about this, but fairly little was accomplished and there are signs of the project in some ways resulting in the opposite of what was aimed for: technology knowledge was strengthened in relationship to the 'softer' knowledge advocated in the programme and there were signs of even lower trust in top managers. At the least there was an undermining or contradiction of the espoused ideal, and what was being implicitly expressed and picked up by organizational members was, for example, limited commitment, lack of inspiration, people not taking empowerment seriously in the change programme ('Wait and see if things improve') and not much teamwork visible amongst those working with change. We should not exaggerate these aspects, but just say that there are reasons to take seriously the possibility of a change project reinforcing what it is supposed to change.

One way of understanding the process in a condensed way is expressed in Table 11.2.

Such reinforcement of the existing at the expense of what was aimed for can of course occur through change efforts producing resistance and struggle and if those opposed to the change win then a strengthening of certain 'conservative' orientations and patterns may occur (Smircich 1983b; Sörgärde 2006). Perhaps more novel and interesting is that the change work in itself, apart from 'external' resistance and conflict, can carry elements in which 'non-recognized' (anthropological) culture is active and counteracts the intentions and espoused objectives. In our case the programme was contradicted not so much by organizational participants

Table 11.2 Levels of culture

Ascribed 'bad' cultural features (experienced culture)	Hyperculture (targets for cultural change)	Outcome of programme
Narrow technology orientation	Customer orientation	Reinforced view of nontechnical work as 'fluffy' (an HR thing)
Lack of teamwork, socially introvert organization	Teamwork, communication	Reproduced division of labour mentality
Invisible leadership, low trust in managers	Visible leadership	Limited confidence in management

Distrusting changes

Meanings and expectations of 'anthropological culture' intervening: managerialist thinking and bureaucratic mentality in situations outside the programme but primarily *within* the culture programme, through the acts of those engaged in it.

A problem is that most people active in change work assume – perhaps after input from consultants and thorough analysis – that they have got it right and that cultural change means that others should change. This easily misses key dimensions of culture 'outside' what is targeted that nevertheless are highly relevant and that in various ways interfere with the efforts to get full acceptance for and commitment to the values and ideas targeted. To repeat, culture is best understood as an interconnected and complex set of meanings, values and orientations of which organizational members are not fully aware (Alvesson 2013; Fitzgerald 1988; Schein 1985). As such it is difficult to effectively slice and package and then focus a few abstracted elements for re-targeting.

Of course, it is hardly necessary or productive to try to address all possible aspects of culture in change work – or in the routine management/leadership of which cultural awareness and the reproduction or strengthening of common meanings and orientations are crucial. It is, however, important to work with a wider set of cultural considerations than just the targeted values. Based on our case in Chapter 10 we argued for a differentiation between various levels or 'types' of culture: hyperculture, experienced corporate culture and anthropological organizational culture.

While change advocates may be most interested in targeted culture (typically similar to hyperculture), other people may invoke and be guided by other understandings. Grasping the experiences and meanings of employees outside the specific core area targeted is important, as they may determine responses. In the TC case, most employees were positive to the ideas and values summarized as hyperculture (as targets worth striving for), but other meanings triggered scepticism and passivity and led to the view of the change programme as a 'paper product'. Anthropological culture throws additional light on this and helps us understand the context and dynamics behind these responses. Understanding culture on this level is difficult, but grasping the elements that influence the specific themes in focus is necessary. Otherwise, the risk of the surface change efforts being undermined by much stronger, unrecognized forces is high. If one is unfortunate, as in the TC case, the result may be a reinforcement of the orientations that were targeted for change. A 'wait-and-see' culture, where people complain but are passive in terms of trying to improve the organization, becomes reinforced.

Conclusions

There is a great interest in seemingly successful cases of organizational change, but it is equally if not more valuable to learn from 'negative' or ambiguous cases – not least because change efforts often lead to unexpected outcomes. There is a desire for people involved in change projects to present these as successful, for psychological and political reasons. This underscores the need to focus on organizational change in depth and elaborate carefully on the micro-processes involved.

The case study, backed up by literature reviews and broader considerations, points to the following fallacies in change work:

- a domination of managerialism, that is, the belief that management is the central and superior actor and its intentions and acts will drive outcomes;
- an overemphasis on planning and design and a neglect of energy, resources, attention and sensitivity in the process of 'implementation' or working with the transformation project;
- a tendency to reify the organization and assume that the organization and its members respond in a unitary way, leading to a neglect of the need to consider and work with the diversities of meanings;
- the translating of complex phenomena like leadership and teamwork into seemingly simple representations, which hides the complex and multifaceted qualities of those phenomena and gives a false impression of what can easily be dealt with;
- a belief in the quick fix, where rather limited instructions, resources and time are supposed to bring about great improvements, whether these are seen in terms of an eye-opener (a major aim) or cultural transformation into new values and practices (a huge aim);
- an underestimation of the need for expressiveness and capturing the hearts and imaginations of people, partly connected to an overreliance on planning and instrumentalism.

Another key point, partly related to the issue of overemphasis on planning and design, concerns the overall images of organizational change work. We have identified a kind of 'root metaphor' (not explicitly expressed) of change work as a passing on of the baton. This is not directly recommended by, but fairly well in line with, much of the normative literature on organizational change, emphasizing the steps that successful projects must go through (so-called n-step thinking). This is clearly problematic in many cases, as it neglects the need for interaction and involvement of the various authors dealing with the unexpected, typically characterizing change work. It definitely underplays the need for ongoing clarification of meaning, including the need to revise and re-synchronize understandings amongst the actors involved. We suggest the football game root metaphor as a better way of conceptualizing change work. It points to how key actors are involved during the entire process, seeing what is happening and intervening when necessary.

Another partly related issue concerns the importance of paying attention to the identities of the people involved in change work. (Roles are important, but we move one step further and focus less on external expectations and more on self-image.) The actors involved seemed to shape their respective parts of the overall project, guided by how they defined themselves in the context of the change project. Crucial here are the actors':

- understanding of the overall meaning of the project;
- own situated identities, for example how they defined themselves in this context;

- ascriptions of positions to others; and
- own models of how the organizational world looked and their own (limited) place in it.

Behind these meanings and identities in the context of the change work is the organizational cultural context. Organizational culture works to a high degree non-consciously, behind the backs of people's identities, informing them in terms of thinking and acting. Our case shows how bureaucratic meanings and beliefs affected organizational members in ways that created severe decoupling and disconnections in terms of the sense making of the key actors. Overreliance on hierarchy, division of labour and rigid distinctions between roles and job tasks followed.

Change work needs not only to address the substance (ideals, values, practices) of what is supposed to be changed, but also to include the management of meaning and understanding of the roles and identities of those to be mobilized in the work. For those who are initiators or key actors in other ways this means sense giving (managing understanding and influencing identities) (Alvesson and Willmott 2002; Alvesson *et al.* 2017; Sandberg and Targama 2007). Such work includes efforts to aid the majority in making sense of how they productively can see key dimensions of change work, for example division of labour, initiative and cooperation, in relationship to themselves.

Considering these subtle aspects is not always easy – the unfortunate people at TC are not alone in missing this.

Note

1   Exceptions include Balogun *et al.* (2015) Dawson (2003), Preece *et al.* (1999) and Stensaker *et al.* (2021).

12 Lessons for cultural change actors and others

In this final chapter, we will more explicitly address issues that we believe are of relevance for practitioners that are interested in engaging with organizational change management. We refrain from producing lists of n-steps to take or technical recipes for how to do things. There is more than enough of this already and we are more interested in themes for reflection and encouraging thinking through the pitfalls and complexities of change work. We proceed from our case, but broaden our approach.

This chapter is divided into three parts. The first concerns traps and we discuss four of these: hyperculture, symbolic anorexia, an over-focus on values and a denial of ignorance. The second goes through the images of the change programme held by a variety of actors. We discuss various images of change projects and the need for and possibility of developing a shared view and a common language around the specific change project. The third part more directly tries to offer fifteen lessons, through indicating not just traps to escape, but also themes worthy of more 'positive' attention in working with change. We end the chapter and thereby the book by mobilizing support for the significance of the fifteen lessons based on a more positive example of organizational change in a large hospital organization (Norbäck and Targama 2009).

Some potential traps in work with organizational cultures

Having mainly addressed issues around understanding the dynamics of organizational culture, including how assumptions and meanings operate non-consciously, we now continue with addressing how change workers can deal with problems in working with culture and cultural change. Suggested ideas have a bearing on what to try to steer around.

Hyperculture

One problem with work on culture is that it is difficult to capture values and meanings. As seen in the case study, there was considerable ambiguity about what the values were supposed to represent and also how they related to all the ideas and

DOI: 10.4324/9781003474555-16

proposals expressed in workshops and consultancy interviews forming the input to the formulation of the five values.

The point of the hyperculture is, however, probably not a matter of precise representation; the idea is more to have something to work with or possibly to have something to present in activities around organizational culture. As such it needs to look good and be easy to present. It needs to be packageable. So people seem to think.

Hyperculture tends to follow the examples of others and use the labels and themes currently popular in the business press and corporate visions, representations of corporate cultures being circulated at a particular time (Thurlow and Helms-Mills 2015). As this facilitates pedagogy and legitimacy, a heavy dose of following standards makes stated values easy to recognize and, as others are expressing these values, people are more inclined to perceive them as right.

So far so good. The problem with hyperculture is that it tends to be disconnected from the specific organizational context it is supposed to refer to. This contributes to our understanding of why the cultural ideal and vocabulary remained at the 'distanced' symbolic level, coexisting for a while with other (more highly prioritized) organizational activities, but did not really make people think through their everyday experiences and how work was done in relationship to the (target or hyper-) culture. An additional problem with hyperculture is that it suggests the possibility of 'big bites': it uses a set of very broad and multidimensional terms which cover almost 'everything'. This makes them appear to be addressing important and legitimate issues, but they risk covering everything and nothing, that is, to be lacking focus, direction and connection to meaning and experiences in everyday work. This overlaps with a tendency for people in organizations to want to accomplish too much in change projects (Dawson 2003).

While hyperculture may be good for some consultants and communication specialists producing documents with the right vocabulary and for top managers giving public speeches, it has some drawbacks when it is the claimed substance of change projects and potential learning and development. Here perhaps it is more appropriate to try to put into words more locally grounded and concretely experienced themes – although it is often very difficult to capture these and formulate them briefly.

Symbolic anorexia

Another key issue, salient in the TC case but also in many other organizations, is the absence of the use of symbolically rich material in the change work. As explored in Chapter 3, culture as a theoretical concept is about shared meanings and symbols. Symbolism is of interest as it summarizes and expresses meaning in a rich and condensed way (Morgan *et al.* 1983). Symbols can be events, actions, material objects, expressions and stories. These make things specific, appeal to experience, illustrate abstractions and are often easy to remember. They often appeal to the entire person: not just brains, but also emotions and fantasy (Alvesson and Berg 1992; Frost *et al.* 1985; Jaeger and Selznick 1964).

As Buchanan and Badham (2020) point out, contemporary leaders are encouraged to be motivational and exciting. They are expected to mobilize support or inspire action by communicating meaning and purpose, through the skilful use of symbolism, for example in the use of inspiring verbal symbols and storytelling. They tell tales of heroes and anti-heroes involved in lively struggles characterized by drama.

Storytelling is often seen as an important element in transformational leadership aiming for organizational change through painting a more desirable, sometimes glamorous or at least uplifting future. Sometimes the content of this storytelling is quite vague, but possibly still emotionally inspiring; sometimes it includes more of an articulation of how the future can be reached, setting an example for followers, and showing the right kind of determinant and confident leadership, embodying the spirit of the change trajectory.

However, this is the ideal in the management and change literature. Often, as in our case, efforts in this direction do not really take off. We have labelled this some-what impoverished practice *symbolic anorexia*. Symbolism is not experienced as rich and inspiring, but as thin and falling flat. One could imagine actors telling horror or success stories with a clear relevance for the organization, perhaps picked up on the organizational grapevine or from other familiar organizations similar to TC (e.g. competitors); or workshops being prepared and framed in ways consistent with the message, which might call for other social and temporal spaces for inter-action than the common ones; or messages about commitment and trust in leader-ship being accompanied by engaged, lively and personal appearances. (Of course, not everyone is capable of appearing charismatic – and this is probably not very important – but presumably everyone has personal examples from their life history of something relevant for underscoring a specific message of a value.) Credible and pedagogical examples that capture something in a way that appeals to experience and thus 'sticks' are vital.

There is a problem with symbolic effectiveness in that it is tempting and easy to use the standard examples that are in circulation. One example could be the story of the railway companies that thought their business was running trains rather than fulfilling people's needs for transport and therefore was lost when cars and then aeroplanes came along. Another could be the example of a person in the Middle Ages seeing two men cutting stones. 'What are you doing?' he asked them. The first responded, 'I am a stone-cutter.' The other said, 'I am building a cathedral.' Such stories are often powerful and seductive – for people who have not heard them before. They may not be so locally relevant and thus not connect to the expe-riences of the people in the organization.

There is a risk that the use of symbolism might come close to the problems with hyperculture, as already pointed out. It may be wise to try to use symbolism that is locally relevant and with a reasonably clear connection to local practices. The use of symbols may easily appear as arbitrary and inauthentic. One possibility is then to search for examples – stories, episodes, failure or success examples, verbal expressions – in the industrial, organizational or professional context that people are familiar with and that may be utilized in a pedagogical way. These may need to be 'scaled up' and connected to concepts reaching beyond the specific illustration. One example could be people adding too many technical details to a product –

making it costly and harder to use for many consumers. This can be conceptualized as 'feature creep'. The bad habit of overdoing things – not only technical details but also policies, meetings, training sessions – with limited value is very and increasingly common in organizations (Alvesson and Spicer 2025).

To capture this and other issues, one wants to draw attention to areas or themes in an imaginative way; the combination of concepts and illustrations are thus important. The feature creep concept may be supplemented by a specific example of an expert, a team or a project characterized as too much of a nerd or perfectionist mentality at work or an outcome in the form of a specific product that consumers found too complicated or expensive. The stone-cutter story – or other examples where people are mindlessly carrying out work – can be seen as illustrating the broader concept of 'clarifying meaning and purpose', a key leadership task sometimes forgotten as people are very much into either technical details or using fluffy business lingo (excellence, value creation) that some people may see as 'business bullshit' (Spicer 2017).

The limited value of values

Our third flag in this section concerns the use of values. Most practitioners and many researchers view values as the key element in organizational cultures (see for example Barrett *et al.* 1995; Schein 1985; van Hulst and Ybema 2019). We believe that values are less valuable than most people seem to think in understanding and influencing culture. This is not to say that values are irrelevant. They are indispensable in work with organizational culture and the changing of it. But there are some basic shortcomings. We think this is well illustrated in our case. Here statements about values often lead to two types of responses: 1) they sound good and, as everybody seems to agree, there are difficulties in getting any further (yes, customer orientation is a good thing); and 2) they sound good, but any closer scrutiny leads to problems and uncertainties (yes, our customers should come first, but what does this actually mean?).

Values are normally framed in such ways that they sound good (occasionally bad) and it is too easy to agree with the good things (and disagree with the bad). The problem is that it is the conflictual relationship between various good things that needs to be sorted out – priorities need to be set – and within the focus on a specific value this is easily lost from sight. Customer orientation, yes – but does this mean that technology orientation should be downplayed? Improved leadership, yes – but would this lead to non-managerial employees receiving less attention (less status, less resources for development, etc.) and being trained to obey the leader?

Another and perhaps more important aspect concerns meaning. Values tend to sidestep this issue. But meaning is crucial and should perhaps be upgraded in management, leadership and change work (Sandberg and Targama 2007), including at the expense of the theme of values. That customer orientation, visible leadership, trust in management, teamwork, etc. are valuable is one thing; more crucial is to sort out the meaning of these values, seldom investigated even in studies claiming to take a more social constructionist view, as suggested in Chapter 2. As became clear in the workshop discussion at Satellite, not only was the degree of customer orientation of the unit difficult to sort out and agree upon, but so too was what is actually meant by a 'customer'. This appears to be much more fundamental than the degree of customer orientation, as the latter is totally meaningless without a shared understanding of the former. And an understanding of a customer is not just a matter of identifying the category (or bodies) one is addressing; presumably some deeper understanding of the meaning of this group – when finally identified – is significant. How, more precisely, are customers defined and what does it mean to be oriented towards them?

Similar questions can be raised about leadership, as discussed in Chapter 2. The meaning of leadership needs to be clarified before one tries to make leadership more visible, which is regularly suggested as significant in change literature. Is it about managers popping up occasionally, engaging in small talk with people? Or is it about something much more distinct, like the charismatic leader pointing at the overall direction of the organization and inspiring the masses with engaging talk? Or is it about taking command, making decisions and, if necessary, being tough? In other words, is 'visible leadership' a matter of managers being more visible, for example being around chatting with co-workers and showing an interest in them, or is it a specific type of act – 'leadership' – that should be more visible? Is it about frequent small talk and meetings or big and clear acts? Or is it generally about fixing things, that is, making certain that the preconditions for employees being able to do their work are there? As leadership (and teamwork and other possible good things) can be given a wide variety of different meanings, a clear idea of what it is supposed to be about – and here the concept of meaning is crucial – should precede and possibly receive more attention than values (Alvesson *et al.* 2017).

Other important themes perhaps calling for a focus on meanings and understandings rather than values are managerialism and bureaucracy. We have tried to show the significance of assumptions and expectations about senior managers being active and others passively waiting and seeing before following a change, and people viewing themselves as functioning within their place in organizational formal structure ('box thinking'). That managerialism and bureaucratic culture inform how people relate to their organization is about meaning, not necessarily that they value managerialism and bureaucracy. Actually, they may even devalue these, but still see them as natural and as guiding principles to be followed. A value focus thus draws attention away from profound cultural phenomena around understanding, meanings and beliefs, difficult to grasp in terms of what is seen as good and leading to positive outcomes, that is, values.

This is of course not to say that value talk is unrelated to efforts to clarify meaning, but the latter is typically underplayed and may occasionally be neglected. One can imagine situations where people agree upon for example customer orientation as the value, but may interpret this in totally different ways, indicating that there is actually profound disagreement about what this means.

Working with culture as an 'it' rather than 'we'

When a group of people set out to change culture, do they then try to change *it* or *others* or do they also include *themselves* in the change project? In the TC case, there were few, if any, references to people acknowledging any need to think through and change their own values and meanings. This is probably very common. The principal thought model seems to be: top management, perhaps together with a consultant, have spotted what needs to be changed – the challenge is to get the targeted mass of people to be transformed into having the appropriate set of values and beliefs.

There are many examples of this in the business press, sometimes re-reported also in otherwise thoughtful books (e.g. Palmer *et al.* 2022). A popular example is to report the story that a new CEO starts the job, discovers enormous problems, finds out how to deal with them and then launches a large-scale and fantastic change programme holding the promise of great transformation and great success. He came, he saw, he acted and improvement followed (perhaps). All this happens quite quickly and one must admire the speed, self-confidence, insightfulness and forcefulness that the new CEO and his or her helpers can mobilize (see Beer and Nohria 2000).

We could, of course, also produce a hero story like the one in the preceding story, based on TC. It would be something like this: John Howard became CEO of TC, a former R&D unit of a large high-tech firm. The unit now had to stand on its own feet. John thought deeply about the situation with his closest managers. Based on their own insights and a number of measurements and studies within the firm it was clear to them that there were major problems in terms of a narrow focus on technology at the expense of interest in customers and markets. There were also signs of problems with leadership – it was weak and invisible – and with teamwork. Action was to be taken immediately. A consultant from a leading management firm was used, a task force was organized and a number of workshops with managers at various levels were launched. A change programme making all employees aware of the new corporate situation and engaging them in realizing values crucial for success and survival was started. About here most business press reports, and those textbooks drawing upon these, stop and they offer no knowledge of what happens after the start-up phase.

Of course, in some cases, there may be a group of exceptionally insightful people who have seen the light and embarked on a journey to show it to the larger groups in need of new guiding principles in the form of assumptions, values and ideas. But perhaps more often the difference between change agents and others is not so self-evident and the former group might also benefit from modesty and engaging in struggles with their own taken-for-granted assumptions and values in use. Addressing culture change as a matter of '*We* need to change' – including those taking the initiative and pushing for change – rather than 'they' or 'it' (the rest of the organization) being targeted for change is probably helpful here. Cultural change may productively be seen as a transformation process involving an organizational collective, and even those who have thought more about it and who are in positions responsible for driving change are included in this collective. Changing culture can therefore be read as changing ourselves. Steps on how to improve the others may be valuable, but as the TC story indicates it is very much those who are supposed to lead the journey to a better organizational culture who need to think through, challenge and revise their own assumptions, beliefs and meanings (just consider their ideas around hierarchy, technocracy, the relay race-like change work, the post office metaphor, etc.).

Limited knowledge

Our last point indicates the final trap that we want to address: self-confidence combined with ignorance in the case of those doing change work. Generally, and we base this view on a number of in-depth studies, it is our impression that many key actors in organizations have surprisingly little knowledge of what goes on or what they themselves actually are up to (e.g. Alvesson and Sveningsson 2003). Being a bit confused about one's own and subordinates' practice is relatively common among managers (Sveningsson and Alvesson 2016). Occasionally it may seem as if a certain ignorance is cultivated (Jackall 1988; Schaefer 2014). People occasionally protect themselves by avoiding gathering knowledge or inquiring about issues that may be potentially negative for them. One obvious example of ignorance in our case was how most of those involved thought that someone else should carry the cultural change. Perhaps people may want to circumvent involvement in complex matters because it is time- and cognitively demanding to have a good overview of the broader picture and/or specific problematic issues – and possibly they realize that one is expected to perform more on certain tasks or confront people. Knowing is occasionally risky.

Despite the overwhelming indications of the misfortunes of the change programme, key people thought – or perhaps rather navigated themselves into thinking/hoping that – it was in vital respects successful:

> A valuable thing with the cultural programme was the feedback that we received. We in the senior management group could see all the action plans from groups compiled in a helpful way. So we saw what people were proud about, what they were frustrated about, where we were insufficient. This gave us a very good picture of the situation in the company.
>
> (Allen, CTO)

In a meeting with two of the people responsible for the implementation work, Aldridge and Duncan, some time after the workshops, they started somewhat cautiously by saying that they had understood that most people in the organization viewed the programme in a positive light and that it was broadly seen as successful. After we had diplomatically reported the much more negative views of most people, they retreated from their first position, saying that they knew about the problems, and emphasized that they had not been involved from the start and had actually only participated to a modest degree in the programme.

On the whole, there were many other instances of limited awareness of what was going on, from Neville's belief (in stark contrast to that of his subordinates) that he had an involved and supportive leadership style to most employees having problems in understanding what the values included in what we refer to as hyperculture actually referred to. In general, the problem of ignorance is, of course, fundamental, but it is relevant to point to situations where listening would be helpful. Invoking modesty and curiosity, opening up channels for feedback and critique, checking assumptions as far as possible and trying to be close to those targeted for 'improvement' and listening to their views and meanings all seem important in order to reduce the chance of change work becoming a fantasy project.

It seems to be a good guess that many of the heroic new CEOs seeing bad practices and embarking on the journey to a superior organization, as portrayed in the business literature, have jumped to conclusions prematurely and that their change journeys might 1) be revised or cancelled or 2) be less fantastic when more is learned about the corporation and its situation. But as most writers are not following the journeys for very long, this is seldom documented and might not fit into the hero/success or scapegoat/failure stories that are most popularly produced (and perhaps read about).

We saw a glimpse of this in TC when, some time after the starting of the cultural change programme, the CEO, John Howard, met some customers complaining about a delivery not being on time. John became upset and worried and launched a new programme focusing on time schedules, which suddenly appeared more important than the more general ideals focused on in the corporate culture formulations. One may suspect that John is not the only new CEO unable to stick to the direction he had pointed out for the entire organization. We may guess that not a few of the heroic CEOs reported to have launched bold change projects shortly after starting their employment may not have stuck to these after a time, when new issues turned up and they had broader experience of their new corporations.

On the basic images of change

A key question for change projects is how all those who are supposed to play an active role in the work define and understand the basic nature of the project. What is it, at a more fundamental level, about? We do not have the objectives or procedures in mind, but the overall definition and understanding of the character of the change project.

As suggested in Chapter 11, we think that efforts to produce clarity and agreement – to reduce unrecognized variety – are necessary here. The confusion and diversity of meanings seen at TC illustrates this.

As seen from Chapter 2, some literature addresses this in terms of the image of the change manager. As reviewed there, Palmer *et al.* (2022) combine two dimensions. One is whether the manager is in control or merely contributes to the shaping of the change process. The other is the outcomes of this, where three positions are identified: predictable, partly predictable and unpredictable. They then point out six images: director, navigator, caretaker, coach, interpreter and nurturer. This framework is valuable, but gives more emphasis to the single, solitary manager in charge, supposedly running the project – or in the more modest versions (caretaker, interpreter, nurturer) still playing a key role. Our contribution is different, as we think that the collective nature of change work and the views of those targeted need to be taken seriously. As also discussed in Chapter 2, others address the nature of change from the dimensions of planned or emergent and incremental or radical. These are of course often treated as objective characteristics, but are perhaps often best addressed in terms of the various people involved and their understandings, as noted in Chapter 2 ('Images of organizational change', p. 21). Sörgärde (2006) for example studied a firm where those responsible for the change effort thought that this was a matter of moderate adjustment and improvement of structure while those targeted thought the change revolutionary and an attack on the integrity and identity of the organization. Of course, such varied meanings make the entire project impossible, but even less extremely diverse meanings may create problems.

We will follow this line of thinking and look at the meanings that various groups of people held in relationship to the change programme. We don't think that most people necessarily had one clear and consistent image. They may have had more, oscillated between these or changed image over time. They may in retrospect have reinvented their images of earlier stages according to how the change efforts were experienced by themselves and others. It is important to consider both more stable and fluctuating meanings. People being responsible for change can't assume stable or consistent meanings but need to try to grasp meanings and how they may change and drift, and work towards a level of shared or uniform meanings, either stable or changing in coordinated ways.

Transformation, eye-opener and wave

The images expressed by the change managers in our case included those of fundamental transformation project and eye-opener. These indicate quite diverse aims, the first being far-reaching and radical and implying the organization would be functioning in new ways, the second being more a kind of inspiration for rethinking. The latter surfaced at the end of the project: 'This was thought very much to be an impulse to the organization, an eye-opener' (Allen). But the earlier emphasis on workshop leaders reporting their results and talk of careful following up indicate a higher level of ambition, which somehow was dropped.

The expressed view of the change as a wave concerned not the purpose, but the way it was supposed to work. Some powerful and inspirational acts were supposed to start a movement and then people were expected to be engaged and to continue the change work:

> The basic idea was to transfer a new way of thinking down the organization and also to encourage suggestions from below. The idea was to create a kind of wave

within the company like 'Yes, we understand that this is a challenge and that this is business that we shall commit ourselves to.'

(Aldridge)

The wave can be seen as the opposite to the top-down implementation of change, where the force of the change initiative is supposed to create the dynamic.

The eye-opener and wave images were presented in interviews *after* the change programme was active and may reflect a desire to adjust the views of the purpose and logic to the quite meagre outcomes. The impression was that top management in the planning and start-up phases, and possibly throughout the active change work, saw the programme as a basic transformation project, turning an internal R&D unit with bureaucratic managers into a market-oriented business run by leaders. Presumably a clarification of revisions of the basic view of the change programme would have been beneficial.

Quite different images were those of post-delivery, held by HR in particular, and the carrying out of instructions and ticking them off, as held by many middle managers.

The diversity of images amongst various change managers was thus profound. Of course, an extreme optimist might believe that an eye-opening exercise would lead to radical transformation, more or less the idea with Marshak's (2009) metaphor of change as 'liberate and re-create', and the idea of a message in a bottle may be a synthesis of the wave and post-delivery views but the confusions and contradictions involved are worth emphasizing. When the wave hits the post office the movement stops.

These images are then contradicted by the images reported by those targeted for change. Here we can note images such as:

- *Hypocrisy – hard selling of an untrustworthy ideal*: 'You don't live the way you learn. Managers say "We shall have this corporate culture", but they don't work like that in their daily work, not from the management part at all. I really think this material [the cultural programme] is very good, I'm not critical towards that, but I'm critical towards the way they push it. It feels like they shove it down the throat of people like "Don't do what I do but what I say"' (Price, middle manager).
- *Show for the people*: 'We had our kick-offs as we became an independent company and managers said "We have a new corporate culture", but they didn't tell us what it was about so it all came to nothing. There was no substance to it. They talked extensively but without substance, and you didn't get any the wiser about it. They created some sort of ideal image that we don't have. We have a very long way to go there. It feels like they are not really working according to it but that it is some kind of show for the people' (Price, middle manager).

While these meanings are negative and emphasize deception and manipulation, others see the change activities as less morally problematic but weaker and emptier:

- *Empty ritual*: 'At the bigger meetings, they have someone who is responsible for the culture and they come on the stage and say something but then it sort of becomes unimportant' (Henley, engineer). This was under-scored by the low status of culture issues in the organization. These were viewed as unimportant reshuffling within the organization: 'At GT [the par-ent company] one can say that corporate culture issues have an extremely low status among the technicians, because as long as I have been working at GT every organizational change has meant that they only take the deck of cards and re-sort among the existing managers' (Cook, engineer). This image was also expressed in statements about the change programme refer-ring only to talk and paper, with no action, or to good ideals far removed from reality.

We can thus point to the various images used – or at least suggested – by the people involved. Change managers and others then held or developed images as shown in Table 12.1.

These images emerged from the field and may be quite specific to our case. But they still say quite a lot about the problems around diverse meanings and the need to take seriously the images held on change management – by all involved, not least those to be operated upon.

The images guiding how people relate to change programmes and their com-munication around these are thus key elements in the process and a major source of the failure in our case. It is important to clarify one's own view, confront it with that of other significant people and develop a joint understanding – or at least reduce variation and clarify alternative understandings. Coherent communication appears vital. Otherwise, the confusions of messages emerging from the transfor-mation, eye-opener and post office views may easily fuel the more negative images. A problem here is that this calls for some ongoing work and close scrutiny of how images change. As stated, images are not necessarily static and coherent; they are often emergent, multiple and shifting (Reissner 2011). There are therefore good reasons to re-synchronize understandings of what goes on and the various roles of those involved. In terms of translation, Callon (1986) suggests that, in order to

Table 12.1 The images used

Image	Held by
Transformation process	Initiators of the change effort
Eye-opener	
Wave	
Post office	Administrators of the change work
Tick-off activities	and many junior managers
Managerial hypocrisy	Most employees, including several
Show	middle managers
Paper product	
Far-fetched utopia	
Meaningless reshuffling	

create a process that actors agree upon, that is, enlist key actors, it is important to take seriously and negotiate the terms of commitment and engagement with these, making them develop interests and identities aligned with the change process. This would support the self-image of the change manager as an interpreter and educator (Lawrence *et al.* 2006; Palmer *et al.* 2022).

What can be learned? Fifteen lessons for cultural change projects

We will now address some practical implications for organizational cultural change work – and to some extent for change work in general and for management more broadly. Some general suggestions for business performance, as discussed in Chapter 2, may be seen as relevant here. Beer (2017) claims that the following organizational behaviours lead to high performance: *coordination* between functions, businesses and regions; *commitment* to consumer needs; *competence* in the function most critical for success; *communications* that engage people in honest dialogue; and *creativity* in both technical and administrative areas. Heracleous and Langham (1996) suggest four significant issues in successful change management: visible and clear leadership, clear communication, involvement of employees in the planning phase and developing new skills. Cummings *et al.* (2020) suggest motivating change by creating readiness for change, creating a vision, developing political support by accessing change agents, managing the transition and sustaining momentum by supporting the change by resources etc. Already twenty-five years ago, Beer and Nohria (2000) claimed to have cracked the code for successful change by suggesting a combination of E- and O-type changes, that is, focusing upon both pure economic conditions and organizational capabilities. It is, of course, difficult to object to these quite general prescriptions. Like most efforts to identify key variables, they refer to themes framed in such a way that they are by definition important and seeming to bring about favourable outcomes. They would not stand the 'negativity' test, that is, it would not make sense to claim the opposite, to argue for unclear communication, disinterest in customer needs and neglect of creativity. And if the unfortunate change people in TC had been better at accomplishing for example coordination, commitment, competence, communication and creativity, recommended by Beer and Nohria (and most others in the advice business), the change project would by definition have been perceived in a more positive way.

In terms of the use of principles for change work, it is common and perhaps too easy to produce suggestions where the positive outcome is already present in the words used to accomplish this (cf. Sandelands and Drazin 1989). The action and the outcome are confused – and the statements become tautological. As seen from Chapter 3, Beer (2017) suggests principles such as mobilizing energy for change, developing a new compelling vision and identifying barriers to implementing the new direction (examples of barriers would be for example 'unclear strategy', 'an ineffective top team', 'poor coordination' and 'inadequate leadership'). Similarly,

Kotter (1996/2012) suggests that in order to produce change it is important to establish a sense of urgency, create guiding coalitions, develop and communicate a clear vision and strategy, empower employees, generate and consolidate short-term wins and anchor new approaches in existing culture (counteracting 'no urgency', 'poor guides', 'fuzzy vision and strategy', 'neglect of change progression, potential barriers and existing culture'). Connecting to the OD approaches, Robbins (2003: 566) suggests that the following values should accompany change: 'respect for people', 'trust and support', 'power equalization', 'confrontation' in terms of openly discussing problems and 'participation' (issues to be confronted include 'disrespect', 'mistrust and lack of support', 'hierarchical relations' and 'closed and secret change processes'). These suggestions and issues of change may intuitively sound helpful, but do not necessarily say more than do something positive and get rid of the bad stuff. They are not necessarily very helpful in drawing attention to what it is important to focus upon: an interest in strategy, people, power, communication and engagement, which is perhaps not very surprising (after all, what else could one be interested in?).

Having expressed this scepticism, we realize that we may have painted ourselves into a corner. We probably also deserve a critique when trying to express a few lessons of relevance for practical work with changes. We try, however, to be a bit more cautious than is common and don't claim to provide a recipe for how to work successfully. As many commentators on change suggest, there are no easy or universally valid truths in the business of organizational change. But we do think that our case – combined with general knowledge about organizational cultures and change projects – indicates the importance of seriously considering the following issues. We divide them into five overall themes: framing context, organizing change work(ers), content, tactics and process.

Framing context

1   See organizational transformation as a matter of *self-transformations including everybody, not just those to be 'worked upon' for improvement*. The entire organization is then included in the change process; it is not just a matter of an enlightened elite getting the organization or 'them' to change. People active in changing need to think through their ideas, beliefs, meanings and self-views – avoiding assuming that they have got it right and now it is a matter of getting others to transform. This assumption is common in the practitioner-oriented change literature.

2   Work with *moderate* (realistic) *aims* and proceed from the experiences of existing culture, realizing that only some progress can be made within the near future. Avoid getting caught in a huge gap between ideals and reality. As seen throughout the book, there is an assumption in much of the practitioner-oriented literature that top and senior managers can direct change. However, the basis of cultural change should be the meanings and orientations of the large group of employees, not the dream worlds of senior managers and consultants with

little contact with the meanings and orientations expressed in everyday organizational life.

3   There is a need for endurance and *a long-term view*. Culture is a slow-moving phenomenon; persistence in coming back to, varying and pushing for the ideas, meanings and ideals that are advocated is an absolute must. Quick fixes do not work. Of course, the more persistent and enduring the approach, the better the aims make sense, given sustained effort. (So points 2 and 3 correspond.)

Organizing change work(ers)

1   Cultural change work calls for accepting the need for *integration* of conceptualization and implementation and ongoing follow-up work. Change work calls for those involved to consider the whole project – division of labour, commonly advanced in much change literature leads to unanticipated problems (Ghoshal and Bartlett 1996; Kotter 1996/2012, 2018; Lawrence *et al.* 2006).
2   It is important not only to manage and clarify the roles and relationships between those engaged in change work but also to address their *identities*. People need to clarify how they view themselves in the specific context of the change programme and make sure that this view is understood by others, as identities often vary quite considerably also within the same organization as discussed in Chapter 2 (Stensaker *et al.* 2021). Callon and Latour (1981) suggest 'enlisting key actors' by clarifying terms of involvement such as roles and identities of participants. Role expectations need to be aligned with identities and discrepancies clarified.
3   Equally important, and related to identity clarification, is the theme of developing and, when called for, revising *the basic image* of the change programme. Is it an eye-opener or a profound transformation effort? Is it manager driven and unitary or is it supposed to include local initiative and variation? Coherence in communication needs to be thought through here and, as far as possible, accomplished. The success of the change work is presumably partly a matter of a number of people having a broadly similar view of what the work is basically about. This suggests recognizing the value of dialogue, as discussed in Chapter 2 (Hastings and Schwartz 2022).
4   There is a need for a *strong sense of 'we'* in change work – if those promoting and seen as symbolizing the cultural change are viewed as outsiders or on the periphery of an organization, then the change project's credibility and experienced relevance will be questioned. In particular it is important to avoid a negative symbolism being ascribed to those working with organizational and cultural change.[1] If large groups of employees have low confidence in for example senior executives, HR people or consultants and see these as 'peripheral' or outsiders, at the same time as they are viewed as central in the change work, then this will not be convincing. It may, as in our case, easily be interpreted as another 'HR thing'. An obvious solution would be to ask some typical employees or middle managers to work with the project, together with HR people, consultants and senior managers. This would suggest that the

project is of concern also for people belonging to and symbolizing 'us' – the broad, core groups in the firm – and not only people easily viewed as outside the group that most people identify with.

Content

1 *Avoid the self-evidently good.* Cultural change work is in vital respects facilitated by a critique of some dominant, existing orientations and the proposal of something controversial. Promoting the self-evidently good – such as agile, customer orientation, digitalization, respect for people, etc. – easily leads to no effects (yawn). Instead, what tends to shake people up a bit and spark discussion and questioning has a better chance of leading somewhere (e.g. 'We believe in the well-run-machine bureaucracy'). Once again this relates to the theme of being careful about hyperculture.

2 Focus on *meanings*, rather than – or at least more than – values. Many writers on change discuss the importance of having credos and values of organizational change that reach beyond the everyday lives of employees in order to trigger creative tensions and subsequent action on the part of employees (Cummings *et al.* 2020; Kotter 1996/2012, 2018). It is, of course, important to have some idea of the change direction, but we think that a one-sided focus on values easily invokes a preference for ideals rather than what is realized and what people mean – the projection of an ideal world confused with what exists (hyperculture). The meaning and understanding of the basic elements of organizational culture that are targeted for rethinking need to be clarified. Ask questions such as 'What is going on here?' and 'What is wrong with this place?' before seeking ideals. Clarifying problematic assumptions and wishful thinking calls for investigations and self-critique around meanings.

Tactics

1 *Combine pushing and dialogue.* In order to create both push and pull, paying close attention to the interplay between central agents – who are highly committed – and others is vital. Selected other groups need to be called upon to contribute, convince, inspire and remind larger groups (and to report back and take seriously the views of these larger groups). These selected others must be mobilized and encouraged to mobilize themselves. But they may need input and some push. Follow-up meetings with a mix of pushing and dialogue are important here. This amounts to something beyond what many authors of organizational change refer to as clear and one-sided communication of visions, strategy or direction of change efforts to core groups (Beer 2017; Kotter 2018). In addition, we address issues of intimate and frequent interaction, in terms of dialogue, sense giving and sense making, reporting, follow-up and feedback, in and between various core groups in order to support encouragement for

changes. Reminding and 'nagging' also appear important. The relay race here offers an 'anti-model' or negative example.

2   Working with organizational culture calls for skilful work with *emotions and symbolism* – the formulation of messages that appeal not only to reason and intellect but also to emotion and imagination is important. Formulated in negative terms, this means that cultural thinness/symbolic anorexia must be avoided. It also calls for a level of expressiveness and emotionality that is at odds with a bureaucratic style. We are not suggesting that cultural work calls for charismatic performances or singing-and-dancing sessions. But the idea of targeting values goes beyond the instrumental working through of procedures and calls for a higher level of demonstrated enthusiasm to be credible and have a chance of 'sticking'. To just follow the flow contingent upon a bureaucratic cultural mentality does not seem to be effective in this kind of project.

Process

1   It is important to take seriously the local sense making that takes place in organizations during change. Cultural change efforts call for *connecting to people's experiences* in a positive sense. This means that one should ground ideas and ideals in the local organizational context and try to avoid the repetition of standard formulas. The temptation to follow the example and style of others and produce hyperculture should be resisted. Expressed differently, it means another trade-off than that which seems to be common between ideas, meanings and values close to experience on the one hand and what sounds good in semi-public statements on the other. (See also point 1 under the sub-heading 'Content'.)

2   *Pay careful attention to process and 'reception'.* Here it is important to draw attention to meaning and sense making from a variety of actors involved in the change efforts. This exploration suggests that how the messages about change are interpreted and made sense of by various groups of employees must be carefully followed and listened to. Learning and adapting are crucial. Revisiting plans, reviewing the process and revising the ideas and roles of those active are important ingredients. Cultural change work can't follow a rationally decided design. This is an area with very strong limits to rationality – close attention to process is called for. For this reason, a model strictly dividing up the change work in planning and implementation is problematic.

3   *Keep cultural themes on the agenda.* There is a need for ongoing work. Avoid 'ticking off' culture work – 'now over to something else'. Leadership partly means putting important things on the agenda – and keeping them there (Alvesson *et al.* 2017). Of course, many of the 'conventional' tasks of managers can be ticked off, and certain types of change projects dealing with technical and administrative systems may include more of such elements than cultural change efforts. Cultural themes like values and meanings are not discrete, permanent, easy to grasp or in other ways possible to package and deal with once and for all or for a time, as suggested in the literature on

change that emphasizes a list of successive steps (n-step thinking). Values and meanings are slippery, uncertain, vague and sensitive to drifting. They call for continuous attention and explicit and symbolic work. This does not mean that a lot of time needs to be allocated to 'value talk' and the discussion and clarification of meaning. But to (briefly) point to, remind, illustrate and bring the issues on track at various times is important in order to drive cultural change. Using cultural change-facilitating language is, of course, by definition important.

Finale and conclusion

1   Be careful with engaging in change projects. It is merely a myth that change is always good, and senior managers frequently have unrealistic assumptions and expectations. They start too many projects and too many are soon dropped or carried out weakly (Amundsen 2003; Dawson 2003; Jackall 1988). The result is often cynicism, waste of time and the institutionalization of negative expectations and 'wait-and-see-if-something-is-happening' thinking. This makes change more difficult next time. Managers starting too many initiatives and overburdening people with demands and assignments sometimes produce 'wait-and-see' cultures – and complain about the scepticism and inertia resulting from this. Better change work often calls for fewer change work initiatives. There is a large mass media- and consultancy-driven change management industry propagating the need for drastic changes and promises of great accomplishments if the 'right' change model or change consultant is used. A new fashion introduces a gap between the ideal and what exists. Critical and selective responses to these are indicated. Fewer and – as more thinking, effort, energy and resources can be put into these – probably better change projects are to be recommended. We do confess, however, that it is not easy to know when to embark on a change journey. Frequently, one discovers too late that other important and urgent tasks are undermining the change project and this leads to mainly negative consequences. An insightful manager may think: 'I know that only one out of three change initiatives will lead anywhere, but I don't know which.' Perhaps our book has given a modest input to thinking and reflection, increasing the likelihood of a reasonably successful change project.

A supporting case, additional lesson and closing comment

The preceding lessons have been generated from a comparatively negative case. Learning from mistakes and failures is valuable and often offers the best input for understanding and getting ideas for what to do – or at least be careful about. Based on a negative example, we think it is possible to generate some significant principles that may guide change work, primarily in cultural change but also, to some extent, more generally.

The significance of the preceding lessons is discussed by Norbäck and Targama (2009) in an extensive study of organizational change work at a hospital in Sweden. The authors in question compare and relate their case – a more successful one – to ours and conclude their analysis by strongly supporting our lessons and recommendations for change work. (Their book was written after the publication of the first edition of our book.)

Based on a three-year leadership development programme the researchers (Norbäck and Targama 2009) participated in a change programme between 2003 and 2005 at a large regional hospital that included all senior managers such as physicians and other staff. The purpose of the programme was to improve the managerial practice at the hospital by establishing a new management system; the latter specifically aimed at what was termed continuous improvements – a form of organizational development through incremental learning – of the work environment and tasks at the hospital. The leadership development and organizational learning improvement activities were guided by three central objectives:

1   Create unity in the leadership about the significance of a management system for managerial practice.
2   Engage everyone in the change work.
3   Create follow-up routines for facilitating development and learning.

The change programme thus bears strong resemblances with what we in Chapters 2 and 3 refer to as a process approach – such as reframing and development of everyday practices – of an O-type of change, rather than a rationally designed and large technocratic project of an E-type.

The authors also suggest that the change programme in most important respects followed the fifteen lessons formulated earlier. In addition to these, Norbäck and Targama also add a lesson by emphasizing the significance of establishing supporting structure in change work. Later we briefly discuss the authors' story of the change work at the hospital on the basis of our fifteen lessons, here organized according to the five broader themes drawn upon earlier.

In terms of *context* Norbäck and Targama suggest that they managed to create a unity of understanding in the senior management group about the importance of everyone's participation in change, in line with the overall objectives. Facilitating broader understanding of the leadership within the hospital as well as engaging all employees in various seminars aimed at guiding local sense making of the ideas in the programme was central. The change programme in its entirety aimed at backing long-term development of the learning capacity of the hospital rather than short-term efficiencies.

When discussing the *change workers*, Norbäck and Targama conclude that they worked quite in line with the preceding lessons. Integration of planning, implementation and continuous work with follow-up is said to have been an integral part of the pedagogic model of the change work. In doing that they also considered identities and roles that helped in making challenges with subcultures more visible, in particular among the professional actors such as physicians and nurses.

With the exception of some minor variation among a small group of physicians Norbäck and Targama also suggest that they managed to create a common image about the significance of the change work among all the key participants. The mentioned small group of physicians were less convinced about the direction of change and this had a minor negative impact on the we-feeling among everyone and may also have reduced the physicians' confidence in the management group somewhat. These views of some physicians were, however, not large enough to undermine the impact of the effect of the cultural change in most parts of the organization.

In terms of *content* Norbäck and Targama conclude that, in contrast to the usual banalities and clichés often expressed in these situations, the change programme was initially regarded as controversial and subsequently quite challenging in many respects. Those managing the change also put strong emphasis on the meaning and understanding of the programme by focusing upon local interpretation of central terms and concepts. This enabled local problematization of some of the central assumptions of the programme and contributed to the identification of several areas in need of improvements, especially the need for increased coordination of occupational groups over professional and departmental borders.

The *tactics* used in the organizational development are suggested to have been a combination of push and pull. This is also said to have been a characteristic of the whole programme and something often discussed quite consciously at the change seminars that constituted a vital part of the change work. Also, in terms of emotional commitment, it is proposed that the change programme came close to our lessons. Initiatives in the change process always started in open discussions with strong focus on ideas, meaning and motives behind the initiative rather than on formal methods and techniques for implementation. Questions of why they had to engage in the change work were always quite intensively discussed among those involved in the change process. This made it possible to avoid an early bureaucratization of the programme and, in contrast, maintain engagement, motivation and creativity.

In terms of the *process*, we suggest in our lessons that it is vital to acknowledge the local sense making and interpretation. This is argued by Norbäck and Targama to have been central in the leadership development programme where they tried to avoid routine distribution of overheads and other forms of documentation that often lead to concepts of the participants being more mechanically appropriate, without relating them to their own local work environment. Based on this, the authors suggest that lesson 13 – about the significance of focus on meaning creation, learning and flexibility – could almost be seen as an overall declaration of the whole leadership development programme. The authors suggest that the programme followed a classic organizational development logic rather than a rationally designed plan. They also suggest that this approach – focus on local interpretation and understanding – came naturally in the development programme since they were particularly eager to avoid change work consisting of the ticking off of activities in a mechanical manner. The three guiding objectives of the change work – unity, broad engagement and follow-up for learning and development – were expressed continuously during the whole change programme.

When it comes to the last lesson about the *myths of changes* the authors suggest that leader development constitutes a sustainable change programme aimed at facilitating for change as an integrated part of daily work activities. Arguably the programme expressed an organizational development philosophy – change of O-type – with the purpose of improving an organization's long-term ability to learn and with the aim of accomplishing distinctive results and outcomes.

In addition to these lessons the authors also emphasize the significance of what they call *supporting structures* in change work. This may involve groups of actors possessing different and thus complementary competences and having the ability to monitor and evaluate the progression of change work in terms of ambitions fulfilled. These groups should also assure credibility for the change work and for those involved.

All in all, Norbäck and Targama (2009) suggest that change work that involves a common understanding of management systems and an organization's learning capacity should draw upon an organization development change ideal which in many ways contradicts the classic instrumental change rationality, what we in previous chapters have characterized as technocratic change projects.

A closing word

As a finale we would argue, once again, that established and dominating knowledge is not always reliable and useful in all situations. What seems convincing on paper and in sales pitches to management teams looking for quick solutions does not always work very well in complex organizational situations. By uncritically and single-mindedly following a technocratic logic in a cultural change context even the most convinced change supporter might actually end up as his/her own change enemy.

Note

1 For example, in a study of the establishment of Total Quality Leadership (TQL) practices in the American Navy, Barrett et al. (1995) reported that one of the local commanders implementing the change interpreted the TQL initiative as motivated by higher commanders' interest in climbing up the hierarchy, rather than expressing genuine interest in TQL. This cynicism about the motives of the change efforts initially resulted in some lack of commitment and frustration on the part of local commanders.

Bibliography

Ackroyd, S. and Crowdy, P. A. (1990) 'Can Culture Be Managed? Working with Raw Material: The Case of English Slaughtermen'. *Personnel Review*, 19(5), 3–13.

Adler, P. (1999) 'Building Better Bureaucracies'. *Academy of Management Executive*, 13(4), 36–47.

Agar, M. (1986) *Speaking of Ethnography*. Beverly Hills, CA: Sage.

Allen, K. S., Grelle, D., Lazarus. E. M., Popp, E. and Gutierrez, S. L. (2024) 'Hybrid Is Here to Stay: Critical Behaviors for Success in the New World of Work'. *Personality and Individual Differences*, 217, 1–11.

Alvesson, M. (1995) *Management of Knowledge-Intensive Companies*. Berlin: de Gruyter.

Alvesson, M. (2002) *Postmodernism and Social Research*. Buckingham: Open University Press.

Alvesson, M. (2013) *Understanding Organizational Culture* (2nd ed.). London: Sage.

Alvesson, M. (2022) *The Triumph of Emptiness* (2nd ed.). Oxford University Press.

Alvesson, M. and Berg, P. O. (1992) *Corporate Culture and Organizational Symbolism*. Berlin and New York: de Gruyter.

Alvesson, M., Blom, M. and Sveningsson, S. (2017) *Reflexive Leadership*. Sage.

Alvesson, M. and Sköldberg, K. (2017) *Reflexive Methodology. New Vistas for Qualitative Research* (3rd ed.). Sage.

Alvesson, M. and Spicer, A. (2012) 'A stupidity-Based Theory of Organizations'. *Journal of Management Studies*, 49, 1194–1220.

Alvesson, M. and Spicer, A. (2016) *The Stupidity Paradox. The Power and Pitfalls of Functional Stupidity at Work*. London: Profile.

Alvesson, M. and Spicer, A. (2025). *The Art of Less: How to Focus on What Really Matters at Work*. London: Bloomsbury.

Alvesson, M. and Sveningsson, S. (2003) 'Good Visions, Bad Micro-Management and Ugly Ambiguity: Contradiction of (Non)Leadership in a Knowledge Intensive Organization'. *Organization Studies*, 24(6), 961–988.

Alvesson, M. and Sveningsson, S. (2011a) 'Management Is the Solution: Now What Was the Problem? On the Fragile Basis for Managerialism'. *Scandinavian Journal of Management*, 27(4), 349–361.

Alvesson, M. and Sveningsson, S. (2011b) 'Identity Work in Consultancy Projects: Ambiguity and Distribution of Credit and Blame'. In C. Candlin and J. Crichton (eds) *Discourses of Deficit*. London: Palgrave Macmillan.

Alvesson, M. and Thompson, P. (2005) 'Post-Bureaucracy?' In S. Ackroyd, R. Batt, P. Thompson and P. Tolbert (eds) *Oxford Handbook of Work and Organization Studies*. Oxford: Oxford University Press.

Alvesson, M. and Willmott, H. (2002) 'Producing the Appropriate Individual: Identity Regulation as Organizational Control'. *Journal of Management Studies*, 39(5), 619–644.

Alvesson, M. and Willmott, H. (2012) *Making Sense of Management: A Critical Introduction* (2nd ed.). London: Sage.

Amundsen, O. (2003) 'Fortellinger om Organisasjonsendringer'. PhD thesis, Norges teknisknaturvetenskaplige Universitet, Trondheim.

Anthony, P. (1994) *Managing Culture*. Buckingham: Open University Press.

Arena, M., Hines, S. and Golden. (2023) 'The Three C's for Cultivating Organizational Culture in a Hybrid World'. *Organizational Dynamics*, 52, 1–10.

Argyris, C. (1982) 'How Learning and Reasoning Processes Affect Organizational Change'. In P. Goodman (ed.) *Change in Organizations*. San Francisco, CA: Jossey-Bass.

Ashforth, B. E. and Mael, F. (1989) 'Social Identity and the Organization'. *Academy of Management Review*, 14, 20–39.

Bacharach, P. and Baratz, M. S. (1962) 'Power, Politics, and Organizational Change'. *American Political Science Review*, 56(4), 942–952.

Badham, R., Garrety, K., Morrigan, V. and Dawson, P. (2003) 'Designer Deviance: Enterprise and Deviance in Cultural Change Programmes'. *Organization*, 10(4), 707–730.

Balogun, J. (2006) 'Managing Change: Steering a Course Between Intended Strategies and Unanticipated Outcomes'. *Long Range Planning*, 39, 29–49.

Balogun, J., Bartunek, J. M. and Do, B. (2015) 'Senior Managers' Sensemaking and Responses to Strategic Change'. *Organization Science*, 26(4), 960–979.

Balogun, J. and Johnson, G. (2004) 'Organizational Restructuring and Middle Manager Sensemaking'. *Academy of Management Journal*, 47(4), 523–549.

Balogun, J. and Johnson, G. (2005) 'From Intended Strategies to Unintended Outcomes: The Impact of Change Recipient Sensemaking'. *Organization Studies*, 26(11), 1573–1601.

Barrett, F., Thomas, G. and Hocevar, S. (1995) 'The Central Role of Discourse in Large-Scale Change: A Social Construction Perspective'. *Journal of Applied Behavioral Science*, 31(3), 352–372.

Bartunek, J., Rousseau, D. M., Rudolph, J. W. and DePalma, J. A. (2006) 'On the Receiving End: Sensemaking, Emotion and Assessments of an Organizational Change Initiated by Others'. *Journal of Applied Behavioral Science*, 42(2), 183–206.

Bate, P. (1994) *Strategies for Cultural Change*. Oxford: Butterworth-Heinemann.

Baudrillard, J. (1981/1995) *Simulacra and Simulation*. Ann Arbor, MI: University of Michigan Press.

Beech, N. and Macintosh, R. (2012) *Managing Change: Enquiry and Action*. Cambridge: Cambridge University Press.

Beer, M. (2017) 'Lead Organizational Change by Creating Dissatisfaction and Realigning the Organization with New Competitive Realities'. In E. Locke (ed.) *The Blackwell Handbook of Principles of Organizational Behaviour*. Oxford: Blackwell.

Beer, M. and Eisenstat, R. (1996) 'Developing an Organization Capable of Implementing Strategy and Learning'. *Human Relations*, 49(5), 597–619.

Beer, M. and Nohria, N. (2000) 'Cracking the Code of Change'. *Harvard Business Review*, 3, 133–141.

Bloom, N., Barrero, J. M., Davis, S., Meyer, B. and Mihaylov, E. (2023) 'Research: Where Managers and Employees Disagree About Remote Work'. https://hbr.org/2023/01/research-where-managers-and-employees-disagree-about-remote-work

Bodell, L. (2022) 'Most Change Initiatives Fail – Here's How to Beat the Odds'. *Forbes*. www.forbes.com/sites/lisabodell/2022/03/28/most-change-initiatives-fail-heres-how-to-beat-the-odds/?sh=fd5024522eea&trk=article-ssr-frontend-pulse_little-text-block

Bommer, W., Rich, G. and Rubin, R. (2005) 'Changing Attitudes About Change: Longitudinal Effects of Transformational Leader Behavior on Employee Cynicism About Organizational Change'. *Journal of Organizational Behavior*, 26, 733–753.

Boorstin, D. (1961) *The Image*. New York: First Vintage Books.

Bradford, D. L. and Burke, W. W. (eds) (2005) *Reinventing Organization Development: New Approaches to Change in Organizations*. San Francisco, CA: Pfeiffer/Wiley.

Bradley, J. and Hastings, G. (2022) 'Leading Change Processes for Success: A Dynamic Application of Diagnostic and Dialogic Organization Development'. *The Journal of Applied Behavioral Science*, 58(1), 120–148.

Brown, A. (1995) *Organizational Culture*. London: Pitman.

Brown, A. and Humphreys, M. (2003) 'Epic and Tragic Tales Making Sense of Change'. *Journal of Applied Behavioral Science*, 39(2), 121–144.

Brown, A. B., Gabriel, Y. and, Gherardi, S. (2009) 'Storytelling and Change: An Unfolding Story'. *Organization*, 16(3), 323–333.

Brunsson, N. (1985) *The Irrational Organization*. Chichester: Wiley.

Brunsson, N. (2019) *The Organization of Hypocrisy. Talk, Decisions and Actions in Organizations* (pocket ver). Copenhagen Business School.

Buchanan, D. and Badham, R. (1999) 'Politics and Organizational Change: The Lived Experience'. *Human Relations*, 52(5), 609–629.

Buchanan, D. and Badham, R. (2011) *Power, Politics and Organizational Change. Winning the Turf Games*. (2nd ed.). London: Sage.

Buchanan, D. and Badham, R. (2020) *Power, Politics, and Organizational Change*. London: Sage.

Buchanan, D. and Dawson, P. (2007) 'Discourses and Audience: Organizational Change as Multi-Story Process'. *Journal of Management Studies*, 44(5), 669–686.

Burke, W. W. (2018) *Organizational Change* (5th ed.). Thousands Oaks, CA: Sage.

Burnes, B. (2004) *Managing Change: A Strategic Approach to Organisational Dynamics*. Harlow: Prentice Hall.

Burnes, B. (2017) *Managing Change*. Harlow: Pearson Education.

Burnes, B. (2020) 'The Origins of Lewin's Three-Step Model of Change'. *The Journal of Applied Behavioral Science*, 56(1), 32–59.

Bushe, G. R. and Marshak, R. J. (2015) 'Introduction to the Dialogic Organization Development Mindset'. In G. R. Bushe and R. J. Marshak (eds) *Dialogic Organization Development: The Theory and Practice of Transformational Change* (pp. 11–32). Berrett-Koehler.

By, R. T. (2020) 'Organizational Change and Leadership: Out of the Quagmire'. *Journal of Change Management*, 20(1), 1–6.

Callahan, J. L. (2002) 'Masking the Need for Cultural Change: The Effects of Emotion Structuration'. *Organization Studies*, 23(2), 281–297.

Callon, M. (1986) 'Some Elements of a Sociology of Domestication'. In J. Law (ed.) *Power, Action and Belief: A New Sociology of Knowledge?* London: Routledge & Kegan Paul.

Callon, M. and Latour, B. (1981) 'Unscrewing the Big Leviathan: How Actors Macro-structure Reality and How Sociologists Help Them to Do So'. In K. Knorr-Cetina and A. V. Cicourel (eds) *Advances in Social Theory and Methodology: Toward an Integration of Micro- and Macro-Sociologies*. London: Routledge.

Caprar, D., Walker, B. and Ashforth, B. (2022) 'The Dark Side of Strong Identification in Organizations: A Conceptual Review'. *Academy of Management Annals*, 16(2), 759–805.

Child, J. (2015) *Organizations: Contemporary Principles and Practice* (2nd ed.). Chichester: Wiley.

Choudhury, P., Tarun Khanna, T., Makridis, C. and Kyle Schirmann, K. (2024) 'Is Hybrid Work the Best of Both Worlds? Evidence from a Field Experiment'. *Review of Economics and Statistics*, (Forthcoming) 1–24. doi:10.1162/rest_a_01428.

Collins, D. (1998) *Organizational Change: Sociological Perspectives*. London: Routledge.

Collins, D. (2018) *Stories for Management Success: The Power of Talk in Organizations*. London: Routledge.

Cummings, T. G., Worley, C. G. and Donovan, P. (2020) *Organization Development and Change*. Andover: Cengage Learning EMEA.

Dawson, P. (2003) *Understanding Organizational Change*. London: Sage.

Dawson, P. (2014) 'Reflections: On Time, Temporality and Change in Organizations'. *Journal of Change Management*, 14(3), 285–308.

Dealy, M. and Thomas, A. (2005) *Change or Die: How to Transform Your Organization from the Inside Out*. Praeger Books.

de Rond, M., Holeman, I. and Howard-Grenville, J. (2019) 'Sensemaking from the Body: An Enactive Ethnography of Rowing the Amazon'. *Academy of Management Journal*, 62(6), 1961–1988.

DiMaggio, P. J. and Powell, P. P. (1991) 'The Iron Cage Revisited: Institutional Isomorphism and Collective Rationality in Organizational Fields'. In W. W. Powell and P. J. DiMaggio (eds) *The New Institutionalism in Organizational Analysis*. Chicago, IL: University of Chicago Press.

Edmondson, A. C. and Besieux, T. (2021) 'Reflections: Voice and Silence in Workplace Conversations'. *Journal of Change Management*, 21(3), 269–286.

Elsbach, K. D. and Stigliani, I. (2018) 'Design Thinking and Organizational Culture: A Review and Framework for Future Research'. *Journal of Management*, 44, 2274–2306.

Endrejat, P. and Burnes, B. (2022) 'Draw It, Check It, Change It: Reviving Lewin's Topology to Facilitate Organizational Change Theory and Practice'. *The Journal of Applied Behavioral Science*. doi:10.1177/00218863221122875..

Erwin, E. and Garman, A. (2010) 'Resistance to Organizational Change: Linking Research and Practice'. *Leadership & Organization Development Journal*, 31(1), 39–56.

Fine, G. A. and Hallett, T. (2014) 'Group Cultures and the Everyday Life of Organizations: Interaction Orders and Meso-Analysis'. *Organization Studies*, 35(12), 1773–1792.

Fitzgerald, T. H. (1988) 'Can Change in Organizational Culture Really Be Managed?' *Organizational Dynamics*, 17(2), 117–134.

Fleming, P. (2005) 'Workers' Playtime? Boundaries and Cynicism in a "Culture of Fun" Program'. *Journal of Applied Behavioral Science*, 41(3), 285–303.

Fleming, P. and Spicer, A. (2014) 'Power and Management in Organization Science'. *Academy of Management Annals*, 81(1), 237–298.

Fleming, P. and Sturdy, A. (2009) '"Just be Yourself": Towards Neo-Normative Control in Organizations'. *Employee Relations*, 31(6), 569–583.

Ford, J. D. and Ford, L. W. (1995) 'The Role of Conversations in Producing Intentional Change in Organizations'. *Academy of Management Review*, 20, 541–570.

Forester, J. (2003) 'On Fieldwork in a Habermasian Way: Critical Ethnography and the Extraordinary Character of Ordinary Professional Work'. In M. Alvesson and H. Willmott (eds) *Studying Management Critically*. London: Sage.

Francis, H. and Sinclair, J. (2003) 'A Processual Analysis of HRM-Based Change'. *Organization*, 10(4), 685–706.

Frost, P. J., Moore, L. F., Louis, M. R., Lundberg, C. C. and Martin, J. (eds) (1985) *Organizational Culture*. Beverly Hills, CA: Sage.

Gagliardi, P. (1986) 'The Creation and Change of Organizational Cultures: A Conceptual Framework'. *Organization Studies*, 7(2), 117–134.

Geertz, C. (1973) *The Interpretation of Cultures*. New York: Basic Books.

Ghoshal, S. and Bartlett, C. A. (1996) 'Rebuilding Behavioral Context: A Blueprint for Corporate Renewal'. *Sloan Management Review*, 37(2), 23–36.

Gioia, D., Patvardhan, S., Hamilton, A. and Corley, K. (2013) 'Organizational Identity: Formation and Change'. *The Academy of Management Annals*, 7(1), 123–193.

Gleeson, B. (2017) '1 Reason for Why Most Change Management Efforts Fail'. *Forbes*. www.forbes.com/sites/brentgleeson/2017/07/25/1-reason-why-most-change-management-efforts-fail/?sh=2527d5ee546b&trk=article-ssr-frontend-pulse_little-text-block

Grant, D. and Marshak, R. (2011) 'Towards a Discourse-Centered Understanding of Organizational Change'. *Journal of Applied Behavioral Science*, 47(2), 204–235.

Grant, D., Wailes, N., Michelson, G., Brewer, A. and Hall, R. (2002) 'Editorial: Rethinking Organizational Change'. *Strategic Change*, 11, 237–242.

Hart, H. (1999) 'Ständiga Förbättringar som Kompenent i en Ledningsstrategi för Förändring'. In T. Nilsson (ed.) *Ständiga Förbättring – om Utveckling av Arbete och Kvalité*. Solna: Arbetslivsinstitutet.

Hastings, B. and Schwartz, G. (2022) 'Leading Change Processes for Success: A Dynamic Application of Diagnostic and Dialogic Organization Development'. *The Journal of Applied Behavioral Science*, 58(1), 120–148.

Hatch, M. J. and Schultz, M. (2002) 'The Dynamics of Organizational Identity'. *Human Relations*, 55(8), 989–1018.

Helms Mills, J. (2003) *Making Sense of Organizational Change*. New York: Routledge.

Heracleous, L. (2001) 'An Ethnographic Study of Culture in the Context of Organizational Change'. *Journal of Applied Behavioral Science*, 37(4), 426–446.

Heracleous, L. and Barrett, M. (2001) 'Organizational Change as Discourse: Communicative Actions and Deep Structures in the Context of IT Implementation'. *Academy of Management Journal*, 44, 755–778.

Heracleous, L. and Langham, B. (1996) 'Strategic Change and Organizational Culture at Hay Management Consultants'. *Long Range Planning*, 29(4), 485–494.

Hislop, D., Bosua, R. and Helms, R. (2018) *Knowledge Management – A Critical Introduction*. Oxford University Press.

Hofstede, G., Bram, N., Daval, O. D. and Geert, S. (1990) 'Measuring Organizational Cultures: A Qualitative and Quantitative Study Across Twenty Cases'. *Administrative Science Quarterly*, 35, 286–316.

Howard-Grenville, J. (2020) 'How to Sustain Your Organization's Culture When Everyone Is Remote'. *Sloan Management Review*, 1–4.

Hughes, M. (2010) *Managing Change: A Critical Perspective*. London: Chartered Institute of Personnel and Development.

Hughes, M. (2011) 'Do 70 Per Cent of All Organizational Change Initiatives Really Fail?' *Journal of Management*, 11(4), 451–464.

Hughes, M. (2016) 'Leading Changes: Why Transformation Explanations Fail'. *Leadership*, 12(4), 449–469.

Hurley, R. F., Church, A. H., Burke, W. W. and Van Eynde, D. F. (1992) 'Tensions, Change and Values in OD'. *OD Practitioner*, 29, 1–5.

Ibarra, H. (2020) 'Take a Wrecking Ball to Your Company's Iconic Practices'. *Sloan Management Review*, 61(2), 12–16.

Jabri, M. and Jabri, E. (2022) *Managing Organizational Change: Process, Social Construction and Dialogue* (3rd ed.). Bloomsbury Academic.

Jackall, R. (1988) *Moral Mazes: The World of Corporate Managers*. Oxford: Oxford University Press.

Jaeger, G. and Selznick, P. (1964) 'A Normative Theory of Culture'. *American Sociological Review*, 29, 653–669.

Jian, G. (2011) 'Articulating Circumstance, Identity and Practice: Toward a Discursive Framework of Organizational Changing'. *Organization*, 18(1), 45–64.

Johnson, G. (1987) *Strategic Change and the Management Process*. London: Blackwell.

Kanter, R. M. (1983) *The Change Masters*. London: Unwin-Hyman.

Kärreman, D., Sveningsson, S. and Alvesson, M. (2002) 'The Return of the Machine Bureaucracy? Management Control in the Work Settings of Professionals'. *International Studies of Management and Organizations*, 32(2), 70–92.

Knights, D. and Vurdubakis, T. (1994) 'Foucault, Power, Resistance and All That'. In J. Jermier, D. Knights and W. Nord (eds) *Resistance and Power in Organizations* (pp. 167–198). London: Routledge.

Kotter, J. P. (1996/2012). *Leading Change*. Boston, MA: Harvard Business School Press.

Kotter, J. P. (1999) 'What Effective General Managers Really Do'. *Harvard Business Review*, 77(2), 145–158.

Kotter, J. P. (2014) *Accelerate*. Boston, MA: Harvard Business Review Press.

Kotter, J. P. (2018) 'Eight Steps to Accelerate Change in Your Organization'. www.kotterinc.com/wp-content/uploads/2019/04/8-Steps-eBook-Kotter-2018.pdf (accessed 4 March 2024).

Kunda, G. (1992) *Engineering Culture: Control and Commitment in a High-Tech Corporation*. Philadelphia, PA: Temple University Press.

Latour, B. (1986) 'The Powers of Association'. In J. Law (ed.) *Power, Action and Belief: A New Sociology of Knowledge?* London: Routledge & Kegan Paul.

Latour, B. (1988) *The Pasteurization of France.* Cambridge, MA: Harvard University Press.

Latour, B. (2005) *Reassembling the Social.* Oxford: Oxford University Press.

Lawrence, T., Dyck, B., Maitlis, S. and Mauws, M. K. (2006) 'The Underlying Structure of Continuous Change'. *Sloan Management Review,* 59–66.

Leavitt, H. J. (1964) 'Applied Organizational Change in Industry: Structural, Technical and Human Approaches'. In W. W. Cooper, H. J. Leavitt and M. W. Shelly (eds) *New Perspectives in Organization Research.* New York: Wiley.

Legge, K. (1995) *Human Resources Management Rhetorics and Realities.* London: Macmillan.

Lewin, K. (1951) *Field Theory in Social Science.* New York: Harper & Row.

Lindblom, C. E. (1959) 'The Science of Muddling Through'. *Public Administration Review,* 19(2), 79–88.

Lukes, S. M. (1974) *Power: A Radical View.* London: MacMillan.

Lundberg, C. (1985) 'On the Feasibility of Cultural Interventions in Organizations'. In P. J. Frost, L. F. Moore, M. R. Louis, C. C. Lundberg and J. Martin (eds) *Organizational Culture* (pp. 381–389). Beverly Hills, CA: Sage.

Mackenzie, E., McGovern, T., Small, A., Hicks, C. and Scurry, T. (2021) '"Are They Out to Get Us?" Power and the "Recognition" of the Subject Through a "Lean" Work Regime'. *Organization Studies,* 42(11), 1721–1740.

Magala, S. (2005) *Cross-Cultural Competence.* London: Routledge.

Marshak, R. J. (2009) *Organizational Change: Views from the Edge.* Bethel: Lewin Center.

Martin, J. (2002) *Organizational Culture.* Thousand Oaks, CA: Sage.

Martin, J., Feldman, M., Hatch, M. and Sitkin, S. (1983) 'The Uniqueness Paradox in Organizational Stories'. *Administrative Science Quarterly,* 28, 438–453.

Martin, J. and Meyerson, D. (1988) 'Organizational Cultures and the Denial, Channeling and Acknowledgement of Ambiguity'. In L. R. Pondy, R. J. Boland and H. Thomas (eds) *Managing Ambiguity and Change.* New York: Wiley.

McGregor, D. (1960) *The Human Side of Enterprise.* New York: McGraw-Hill.

McMenemy, L. (2018) 'What Is a Chief Storyteller? Five Business Leaders Share Their Stories'. *Skyword,* 22 March. www.skyword.com/contentstandard/marketing/what-is-a-chief-storyteller- five-business-leaders-share-their-stories/ (accessed 15 March 2024).

Meyer, J. W. and Rowan, B. (1977) 'Institutionalized Organizations: Formal Structure as Myth and Ceremony'. *American Journal of Sociology,* 83(2), 340–363.

Mintzberg, H. (1998) 'Covert Leadership: Notes on Managing Professionals'. *Harvard Business Review,* 140–147.

Mirfakhar, A., Trullen, J. and Valverde, M. (2018) 'Easier Said Than Done: A Review of Antecedents Influencing Effective HR Implementation'. *The International Journal of Human Resource Management,* 29(22), 3001–3025.

Monteiro, P. and Adler, P. (2022) 'Bureaucracy for the 21st century: Clarifying and Expanding Our View of Bureaucratic Organization.' *Academy of Management Annals,* 16(2) 427–475.

Morgan, G. (1997) *Images of Organization* (2nd ed.). Thousand Oaks, CA: Sage.

Morgan, M., Frost, P. J. and Pondy, L. R. (1983) 'Organizational Symbolism'. In L. R. Pondy, P. J. Frost, G. Morgan and T. C. Dandridge (eds) *Organizational Symbolism.* Greenwich, CT: JAI Press.

Murdoch, Z. and Geys, B. (2014) 'Institutional Dynamics in International Organizations'. *Organization Studies,* 35(12), 1793–1811.

Musson, G. and Duberley, J. (2007) 'Change, Change or be Exchanged: The Discourse of Participation and the Manufacture of Identity'. *Journal of Management Studies,* 44(1), 143–164.

Newell, S., Robertson, M., Scarbrough, H. and Swan, J. (2009) *Managing Knowledge Work and Innovation* (2nd ed.). Red Globe Press.

Nikpour, A. (2017) 'The Impact of Organizational Culture on Organizational Performance: The Mediating Role of Employee's Organizational Commitment'. *International Journal of Organizational Leadership*, 6, 65–72.

Norbäck, L.-E. and Targama, A. (2009) *Det Komplexa Sjukhuset: Att Leda Djupgående förändringar i en Multiprofessionell Verksamhet*. Lund: Studentlitteratur.

Normann, R. (1977) *Management for Growth*. Chichester: Wiley.

Nörmark, D. and Fogh Jensen, A. (2021) *Pseudowork*. Copenhagen: Gyldendahl Trade.

Ogbonna, E. and Harris, L. (1998) 'Managing Organizational Culture: Compliance or Genuine Change?' *British Journal of Management*, 9, 273–288.

Ogbonna, E. and Wilkinson, B. (2003) 'The False Promise of Organizational Culture Change'. *Journal of Management Studies*, 40, 1151–1178.

Ouchi, W. G. (1980) 'Markets, Bureaucracies and Clans'. *Administrative Science Quarterly*, 25, 129–141.

Palmer, I., Dunford, R. and Buchanan, D. (2022) *Managing Organizational Change: A Multiple Perspectives Approach* (4th ed.). Maidenhead: McGraw-Hill.

Palmer, I. and Hardy, C. (2000) *Thinking About Management*. London: Sage.

Pathiranage, Y., Jayatilake, L. and Abeysekera, R. (2020) 'A Literature Review on Organizational Culture Towards Corporate Performance'. *International Journal of Management, Accounting and Economics*, 7(9), 522–544.

Pettigrew, A. M. (1985) *The Awakening Giant*. Oxford: Basil Blackwell.

Pettigrew, A. M. (2012) 'Context and Action in the Transformation of the Firm: A Reprise'. *Journal of Management Studies*, 49(7), 1304–1328.

Pettigrew, A. M., Woodman, R. and Cameron, K. (2001) 'Studying Organizational Change and Development: Challenges for Future Research'. *Academy of Management Journal*, 44(4), 697–713.

Pfeffer, J. (1992) *Managing with Power: Politics and Influence in Organizations*. Boston, MA: Harvard Business School Press.

Pieterse, J., Caniëls, M. and Homan, T. (2012) 'Professional Discourses and Resistance to Change'. *Journal of Organizational Change Management*, 25(6), 798–818.

Prasad, P. and Prasad, A. (2000) 'Stretching the Iron Cage: The Constitution and Implications of Routine Workplace Resistance'. *Organization Science*, 11(4), 387–403.

Preece, D., Steven, G. and Steven, V. (1999) *Work, Change and Competition*. London: Routledge.

PwC (2018) 'SDG Reporting Challenge 2018. From Promise to Reality: Does Business Really Care About SDGs?' *PwC Global Study*. www.pwc.com/gx/en/sustainability/SDG/sdg-reporting-2018.pdf (accessed 18 March 2024).

Ray, C. A. (1986) 'Corporate Culture: The Last Frontier of Control'. *Journal of Management Studies*, 23(3), 287–297.

Reichers, A., Wanous, J. and Austin, T. (1997) 'Understanding and Managing Cynicism About Organizational Change'. *Academy of Management Executive*, 11(1), 48–59.

Reissner, S. C. (2011) 'Patterns of Stories of Organizational Change'. *Journal of Organizational Change Management*, 24(5), 593–609.

Rennstam, J. (2007) 'Engineering Work'. PhD thesis, Lund Business Press, Lund.

Robbins, S. P. (2003) *Organizational Behavior* (Int. ed.). Upper Saddle River, NJ: Prentice Hall.

Roethlisberger, F. and Dickson, W. (1950) *Management and the Worker: An Account of a Research Program Conducted by the Western Electric Company, Hawthorne Works, Chicago*. Cambridge, MA: Harvard University Press.

Rouleau, L. (2005) 'Micro-Practices of Strategic Sensemaking and Sensegiving: How Middle Managers Interpret and Sell Change Every Day'. *Journal of Management Studies*, 42(7), 1413–1441.

Sandberg, J. and Targama, A. (2007) *Managing Understanding in Organizations*. London: Sage.

Sandelands, L. and Drazin, R. (1989) 'On the Language of Organization Theory'. *Organization Studies*, 10, 457–478.

Schaefer, S. (2014) *Of Images, Ignorance and Bliss: A Study of Managerial Work When Organising for Creativity*. Lund: Lund Business Press.

Schein, E. H. (1985) *Organizational Culture and Leadership*. San Francisco, CA: Jossey-Bass.

Scott, W. R. (1994) 'Institutions and Organizations: Toward a Theoretical Synthesis'. In J. W. Meyer and W. R. Scott (eds) *Institutional Environments: Structural Complexity and Individualism*. Beverly Hills, CA: Sage.

Scott, W. R. and Meyer, J. W. (eds) (1994) *Institutional Environments: Structural Complexity and Individualism*. Beverly Hills, CA: Sage.

Sculley, J. (1987) *Odyssey: Pepsi to Apple*. New York: Harper & Row.

Senge, P. (1996) 'The Leaders' New Work: Building Learning Organizations'. In K. Starkey (ed.) *How Organizations Learn*. London: Thomson Business Press.

Sennett, R. (1998) *The Corrosion of Character*. New York: W.W. Norton.

Siehl, C. (1985) 'After the Founder: An Opportunity to Manage Culture'. In P. J. Frost, L. F. Moore, M. R. Louis, C. C. Lundberg and J. Martin (eds) *Organizational Culture*. Beverly Hills, CA: Sage.

Sminia, H. (2016) 'Pioneering Process Research: Andrew Pettigrew's Contribution to Management Scholarship, 1962–2014'. *International Journal of Management Reviews*, 18, 111–132.

Smircich, L. (1983a) 'Concepts of Culture and Organizational Analysis'. *Administrative Science Quarterly*, 28, 339–358.

Smircich, L. (1983b) 'Organizations as Shared Meanings'. In L. R. Pondy, P. J. Frost, G. Morgan and T. C. Dandridge (eds) *Organizational Symbolism*. Greenwich, CT: JAI Press.

Smircich, L. (1985) 'Is Organizational Culture a Paradigm for Understanding Organizations and Ourselves?' In P. J. Frost, L. F. Moore, M. R. Louis, C. C. Lundberg and J. Martin (eds) *Organizational Culture*. Beverly Hills, CA: Sage.

Smircich, L. and Morgan, G. (1982) 'Leadership: The Management of Meaning'. *Journal of Applied Behavioral Science*, 18, 257–273.

Smyth, N. (2018) 'What Is a Chief Storyteller and Do You Need One?' *Techmarsec*, 24 October. www.techmarsec.com/what-is-a-chief-storyteller-and-do-you-need-one/ (accessed 2 January 2019).

Sörgärde, N. (2006) *Förändringsförsök och Identitetsdramatisering: En Studie Bland Nördar och Slipsbärare i ett IT-företag*. Lund: Lund Business Press.

Sorge, A. and van Witteloostuijn, A. (2004) 'The (Non)Sense of Organizational Change: An Essay About Universal Management Hypes, Sick Consultancy Metaphors, and Healthy Organization Theories'. *Organization Studies*, 25(7), 1205–1231.

Spicer, A. (2017) *Corporate Bullshit*. London: Routledge.

Spicer, A. (2020) 'Organizational Culture and COVID-19'. *Journal of Management Studies*, 57(8), 1737–1740.

Stensaker, I. G., Balogun, J. and Langley, A. (2021) 'The Power of the Platform: Place and Employee Responses to Organizational Change'. *The Journal of Applied Behavioral Science*, 57(2), 174–203.

Sturdy, A. and Grey, C. (2003) 'Beneath and Beyond Organizational Change Management: Exploring Alternatives'. *Organization*, 10(4), 651–662.

Sutton, R. and Rao, H. (2024) *Rid Your Organization of Obstacles That Infuriate Everyone*. Harvard Business Review. January–February.

Sveningsson, S. and Alvesson, M. (2003) 'Managing Managerial Identities'. *Human Relations* 56(10), 1163–1193.

Sveningsson, S. and Alvesson, M. (2016) *Managerial Lives: Leadership and Identity in an Imperfect World*. Cambridge: Cambridge University Press.

Sveningsson, S. and Sörgärde, N. (2013) 'Organizational Change Management'. In L. Strannegård and A. Styhre (eds) *Management: An Advanced Introduction*. Stockholm: Studentlitteratur.

Sveningsson, S. and Sörgärde, N. (2023) *Managing Change in Organizations*. London: Sage.

Tasler, N. (2017) 'Stop Using the Excuse "Organizational Change Is Hard"'. *Harvard Business Review*, 19.

Thomas, R., Sargent, L. D. and Hardy, C. (2011) 'Managing Organizational Change: Negotiating Meaning and Power-Resistance Relations'. *Organization Science*, 22(1), 22–41.

Thurlow, A. and Helms-Mills, J. (2015) 'Telling Tales Out of School: Sensemaking and Narratives of Legitimacy in an Organizational Change Process'. *Scandinavian Journal of Management*, 31(2), 246–254.

Tichy, N. M. (1982) 'Managing Change Strategically: The Technical, Political, and Cultural Keys'. *Organizational Dynamics*, Autumn, 59–80.

Tichy, N. M. (1983) 'Managing Organizational Transformations'. *Human Resource Management*, 22(1/2), 45–61.

Todnem, R., Kuipers, B. and Procter, S. (2018) 'Understanding Teams in Order to Understand Organizational Change'. *Journal of Change Management*, 18(1), 1–9.

Trevor, J. and Holweg, M. (2023) 'Managing the New Tensions of Hybrid Work'. *Sloan Management Review*, 64(2), 34–40.

Tsoukas, H. (2005) 'Afterword: Why Language Matters in the Analysis of Organizational Change'. *Journal of Organizational Change Management*, 18(1), 96–104.

Tsoukas, H. and Chia, R. (2002) 'On Organizational Becoming: Rethinking Organizational Change'. *Organization Science*, 13(5), 567–582.

Van de Ven, A. H. and Poole, M. S. (1995) 'Explaining Development and Change in Organizations'. *Academy of Management Review*, 20(3), 510–540.

Van Hulst, M. and Ybema, S. (2019) 'From What to Where: A Setting-Sensitive Approach to Organizational Storytelling'. *Organization Studies*, 41(3), 365–391. doi:10.1177/0170840618815523

Van Maanen, J. and Barley, S. R. (1984) 'Occupational Communities: Culture and Control in Organizations'. In B. M. Staw and L. L. Cummings (eds) *Research in Organizational Behaviour*, Vol. 7. Greenwich, CT: JAI Press.

Van Maanen, J. and Barley, S. R. (1985) 'Cultural Organization: Fragments of a Theory'. In P. J. Frost, L. F. Moore, M. R. Louis, C. C. Lundberg and J. Martin (eds) *Organizational Culture*. Beverly Hills, CA: Sage.

Van Marrewijk, A., Veenswijk, M. and Clegg, S. (2010) 'Organizing Reflexivity in Designed Change: The Ethnoventionist Approach'. *Journal of Organizational Change Management*, 23(3), 212–229.

Wallander, J. (2003) *Decentralization – Why and How to Make It Work*. Stockholm: SNS.

Wang, Y., Sunghoon, K., Alannah, R. and Sanders, K. (2022) 'Employee Perceptions of HR Practices: A Critical Review and Future Directions'. *The International Journal of Human Resource Management*, 31(1), 128–173. doi:10.1080/09585192.2019.1674360

Weick, K. E. (1995) *Sensemaking in Organizations*. Thousand Oaks, CA: Sage.

Weick, K. E. and Quinn, E. R. (1999) 'Organizational Change and Development'. *Annual Review of Psychology*, 50, 361–386.

Weisboard, M. R. (1987) *Productive Workplaces*. San Francisco, CA: Jossey-Bass.

Whittington, R., Regnér, P., Angwin, D., Johnson, G., Scholes, K. (2020) *Exploring Strategy: Text and Cases* (12th ed.). Harlow: Pearson.

Wilkins, A. L. and Ouchi, W. G. (1983) 'Efficient Cultures: Exploring the Relationship Between Culture and Organizational Performance'. *Administrative Science Quarterly*, 28, 468–481.

Willmott, H. (1993) 'Strength Is Ignorance; Slavery Is Freedom: Managing Culture in Modern Organizations'. *Journal of Management Studies*, 30(4), 515–552.

Ybema, S. and Horvers, M. (2017) 'Resistance Through Compliance: The Strategic and Subversive Potential of Frontstage and Backstage Resistance'. *Organization Studies*, 38(9), 1233–1251.

Young, E. (1989) 'On the Naming of the Rose: Interests and Multiple Meanings as Elements of Organizational Culture'. *Organization Studies*, 10, 187–206.

Index

Note: Page numbers in *italics* indicate figures, **bold** indicate tables in the text, and references following "n" refer notes.

Ackroyd, S. 55
actors 7, 9, 75–76, 176, 181–182
advertising 20
agenda setting 58, 59
Alvesson, M. 123, 133
Anthony, A. 60
anthropological organizational culture 152, **152,** 161, 165, 179
'anti-culture' 123
applauded engineering culture 78
Apple 16
artefacts 44
assumptions 4, 29, 44, 85, 92; change agents 188; cultural web model 26, 28–30, *29*; non-conscious 161; self-motivated agents 155
attitude change 81, 82
autonomy 29, 60

background 69, 77–80
Badham, R. 46, 184
balanced scorecards 14, 15
Balogun, J. 33
Barrett, F. 202n1
Bate, P. 44
baton metaphor 125–129, 131–135, 171–173, 178, 181
Baudrillard, J. 147
BBC *see* British Broadcasting Corporation (BBC)
Beer, M. 3, 32, 54, 55, 194, 195
beliefs 11, 44, 85; cultural web model 28; local sense making 63; socialization and training 53; variety and differentiation 55; *see also* assumptions
benchmarking 16, 17

big bites 169–170, 184
Blow consultant companies 87–88
bottom-up approaches 19
British Broadcasting Corporation (BBC) 39
Brown, A. 51, 167
brutal fact 32
Buchanan, D. 46, 184
bureaucracy 68, 131–134, 156–157, 162, 164, 176, 177, 187
Burke, W. W. 18
Burnes, B. 22, 23
business orientation 81, 126, 129
business success 95

Callon, M. 193, 196
cascade model 169, 177
CEO *see* chief executive officer (CEO)
ceremonialism 141–143, 146, 147
change 3–4, 14–42, 49–53, *75;* assumptions 44; case study method 71–73; change agents 188–189; content 6, 19, 197; context 177–180, 195–196; coordination and prioritization 116–119; design of change project 69–70, 83–92, 121, 170–172; disconnected nature of change project 125–136; E-type *vs.* O-type 32; as expression of organizational culture 153–155, 177–180; failures of change project 115; fatigue 123; football game metaphor 174, 181; four metaphors of 20–21; as grand technocratic project 53–55, 62, 123, 168–171; identities 175–177; images of 21, 190–194, **193,** 196; immobilized engagement 115–116, 122, 182; implementation 94–105;

investigative model 69–71; lack of enthusiasm 111, 120; lessons learned 194–199; need for 6, 26; non-targeted cultural manifestations 151; objectives of change project 80–83; organizational change work 8–10, 36–37, **37,** 166–168, 196–197; paradoxes of 11; politics of 19; poor symbolic performance 120–121; process approach 32–35, 40, 170, 198–199; process-oriented view 54; reception of change programme 105–107; as reframing of everyday life 55–56; resistance to 23, 27, 37–40, **38,** 55, 178, 179; results of change programme 107–111; scale of 17–18; as sequential process 26–31; sources of 18–19; substantive 60–62; tactics 197–198; triggers for 15–17; understanding 5–8; unintentional reinforcement of existing culture 161–163, 179–180; workers 151–165, 201

chief executive officer (CEO) 75, 94, 108, 131, 175, 190

chief technical officer (CTO) 77, 175

Choudhury, P. 61

coercion 58–59

collaboration 24, 46

commitment 10, 162, 194; disassociation of managers from change project 118; shared value 143; target culture 142; winning culture 89

communications 28, 30, 193; consultancy 87–88; digital 15, 61; strategies 87; target culture 85, *86,* 142; winning culture 89

competence 194

compliant implementers 172

confidence 79–80, 87

consultants 29, 54, 63n1, 81, 92, 117, 172; description of 77; design of change project 83–92; HR department disconnection with 125–131; identity construction **176;** values 141

consumer market 101

content 6, 19, 197, 201

context 6, 17, 177–180; change models 31; framing 195–196; investigative model 69–71; unity of understanding 200

continuous change 18, 21, 27

continuous improvement 19, 200

continuous learning 32

conversations 170, 177

coordination 194; organizational performance 194; problems 116–119

corporate culture 19, 80–81, 83–84, 93n1, 141, 145, 192–193; experienced **152**

corporate social responsibility (CSR) 4

costs 127, 128

Courtois, J.-P. 46–47

Covid-19 14, 15

creativity 43, 56, 194

Crowdy, P. A. 55

CTO *see* chief technical officer (CTO)

cultural drivers of change 16

cultural heterogeneity 63

cultural kit 97, 121, 129; design of change project 85, 88, 89; post office metaphor 138, 139; workshops 98–100

cultural themes 111, 198

'cultural thickness' 123

cultural web concept 26, 28–30, *29,* 85

Cummings, T. G. 194

customer orientation 58, 88, 103, 162; attitude change 82; lack of 78, 81; meaning of 82, 186–187; target culture 85

customers: definitions of 102–104, 186; mission statement 100, 101, 104; relations with 144

cynicism 39, 40, 111, 123, 199; *see also* scepticism

Dawson, P. 26, 38, 123–124, 142, 147, 154, 167

decision making 89, 143

delegation 135, 174

democratic leadership 22

demographic forces 16

deregulation 15, 16

design 69–70, 83–92, 122, 168, 170, 173, 181

dialogue 197–198

Dickson, W. 22

diffusion model 34, 37, 50–51, 176

digital communication 15, 61

discontinuous change 18

distinctiveness 49, 80

diversification 16

division of labour 11, 132, 156, 171, 177, 182

Dotcom 103–104

downsizing 19

Eagle consultant companies 87–88

economic drivers of change 15, 16

educators 37
Eisenstat, R. 32
emergent change 18–19
emotionality 119–121, 169, 198
employees 22, 195, 197; bottom-up
    approaches 19; communication to
    30, 96; design of change project 87,
    88; failure of cultural change project
    123–124; Group Dynamics school
    22–23; hyperculture 147, **179**; images
    of change programme 192–193;
    low trust in management 79–80;
    mobilization by top management
    155; motivation 141; Organizational
    Development (OD) 22–23; passivity
    154, 163–164; reception of change
    programme 105–107, 198; resistance
    to change 37–38; targeted culture 105;
    TQM programmes 32, 154; winning
    behaviours 90, 91; *see also* managers
empowerment 27, 143, 179, 195
engineering 78, 168–171
Ericsson 4
evaluation 26
everyday reframing 55–56, 156
evolutionary changes 18, 21, 24
Excellence Ltd. 83–89, 125–128
existing culture 28, 77–80; unintentional
    reinforcement 160–163, 179–180
experienced corporate culture **152**
experienced organizational culture
    152–155, 161, **179**
expressiveness 119–122, 170, 181, 198
eye-opener metaphor 108, 110, 173, 175,
    181, 191–194, **193**

facilitators 171–172
facts 39
feature creep 186
follow-up 105, 107–108, 130, 196, 197
football game metaphor 174, 181
Francis, H. 178
fun 95, 96, 157
functional stupidity 133–135

gap analysis 99
Gates, B. 46
Geertz, C. 8
Gerstner, L. 4
Gleeson, B. 32
globalization 15
Global Tech (GT) 67, 75–80
grandiose fantasies 142–146

grand technocratic project 53–55, 62, 123,
    169–171, 176
Group Dynamics school 22–25

Harris, L. 52
Hawthorne experiments 22
Helms Mills, J. 17
Heracleous, L. 28, 30, 45, 50, 155, 194
Holweg, M. 61
HR *see* Human Resource Department (HR)
HRM *see* human resource
    management (HRM)
Human Relations approach 22
Human Resource Department (HR) 76,
    89–92, 99, 119, 139, 196; disconnection
    with junior managers 129–131;
    diversity of meanings 173; facilitators
    171–172; identity construction **176**;
    scepticism about HR issues 158–159
human resource management (HRM)
    81, 147
hyperculture 12, 137–138, 148n3,
    152, **152**, 161, 163, 183; big bites
    169; ceremonial talk 141–143,
    146; grandiose fantasies 142–146;
    importance of 164; manufactured culture
    140–141, 145; official communication
    147; parcel metaphor 138–140; targets
    for change **179**; unpacked package
    138–140
hyperreality 137, 146
hypocrisy 107, 175, 192, **193**

Ibarra, H. 3, 44, 47
IBM 4
iconic practices 44
identification 11
identity 33–35, 174–177, 181, 196;
    organizational 47–49, 80; positioning
    34, 40
ideological domination 58, 59
ignorance 190
image management 167
immobilized engagement 115–117,
    122, 182
implementation 24, 34, 75, 85, 94–105,
    198; compliant implementers 172;
    HR department disconnection with
    consultant 127, 128; investigative model
    70; other work priorities 119; planning
    distinction 170; problems 105
individualism 29, 30
innovation 17, 100, 101, 156

inspiration, winning culture 89
instrumentalism 120–122, 131, 181
intended cultural change 51–53
internationalization 15, 18
interpretation 33, 40, 70, 105–107
interpretative perspective 8, 73, 93n1
introversion 78–79
investigative model 69–71
isomorphism 146

jigsaw puzzle 96, *98*, 143–144
Jobs, S. 16

kick-off meeting 94–96, 129, 143
Knight, P. 46
knowledge-intensive firms (kifs) 68, 122
knowledge management 147
Kotter, J. P. 27, 28, 31, 194–195

Langham, B. 45, 50, 155, 194
language 44–47, 54, 199; significance of
    35–37; *see also* vocabulary
Latour, B. 9, 33, 34, 176, 196
Lawrence, T. 37
leadership 45, 54, 186–187, 194, 198;
    behaviour 84; change process 30;
    democratic 22; development programs
    57; employee concerns 88; low trust in
    79–80; management of meaning 55;
    messages about 185; participative 22;
    remoteness 157–158, 163; target culture
    83–85, *86*, 143; uninspiring 121–122;
    visible 187; winning culture 89; *see also*
    top management
learning: continuous 32; single-loop 20
levels of analysis 6, 21, 22, 45
Lewin, K. 22–24, 27
limited knowledge 189–190
live culture 159
long-term view 24, 196
low trust, in management 79–80

Magala, S. 40
management 7, 11; communication
    culture 87; culture 11, 89; image 167;
    investigative model 69–71; low trust
    in 79–80; sub-culture 47; *see also*
    managers; top management
management control systems 15, 31, 42,
    45, 81
management forum 96–99, 143
managerialism 111, 164–165, 169,
    179, 187

managers 63n1; adeptness in responding
    to change 4; bureaucratic organization
    156; case study data collection method
    72; change outcomes 36; compliant
    implementers 172; coordination
    problems 116–119; decision-making
    30; diversity of meanings 175;
    everyday reframing 55–56; facilitators
    172–173; grandiose fantasies 142–146;
    HR department disconnection with
    129–131; identity construction **176**;
    images of 190; images of change
    programme 193; immobilized
    engagement 115–117, 122, 182;
    influence of 55; kick-off meeting
    94–96; lack of enthusiasm 111, 120;
    low trust in 161, 165; making sense of
    organizational context 17; management
    forum 96–99, 143; middle 39, 52, 60,
    72–73, 76–77, 83–84, 93n2, 98, 197;
    non-implementers 173; other work
    priorities 119; passivity 163–164,
    177; positive interpretation of change
    programme 167, 190; post office
    metaphor 140; reception of change
    programme 105–107; remoteness
    157–158, 163; scepticism 158–159,
    161; skill development 30; uncertainty
    130; 'wait-and-see' cultures 199;
    workshops 90, 91, 99–101, 109, 118,
    130; *see also* top management
market forces 16
marketing 78, 167
Marshak, R. J. 20, 192
McKinsey 26
meaning 8, 11, 43, 61, 163, 181;
    construction of 63, 170–171; continuous
    attention to 199; diversity of 171,
    173, 175–176, 181, 191; everyday
    reframing 55–56; focus on 197;
    investigative model 70; management
    of 178, 181; openness to new meanings
    62; reproduction of cultural 170;
    shared 153; of values 187; variety and
    differentiation 47
measurement issues 70
meetings 46, 54; case study method of
    observation 72–73; kick-off 94–96,
    129, 143
mergers and acquisitions 18, 19
method 71–72
Microsoft 46, 49
'mindset' 68

Mirfakhar, A. 5
mis-logics 174
mission 88, 90, 92, 100–101, 104, 138
modesty 188, 190
motivation 142, 177
myths 41, 45, 202

networking 19
Nike 46
Nissan 51
Nohria, N. 3, 32, 194
non-implementers 173
Norbäck, L.-E. 200–202
norms 16, 23, 44, 50, 141
'n-step' thinking 40, 124, 135, 157,
    181, 199

objectives 81–83, 90, 100, 200
obvious facts 39
OD *see* Organizational Development (OD)
official communication, hyperculture 146
Ogbonna, E. 6, 52, 60
openness 53, 60, 62
Open Systems school 22, 25–26, 40
Operations Department (OT) 76
organizational behaviours 194
organizational culture 3–4, 11, 42–63;
    background 77–80; ceremonial talk
    141–143, 146; change as expression of
    151, 153–156, 178–180; characteristics
    42, 43; concepts of 152, **152**; context
    of change work 177–180, 195–196;
    cultural web concept 26, 28–30, *29*, 85;
    'culture-affirmative' 123; definitions
    of 43, 50; design of change project
    83–92; drivers for change 17; grandiose
    fantasies 143–145, 147; hyperculture
    183; identity 40–41, 47–49;
    implementation of change programme
    94–105; instrumental view of cultural
    work 131; intended 51–53; language,
    stories and rituals 45–47; lessons
    for change 194–199; limited value
    of values 186–188; as manufactured
    140–141, 146; measurement issues
    69; 'mindset' 68; non-recognized
    166, 179; objectives of change project
    80–83; reception of change programme
    105–107; significance of 142;
    substantive changes 60–62; symbolic
    anorexia 183–186; translation 171;
    unintentional reinforcement of existing
    culture 161–163, 179–180; as unpacked

package 138–140, 146; 'variable view'
    of 26; variety and differentiation 47–48,
    50, 61; *see also* hyperculture
Organizational Development (OD) 22–26,
    40, 92, 178
organizational logic 175
organizational structure 20, 31, 42, 68, 81;
    basic assumptions 45; target culture
    83–87, *86*, 143; winning culture 89
outcomes 5, 6, 36–37, 70–71,
    107–111, **179**
outsourcing 19

Palmer, I. 36, 92, 93, 123, 167, 169, 190
paper product metaphor 106, 107,
    121–122, 145, 180, **193**
parcel metaphor 138–140, 175, 177
participative leadership 22
performance: appraisal 54; organizational
    behaviours 194; poor symbolic
    performance 121–122
Pieterse, J. 39
planned change 4, 18, 21–31, 40,
    56, 123; critique of 31–32; grand
    technocratic project 53–55; process
    approach 32, 37
planning 170, 181, 198
political drivers of change 15
politics of change 19, 167
population ecology 7
post office metaphor 139, 140, 146, 173,
    192, **193**, 193
post-structuralism 73
power 57–59
process approach 5, 32–35, 40, 71, 170,
    198–199, 200
process-oriented view, organizational
    change 54
project work 11, 68, 84–85, 160

quality programmes 19, 147; *see also* total
    quality management (TQM)
quick fixes 169, 181, 196
Quinn, E. R. 21, 82

R&D *see* research and development (R&D)
reception 70, 105–107, 198
recruitment 20, 53
re-engineering 14, 19, 32, 168–171
reframing 55–56, 156
refreezing 23
relay race (baton) metaphor 125–129,
    131–135, 171–174, 178, 181

research and development (R&D) 9, 67, 188, 192
resistance to change 23, 27, 37–40, **38**, 55, 178, 179
responsibility 117–120
restructuring 19, 39–40, 60
revolutionary change 18, 21, 25, 123
reward systems 60, 89
rituals 44–47, 141–143; empty 192
Robbins, S. P. 195
Roethlisberger, F. 22
role models 116, 117, 119, 121, 144, 175
root metaphor 44, 166, 181

Satellite 72–73, 101–105, 129–130, 160
scepticism 99, 101, 158–159, 180, 199; mission statement 100–101; reinforcement of organizational culture 161, 165; *see also* cynicism
Schein, E. H. 44–45
self-critique 130
self-organization 68
self-transformations 195
Sennett, R. 38
sense making 3, 7–8, 17, 25, 31, 33–35, 63, 173; disassociation from change project 118; investigative model 69; lack of conversations 170; local meaning 63; middle-managerial 172; process approach 41; translation model 34
Siehl, C. 52
Sinclair, J. 178
situation analysis 28
skills 30
Smircich, L. 44
'7 S' model 26
social constructionism 140, 187
social introversion 78–79
socialization 53
Sörgärde, N. 191
Spicer, A. 133
standardized terms 42, 146
Stensaker, I. G. 5
stories 45–47, 80, 184
strategic architects 171, 173, 176
strategy 18, 28, 42, 74–75, 195; communications 87; cultural web 26; football game metaphor 174; investigative model 69; making 28; Open Systems school 25–26; unclear 195
subcultures 47–49, 85, 171, 177
subjectification 58, 59

substantive change 60–62
success stories 167
supporting structures 202
sustainable development goals (SDGs) 4
Svanberg, C.-H. 4
SWOT analysis 84
symbolic anorexia 124, 183–186
symbolism 8, 45, 50, 55, 119–121, 184–186, 198; lack of expressive 123; negative 197; preoccupation with 147; variety and differentiation 47, 55
systems theory 25

tactics 197–198, 201
Targama, A. 200–202
target culture 83–87, *86,* 106, 122, 143–146, 148n3, 179
teamwork 81, 89–91, 143, 144, 162, 179
Technocom (TC) 67–69, 72, 76, 78–81
technocratic approach 53–55, 123–124, 169–171
technology 144; technological orientation 77–79, 82, 179
theoretical approaches 7
Tichy, N. M. 26
tick-off activities 175, 177, 192, **193,** 198
time 5–6
Titan 68, 72, 104, 129–130
Todnem, R. 5
top management 6, 9, 24, 49, 51, 153–156; coordination problems 119; delegation 135, 174; disconnectedness 132–133; diversity of meanings 175; grandiose fantasies 142; high involvement 92, 132; hyperculture 144; hypocrisy 107, 175, 192; identity construction 176, **176;** key actors 75–76; local initiatives 55; low trust in 179; personal example 60; remoteness 157–158, 163; shortcomings 119; strategic architects 172, 173; sub-cultures 47, 85; support from 26; values 52, 107; wave metaphor 192; *see also* leadership; managers
Total Quality Leadership (TQL) 202n1
total quality management (TQM) 14, 32, 131, 147, 154
TPC theory 26
TQL *see* Total Quality Leadership (TQL)
TQM *see* total quality management (TQM)
training 53
transformation 191–194, **193,** 196
translation 9, 33–35, 171, 176, 193
Trevor, J. 61

triggers for change 15–17
trivialization 168
trust 79–80, 89, 109, 164, 179, 185

uncertainty 107–108, 118, 121, 178;
    managers 130
unfreezing 23, 24, 31
'uniqueness paradox' 146
urgency 27, 53, 105, 195

values 7, 11, 122, 129, 175, 197;
    basic 84–85, 130, 142–144;
    BBC 39–40; belief in 157;
    ceremonialism 136, 142; changing
    49, 50, 52, 56; continuous attention
    to 199; definitions of organizational
    culture 44; employee responsibility 155;
    engineer-driven culture 165; Group
    Dynamics school 23; HR department
    disconnection with consultant 127–129,
    132; hyperculture 137–138, 152,
    161, 163, **179,** 183; limited value of
    186–188; local sense making 63; one-
    sided focus on 197; openness to new
    62; Organizational Development (OD)
    24; organizational identity 44–45;
    post office metaphor 141; reception
    of change programme 107; shared 79,
    89–91, 101, 132, 143, 153; socialization

and training 53; stories and rituals
    45–46; variety and differentiation 47,
    48, 54, 55; winning behaviour 90, 91;
    winning culture 89
visible leadership 187
vision 27, 88, 90, 92, 195
vocabulary 109, 111, 116, 119, 123;
    hyperculture 138, 184; post office
    metaphor 139, 140; workshop
    discussions 101; *see also* language

'wait-and-see' cultures 161, 180, 199
Wallander, J. 39
wave metaphor 116, 173, 175, 177,
    191–194, **193**
Weick, K. E. 21, 82
Whittington, R. 26, 85
Wilkinson, B. 6, 52, 60
winning behaviours 90, 91
winning culture 85, 89, 96, 143
workshops 83, 90, 99–101, 106, 109,
    185; business orientation 126, 129;
    coordination problems 118, 119; failures
    of 130; immobilized engagement 122,
    178; implementation problems 105;
    kick-off meetings 96; lack of follow-up
    105, 107–108, 130; management forum
    97, 98; poor symbolic performance
    120–121

Printed in the United States
by Baker & Taylor Publisher Services